The

Jewish Mourner's

Companion

the
JEWISH
LEARNING GROUP

The

Jewish Mourner's Companion

FIRST EDITION
Copyright ©2006
The Jewish Learning Group, Inc.

Published By

the
JEWISH
Learning Group

Tel. 1-(888)-56-LEARN
www.JewishLearningGroup.com
Email: info@JewishLearningGroup.com

ISBN 1-891293-21-4

Acknowledgements

A special thanks to Rabbi Sholom Ber Chaikin, for giving selflessly of his valuable time to read, amend, and refine the material presented here, and for ensuring its halachic accuracy.

To Rabbi Levi Garelik of the A.C.C. Chevra Kaddisha, for reviewing the material presented here and offering many suggestions, insights, and clarifications.

To Rabbis Nissen Mangel and Yosef B. Friedman, for the English translations of various Psalms and prayers.

To my wife, for her constant support and ready proof-reading. To Leibel Estrin, Yehudis Cohen, and Rabbi Shmuel Rabin for additional proofing and editing.

To countless others who have assisted along the way, including Rabbis Aaron Goldstein, Yehuda Weg, Yoram Ulman, and all others who have offered their ideas and encouragement.

To everyone else not mentioned above who helped make this book possible. Thank you all!

We have devised the following transliteration system to help readers accurately pronounce the Hebrew words of blessings and prayers presented in this book:

Hebrew:	Transliteration:	Example:
ח or כ	ch	Challah
ָ	ö	Law
־	a	Hurrah
ֱ	ay	Today
ֶ	e	Leg
ְ	'	Avid
ֹ or וֹ	o	Tone
ִ	i	Key
ֻ or וּ	u	Lunar
יִ	ai	Aisle
יָ	öy	Toy

Table of Contents

Author's Note

In Jewish tradition, death is not viewed as the end of life, but as a transition from a time of effort to a time of reward. The soul continues to live on. The days of our life are like stepping stones that lead the soul from this world to the next, where the soul enjoys the spiritual accomplishments of its mortal existence.

Still, the illness and passing of a loved one is a painful experience. For this reason, Jewish law mandates both caring for the ill and deceased with respect and dignity, and comforting the mourner during his or her time of need. In this way, Jewish law provides the means to console both the soul and the mourner.

The present Companion provides an overview of these Jewish laws and traditions. It is designed so that one may know how to respond to issues as they occur. Nonetheless, one is encouraged to consult a rabbi who specializes in these laws to address one's particular situation.

May we merit the day when illness and death will be gone forever!

Rabbi Zalman Goldstein

7

The Journey of Life

An Actual Part of God

According to Jewish tradition, the soul is a portion of God infused in a physical body. The Godly soul animates and enlivens the body. It allows it to see, hear, and interact with the world around it. In Hebrew, the soul is called *Neshama*, which literally means "breath."

Describing the creation of Adam, the first human, the Torah relates, "And God formed man of dust from the ground, and He breathed into his nostrils the soul of life, and man became a living soul" (Genesis 2:7).

Jewish mysticism teaches us that when one blows out air, the breath comes directly from one's essence. It is internal, unchanged and unformed by vocalization.

By stating that God "breathed into Adam's nostrils the soul of life," the Torah is telling us that God imparted His "essence" into man, unlike all other creations, which were brought into being "externally" through His speech (God "*Said*" let there be...).

9

Coming from the essence of God, the soul is perfect and untainted. It is charged with the task of making a "dwelling place for God" in this world, through the fulfillment of *Mitzvot* (Heb. God's commandments), and worthy acts.

During a person's lifetime on earth, he is given the merit and free-choice to partner with his Godly soul. He can affect it, and the world, by either allowing the soul to shine forth through proper thoughts, words and deeds, or, God forbid, by burying it beneath layers and coverings, suppressing and tarnishing its Godly radiance. Thus God, in His infinite wisdom, has given His people the gift of repentance, allowing one to "wipe the slate clean," and begin anew.

The Union of Body and Soul

The soul, being a part of God, shares all the attributes applied to God: It is Infinite, All-Powerful, Holy, and Enduring, to name a few of God's attributes. The body, by comparison, is comprised of physical matter. It is temporary. It is here today, yet begins disintegrating as soon as the soul leaves the body.

We can thus readily understand Judaism's concern with the soul over the body. The soul endures, while the body returns to dust.

This in no way diminishes the importance of the body or of the material world. Only by descending into the physical body and living in this world can the soul accomplish its task. The body enables the soul to impart Godliness to the world, as well as to acquire additional holiness for itself.

This is accomplished specifically by interfacing and interacting with the physical and material, by doing mitzvot and other worthy acts, and by studying His Torah.

At the same time, the soul enables the body to transcend its animal nature by refining it and revealing its innate Godliness and goodness. It creates within the body a yearning to escape the limits of material existence and to connect to the eternal.

The Heavenly Court

After passing from this world, the soul is brought before the Heavenly Court to account for its days and actions (or inactions) during its mortal lifetime.

Jewish tradition speaks of a "Celestial Scale" on which one's positive deeds and negative deeds are weighed against each other. The soul receives its reward or punishment accordingly.

Garden of Eden - Life After Life

In Judaism there is no "After-Life" — because life never ends. As it states in Ecclesiastes (12:7): "And the dust (body) returns to the earth as it was, and the spirit returns to God who gave it."

The Torah teaches that there are two worlds or states: *Olam Hazeh* (this World), and *Olam Habah* (the World to Come). In Olam Hazeh, Godliness is hidden (enabling a person to have free-choice). In Olam Habah, Godliness is completely revealed. In between those two worlds is *"Gan Eden"* (heaven; paradise). There the soul reposes until it is ushered into the World to Come, and re-experiences as its reward the Godliness that it brought into the world. The amount of Godly radiance the soul is capable of absorbing and enjoying in Gan Eden, and in the World to Come, is directly proportionate to the Torah, mitzvot, and worthy acts performed by the person in this world.

If the soul returns "tarnished," it must go through a state of *"Gehinom"* (purging; purgatory), in which it is made to understand the spiritual failings and vacuum caused by its lapses and transgressions, before it can enter Gan Eden. We are taught that being that the Godly soul is pure and good at its essence, the experience of Gehinom never exceeds more than twelve months.

Sweetening the Soul's Judgment

Since all Jews come from one source, all Jews are essentially one Godly entity. Therefore, we are capable of benefiting, and are responsible for, one another.

Thus, even if the soul did not accomplish as much as it could or should have, and must experience Gehinom, family members (especially one's children), friends, and even strangers can sweeten its judgments. This is done by reciting Kaddish, performing mitzvot, giving charity, and studying Torah in merit of the soul (see pages 161 and 277).

The World to Come
The Resurrection of the Dead

One of the cornerstones of Jewish belief is *Techiat Hameitim*, the resurrection of the dead, when each body will be regenerated and its soul restored. According to tradition, this era will be ushered in by *Moshiach*, the Messiah.

Judaism believes that the world is constantly marching to this state, and once it is attained, Godliness will be openly revealed. All negativity, illness, wars, death, and so on, will disappear, and the earth will be filled with the knowledge of

God, as the waters cover the sea. At that time, every Jewish person who ever lived, as well as all righteous gentiles, will be brought back to life to bask in the eternal light of God.

The time of Moshiach is neither far off, nor an impossibility in our lifetime. Moshiach can come in an instant. Each positive deed that is performed in this world can be the one that tips the scales of good over evil and ushers in the era of Moshiach.

Your Soul as Your Guide

The soul serves as a "spiritual compass" which guides the body in its journey through the material world, trying to educate it to appreciate and pursue spirituality. Ultimately, the soul refines the physical until it becomes "one" with the soul. At that point, the body becomes a vehicle for the soul and, ultimately, the Will of God. A person in this state is called a *Tzaddik*, one who is completely righteous.

Nourishing Your Soul

In addition to giving each of us a portion of Himself, God gave us the Torah. The laws and mitzvot of the Torah nourish the soul and promote its full and complete expression. The Torah teaches the soul how to conquer and elevate both the animal nature of the body and the materiality of the world. When the time comes to leave, the soul returns to its source along with the Torah it studied, the mitzvot it performed, and the good deeds that it carried out in this world.

If however, a Jewish person lives life outside of or even in contradiction to the Torah, the pure Godly soul becomes stifled and sullied. Unless one does sincere *Teshuva* (return; repentance) in his lifetime, the soul remains this way until it separates from the body, when it returns to its source "empty-handed."

Your Soul's Unique Contribution

According to *Kabbalah* (Jewish mystical teachings), every soul has a mission to accomplish in this world. Each soul reveals and imparts Godliness to a part of the world that is exclusive to it. No other soul can accomplish its task. Further, fulfilling the task is necessary to the perfection of the world.

Therefore, Judaism takes the concept of individual responsibility to heart. One cannot say that "others are doing what Torah demands, so I need not concern myself with it." Judaism requires one's unique contribution, as does the world, which cannot be spiritually complete without it.

A way to discover your soul's mission and purpose is to search yourself for difficult spiritual hurdles: the mitzva or mitzvot that feel "too hard" or beyond your ability or level. We each have the things that come easy, and those that come only through hard work. Those difficult challenges are your true goal and life-task.

Challenging mitzvot are one kind of indicator. Deriving a deep satisfaction and pleasure from a particular mitzva could indicate that it, too, is germane to your soul's mission. Reviewing the results of your soul-searching with a friend or mentor will assure that the process and conclusions are objective.

Torah Living and the Body

It is no coincidence that we are taught that the 613 mitzvot in the Torah correspond to parts of the human body: The 248 positive commandments ("Do's...") relate to the body's 248 limbs, and the 365 prohibitions ("Dont's...") relate to the body's 365 vessels and sinews.

The Talmud and Kabbalah are full of stories in which a person's state of health reflected his or her state of spirituality. For example, if one had a digestive illness, he would concern himself with verifying the kosher status of the food he was eating. If one was suffering from depression, he would increase in charity. If one had difficulty conceiving, one reviewed the Torah's laws of family purity, and so on.

While the links aren't always as neat and simple as above, these stories illustrate the strong relationship that exists between our physical well-being and the full expression of our life-giving soul.

The ideal life is one in which the spiritual and physical complement each other, with each component getting what it needs to make the most of its time on earth.

Reincarnation and Second Chances

The Torah teaches that the soul is sent into this world to elevate its portion in the physical plane. Should it fail in anyway, or in any particular detail, it will come back to this world, in another body, until the task is complete.

For example, if the person excelled in Shabbat observance in one life but was lax in giving charity, his soul will have to live a completely new life to perfect the practice of giving charity, and the same goes for the rest of the mitzvot.

Keeping Body and Soul Together

As will be explained in the following chapters, Jewish law teaches us that every moment of life is extremely precious, and brings untold benefits to the soul.

Therefore, the Torah obligates each person to do all that is possible to keep body and soul united, prolonging life so that the soul can complete its mission, until God decides it's time to collect the soul.

Life and Illness

"May You Live Until 120..."

Every second of life, from the moment of conception until the completion of one's years in this world, is a gift from God. It is a gift that must not be squandered. Indeed every single day, Jews ask God in prayer that one's life be filled with days that are meaningful, healthy, and truly complete in the eyes of God.

It is common among Jews to wish another to live "until 120." This is because the Torah tells us that "Moses was 120 years old when he died" (Deuteronomy 34:7), and his life was deemed perfect and complete. Other leaders who lived until the age of 120, include Hillel, Rabbi Yochanan Ben Zakai, Rabbi Akivah, and Rabbi Yehudah Hanassi. Each were giants in their time.

Judaism urges that one never tire of life. Instead, one must look forward to each additional year with anticipation, excitement, and determination to make the most of every opportunity at every stage of life. Once again, look at Moses. He grew up a prince in the house of Pharoah. Yet God did not tell him to take the Children of Israel out of Egypt until he was 80!

Guarding One's Life

It is a positive commandment for every Jew to live as long as possible, as the Torah states, "Preserve yourself and your soul diligently" (Deuteronomy 4:9). The practical inference is that one must strive to live and one may not allow one's health to deteriorate or deliberately injure the body.

According to the Torah, a person who has fallen ill must actively seek the best medical help for his or her condition; one cannot simply rely on a miracle. At the same time, one should pray and petition God for a complete and speedy recovery.

A Healing Partnership

Healing ultimately comes from God. But for reasons best known to Him, God has determined that we typically have to draw His healing down through an expert or intermediary. Indeed, our sages taught that the entire field of medical science and its many practitioners are but vessels for God's blessings in this world.

The practice of medicine is so important that the *Code of Jewish Law* states, "the physician's right to heal is a religious duty." In essence, the doctor "partners" with God in restoring health, and his part of the partnership is solely the restoration of the person's health. The actual fate of the person is left to God and the Heavenly Court. Therefore, doctors cannot say that so-and-so only has a number of months to live, nor should a person accept such a prediction.

Practical Steps to Healing

Drawn from the advice of our sages: Find a good doctor and follow his instructions. Dispel any thoughts about illness. Think only healthy thoughts. Strengthen your confidence in the Healer of All Flesh that He will heal you in whatever way He sees fit. And increase your study of the esoteric parts of Torah.

Spirituality and Healing

In seeking a cure, a person should work on both material and spiritual aspects. The material aspect includes finding the best medical help and following the treatments prescribed. But there are a number of things that one can do spiritually to improve the situation.

For example, the prayers of an ill person can be very effective, and thus one should never despair. Even if to all mortal eyes there appears to be no hope, nothing is impossible for God. In addition to prayer, one should increase his or her study of Torah, and performance of mitzvot. This may include giving additional charity, taking on a new mitzva observance, and so on. Some request that a *Tzaddik* (great Torah sage; righteous person) bless them or pray on their behalf, for we are taught that the prayers of a Tzaddik are readily accepted by God.

The Kabbalah of Illness

As mentioned above, the Torah states, "Preserve yourself and your soul diligently" (Deuteronomy 4:9). This indicates that one must take care of the soul just as one must look after one's physical well-being, otherwise the Torah would have simply stated "preserve yourself."

Kabbalah teaches that illness comes when the passageways through which the soul radiates are "clogged." Clear the blockage, explains Kabbalah, and the illness will disappear. *Teshuva*, meaning return and repentance, can help in this regard. For this reason, Jewish Law states that when one is ill, one should check his ways.

If a person's thought, speech and deed are not all that they could be, the person should feel regret over the past and resolve to do better in the future. The person should take on specific deeds that demonstrate one's resolve to improve his or her conduct.

As a part of increasing Torah observance and repairing spiritual defects, it is customary to have an expert scribe examine the *Tefillin* (phylacteries) and *Mezuzot* (parchment scrolls placed on doorposts of Jewish homes and businesses) of the person who is ill. If they are found to be defective, they are corrected at this time.

Indeed, there are countless stories linking the kosher status of one's Tefillin and Mezuzot to the physical state of those around them.

For example, a young man was having serious trouble with his heart and his doctors were very concerned. They felt that the defect was so severe that it was untreatable. At a friend's suggestion, he had the Mezuzot in house inspected by a scribe. The scribe found that the word "*Lev*," Hebrew for "heart," was missing from the text. The family replaced the Mezuzah with a kosher one and the young man was completely cured, leaving the doctors astonished.

Not always is the connection between the physical ailment and the spiritual dimension so clear. Sometimes it remains hidden from us, which is why people seek the advice of a

Tzaddik, in addition to one's doctor, during a time of illness. Often, the Tzaddik can identify the spiritual source of a physical problem and suggest ways to rectify the situation.

Upon Recovery

When one recovers from a serious illness, his thoughts and prayers should immediately turn to thanking God. Many people begin to observe a mitzva they have not yet performed before, or commit to improving a certain aspect of their spiritual life, as a way of thanking God for giving them more days with which to fulfill their soul's mission, and to make the world a better place.

Some have the custom to make a *Seudat Hoda-ah*, a meal of thanksgiving. During this festive meal, the host and guests share Torah thoughts and words designed to inspire those present to further their Torah observance.

Many also give *Tzedaka* (charity) to a worthy cause or needy person to express one's gratitude to God.

Men recite the thanksgiving blessing of *Hagomel* at the conclusion of the reading of the Torah in the synagogue.

The Importance of Life

According to Judaism, life is extremely precious and holy, and thus one cannot treat matters of life and death lightly. God states clearly in the Torah: "Therefore choose life" (Deuteronomy 30:19). While we have the power to make a choice, God enjoins us to choose life over death.

For that reason, Judaism forbids acts that result in "mercy killing" or that grant the "right to end life." Until the moment of natural death, every second that the soul is in the body is inestimably valuable — not just to the body, but to to the Jewish people and the world as a whole.

The mere fact that the soul and body are still together is reason enough to sustain this union by all means possible, regardless of the presumed "quality-of-life" (if one can ever truly estimate someone's quality of life) of the person. For life is of infinite, not relative, value, and mathematically any fraction of infinity must also be infinite.

Additionally, the Talmud states that a person can acquire his entire portion in the World to Come in a *single instant* by thoughts of repentance. No one may deny a person that chance.

In the Hands of God

We find an expression in Jewish writings that even if a "sword is hanging over a person's neck," and death seems certain, one still must not despair. For just as one knows that God created the world and sustains life upon it, one must also know that God can intervene and spare what seems to be a certain fate.

To put it another way, if God did not wish us to be alive right now, we would immediately cease living. This fact alone demonstrates that He *wants* us to live. If we (or our loved ones) cannot see a reason to remain alive, it does not mean that God does not. God is truly in control and we should draw great strength, courage, and comfort from this.

At a Crossroads

When decisions have to be made concerning one's own care or that of a loved one, everyone involved is usually motivated by concern for the patient and the desire to do the right thing.

Often, this is easier said than done. Who can say what is truly "the right thing?" Who are we to make what may turn out to be an irreversible decision? As Jews, we are fortunate to have the Torah. It serves as the guiding light for all matters of life.

As mentioned earlier, the Torah stresses the obligation upon everyone to extend life. In addition to many other reasons, during these extra moments, the soul may yet do *Teshuva*, true repentance, and reach its fulfillment — an opportunity that is lost once the soul leaves this world.

When making decisions that affect the life of a person, one should be sensitive to the needs of the soul, in addition to that of the body. It is imperative to consult with a rabbi *who specializes in this area of Jewish law*. This will ensure that whatever is done is guided by Torah, and one will be at peace knowing that he has done what is right according to God and what is right for his loved one.

Life is Always Worth Living

As mentioned above, every moment that a soul is in the body is extremely valuable. We may not understand what this means in our terms, but one thing is certain: "quality" has to be measured by more than what we see or understand. And for this we have to turn to the Torah and to rabbinic guidance.

The Torah teaches that souls come to earth for many purposes. It could be that the destiny of a soul is to elicit certain responses on our part, to teach us about the meaning of life and love, or to help us relate to the person's essence, not his physical aspect. If we succeed in learning the lesson, then the soul has accomplished its mission and is rewarded for it. If we fail to respond with sensitivity and respect for the unconditional value of that person's life, we not only deny the soul its spiritual fulfillment and reward, we deny a small part of our fulfillment as well.

I Am the Guardian of My Life

When God endows a person with life, the person becomes a guardian who must look after his "gift of life." According to Judaism, we do not "own" our soul or body, nor are we free to end life when we want. Life and death have always been, and remain, the realm of God and the Heavenly Court.

Therefore, if one takes his life, God forbid, he is liable for murder, even if only of himself. This action is so severe that the Torah forbids one who defiantly committed suicide from being buried in a Jewish cemetery or to be mourned by his family.

Dealing with Pain and Suffering

The Torah is both compassionate and understanding. It recognizes that there are times when an ill person is suffering greatly. In such cases, Torah law distinguishes between action and inaction. According to Torah law, everyone involved in the care of the patient must do all in their power to preserve and prolong life. In the case of the terminally ill, for whom no cure is known or possible, and who are in extremely severe pain and discomfort, the Torah permits one to allow nature to "take its course." But one may never withhold or decline food, water, or oxygen. This would be tantamount to murder or suicide

In any given situation, it is imperative to consult with a rabbi *who specializes in this area of Jewish law*, before making any decision for yourself or the person in your care.

Drafting a Living Will

In today's day and age, it is a wise idea to clearly inform relatives and doctors of your desires that Jewish law guide your medical care should you become incapacitated, God forbid.

In addition to gaining peace of mind, having a legal document in hand will spare your loved ones and your medical team unnecessary stress and uncertainty should your desires ever come into question. Sometimes known as a "Health Care Proxy" or an "Advanced Directive," most jurisdictions will recognize a clearly written and signed "Living Will."

It is recommended that you consult with a competent rabbi, and a local estate and trust attorney, when drafting the document, to ensure its halachic and legal validity.

SAMPLE ADVANCE DIRECTIVE WITH RESPECT TO HEALTH-CARE AND POST-MORTEM DECISIONS

1. Designation of Health Care Surrogate

Your Name: (Last) _____ (First) _____ (Middle Initial) ___

In the event that I have been determined to be incapacitated to provide informed consent for medical treatment and surgical and diagnostic procedures, I wish to designate as my surrogate for health care decisions:

Name of Surrogate: (Last) _____ (First) _____

Address: _____ Telephone: _____

If my surrogate is unwilling or unable to perform his or her duties, I wish to designate as my alternate surrogate:

Name of Alternate Surrogate: (Last) _____ (First) _____

Address: _____ Telephone: _____

I fully understand that this designation will permit my designee to make health care decisions, except for anatomical gifts, unless I have executed an anatomical gift declaration pursuant to law, and to provide, withhold, or withdraw consent on my behalf; to apply for public benefits to defray the cost of health care; and to authorize my admission to or transfer from a health care facility. I further affirm that this designation is not being made as a condition of treatment or admission to a health care facility.

2. Jewish Law to Govern Health Care Decisions:

I am Jewish. It is my desire, and I hereby direct, that all health care decisions made for me (whether made by my surrogate, a guardian appointed for me, or any other person) be made pursuant to Jewish law and custom as determined in accordance with strict Orthodox interpretation and tradition. Without limiting in any way the generality of the foregoing, it is my wish that Jewish law and custom should dictate the course of my health care with respect to such matters as the performance of cardiopulmonary resuscitation if I suffer cardiac or respiratory arrest; the performance of life-sustaining surgical procedures and the initiation or maintenance of any particular course of life-sustaining medical treatment or other form of life-support maintenance, including the provision of nutrition and hydration; and the criteria by which death shall be determined, including the method by which such criteria shall be medically ascertained or confirmed.

3. Ascertaining the Requirements of Jewish Law:

In determining the requirements of Jewish law and custom in connection with this declaration, I direct my surrogate to consult with the following Orthodox Rabbi and I ask my surrogate to follow his guidance:

Name of Rabbi: (Last) _____ (First) _____ _____

Address: _____ Telephone: _____

If such Rabbi is unable, unwilling or unavailable to provide such consultation and guidance, then I direct my surrogate to consult with, and I ask my surrogate to follow the guidance of, an Orthodox Rabbi referred by the following Orthodox Jewish institution or organization:

Name of Institution/Organization: _____

Address: _____ Telephone: _____

If such institution or organization is unable, unwilling or unavailable to make such a reference, or if the Orthodox Rabbi referred by such institution or organization is unable, unwilling or unavailable to provide such guidance, then I direct my surrogate to consult with, and I ask my surrogate to follow the guidance of, an Orthodox Rabbi whose guidance on issues of Jewish law and custom my surrogate in good faith believes I would respect and follow.

4. Direction to Health Care Providers:

Any health care provider shall rely upon and carry out the decisions of my surrogate, and may assume that such decisions reflect my wishes and were arrived at in accordance with the procedures set forth in this directive, unless such health care provider shall have good cause to believe that my surrogate has not acted in good faith in accordance with my wishes as expressed in this directive. If the persons designated above as my surrogate and alternate surrogate are unable, unwilling or unavailable to serve in such capacity, it is my desire, and I hereby direct, that any health care provider or other person who will be making health care decisions on my behalf follow the procedures outlined in section three (3) above in determining the requirements of Jewish law and custom. Pending contact with the surrogate and/or Orthodox Rabbi described above, it is my desire, and I hereby direct, that all health care providers undertake all essential emergency and/or life sustaining measures on my behalf.

5. Access to Medical Records and Information; HIPAA:

I direct that all of my protected health information (as such term is defined under the Health Insurance Portability and Accountability Act of 1996 ("HIPAA")) and other medical records shall be made available to my surrogate upon request in the same manner as such information and records would be released and disclosed to me, and my surrogate shall have and may exercise all of the rights I would have regarding the use and disclosure of such information and records. In the event that the authority of my surrogate has not yet been established, I authorize each of my health care providers to release and disclose all my protected health information and other medical records to the individual nominated hereunder as my surrogate for the purpose of determining my capacity to make my own health care decisions, including, without limitation, the issuance and release of any written opinion relating to my capacity that such person may have requested. The foregoing direction and authorization shall supersede any prior agreement that I may have made with any of my health care providers to restrict access to or disclosure of my protected health information or other medical records, and shall expire with respect to any health care provider upon being revoked by me in a writing delivered to such health care provider.

6. Post-Mortem Decisions:

It is also my desire, and I hereby direct, that after my death, all decisions concerning the handling and disposition of my body be made pursuant to Jewish law and custom as determined in accordance with strict Orthodox interpretation and tradition. For example, Jewish law generally requires expeditious burial and imposes special requirements with regard to the preparation of the body for burial. It is my wish that Jewish law and custom be followed with respect to these matters. Further, subject to certain limited exceptions, Jewish law prohibits the performance of any autopsy or dissection. It is my wish that Jewish law and custom be followed with respect to such procedures, and with respect to all other post-mortem matters including the removal and usage of any of my body organs or tissue for transplantation or any other purposes. I direct that any health care provider in attendance at my death notify the surrogate and/or Orthodox Rabbi described above immediately upon my death, in addition to any other person whose consent by law must be solicited and obtained, prior to the use of any part of my body as an anatomical gift, so that appropriate decisions and arrangements can be made in accordance with my wishes. Pending such notification, and unless there is specific authorization by the Orthodox Rabbi consulted in accordance with the procedures outlined in section three (3) above, it is my desire, and I hereby direct, that no post-mortem procedure be performed on my body. I further affirm that this designation is not being made as a condition of treatment or admission to a health care facility.

7. Incontrovertible Evidence of My Wishes:

If, for any reason, this document is deemed not legally effective as a health care proxy, or if the persons designated in section one (1) above as my surrogate and alternate surrogate are unable, unwilling or unavailable to serve in such capacity, I declare to my family, my doctor and anyone else whom it may concern that the wishes I have expressed herein with regard to compliance with Jewish law and custom should be treated as incontrovertible evidence of my intent and desire with respect to all health care measures and post-mortem procedures; and that it is my wish that the procedure outlined in section three (3) above should be followed in determining the requirements of Jewish law and custom.

8. Duration and Revocation:

It is my understanding and intention that unless I revoke this proxy and directive, it will remain in effect indefinitely. My signature on this document shall be deemed to constitute a revocation of any prior health care proxy, directive or other similar document I may have executed prior to today's date.

My Signature: _____ Print Name: _____ Date: _____

Witness 1: _____ Witness 2: _____

Organ Donation

Donating an organ to another, while a noble expression of kindness, is a complicated affair in Jewish law. Donations between living persons are generally permitted, as long as the recipient is ready to receive the organ right away (which excludes organ banks), and the donor does not sacrifice or jeopardize his own life and well-being in the process.

The halachic problems begin when the donor is on the verge of death or has already passed on, as many organs cannot be transplanted once the donor's death occurs. Jewish law prohibits tampering with a person who is in the throes of death, or doing anything that may cause or hasten his or her demise. In such a case, touching the person or even merely removing a pillow is forbidden.

Concerning post-mortem organ transplants, one has to contend with Biblical prohibitions such as *Nivul Hamet* – mutilating the body of the deceased; *Halanat Hamet* – delaying the burial of a body; and *Hana'at Hamet* – deriving any benefit from a dead body, including selling or donating it for research.

A third state is someone who is kept alive artificially and whose brain-stem is considered clinically dead. In this case, one apparently does not have to contend with the issues of hastening death or tampering with the dead. The person seems to be suspended between life and death as long as the machines are connected.

Indeed, contemporary rabbinic authorities differentiate between when a person is "officially dead" and when a person is in the "throes of death." Some rabbis hold that brain-stem death is considered "official death" and one may thus operate to remove the necessary organs for transplantation once that state has been established (but not before). Regarding prohibitions against delaying burial and so on, these rabbis cite the ruling that saving a life overrides most Torah prohibitions.

Other rabbis disagree strongly and state that one is alive for all purposes "until the breath of life has ceased from his lips." Therefore, it is forbidden to tamper with the body at all. In their view, any type of mutilation is unforgivable and interferes with the eternal rest and peace of the soul.

As you can see, donating organs is not a simple matter. In all of these matters, one should seek the guidance of a competent rabbi who specializes in this area of Jewish law, before leaving any unalterable directives.

Visiting the Sick

Bikur Cholim, visiting the sick, is a very great mitzva. The Torah relates how God Himself visited our forefather Abraham during his time of illness through three angles. When visiting the sick, one offers prayers for a speedy recovery, material assistance if possible, and of course, moral encouragement.

In cities around the world, there are special Jewish societies dedicated to this mitzva. Many individuals spend time every week and even every day, visiting total strangers in the hospital or those convalescing at home. Depending on the circumstances, these visitors may be the only ones in touch with the patient on a regular basis.

The Torah Way

• The mitzva of visiting the sick consists of three elements: 1) Seeing to the material needs of the patient; 2) Praying for him or her; 3) Spending time with the patient and offering words of encouragement, and so on.

• It is best to visit with others; but one should not forgo the chance to visit if others cannot come along.

• One should not suddenly enter into the patient's room. One should first make sure that the patient is prepared and able to receive visitors, either by first visiting the nurse's station or by knocking on the door before entering.

• The visitor should speak to the patient in a positive manner, engaging the patient with light, yet meaningful talk.

• The visitor should help the patient give *Tzedaka* (charity), for we are taught "great is charity for it saves from death." The visitor can give the patient a few coins to place in a charity box, or the patient can make a pledge to do so on his own.

• The visitor should assist the patient with observing certain mitzvot (i.e. donning *Tefillin* for males, lighting Shabbat and holiday candles, hearing the blowing of the *Shofar* on Rosh Hashana, making the blessing on and shaking the *Lulav* and *Etrog* on Sukkot, hearing the reading of the *Megilla* on Purim, eating *Matza* on Passover, etc.).

• If one feels close to the patient, he should encourage the patient to do a spiritual self-evaluation and to pray. The visitor should also remind the patient of the great power of repentance and the benefit of dedicating oneself to Torah observance.

• Some have the custom to recite the following short prayer in the presence of the patient:

Ha-mökom y'racheim ölecho   הַמָּקוֹם יְרַחֵם עָלֶיךָ
b'soch köl cholei yisrö-ayl.   בְּתוֹךְ כָּל חוֹלֵי יִשְׂרָאֵל.

May the Almighty have mercy on you, among all the sick of Israel.

• One should limit the amount of time spent with the patient, keeping in mind the patient's condition, doctors' orders, and other factors.

• One should not overstay to the point of becoming a burden.

• If it appears that the patient's days are numbered, a family member, or in the case where there is no family available, a close friend or caregiver, should gently remind the patient to put his or her affairs in order (i.e. take care of debts, decide how to dispose of property, recite the *Viduy*, Confession, etc.).

Other Things One May Do

• On days when the Torah is read in synagogues (Mondays, Thursdays, Shabbat and Jewish holidays), one may request a special prayer for the sick, known as "*Mi Shebairach*," to be recited at the Torah. In this prayer, one pledges to give charity in the merit of the ill. It is preferable to provide the reader with the patient's Hebrew name, and that of his or her mother.

• Some people seek a blessing from a *Tzaddik* (great Torah sage; righteous person) and/or ask the Tzaddik to pray for them. Similarly, some people may send a note to the resting place (gravesite) of great Torah leaders, and ask them to beseech God on behalf of the ill person. Friends can certainly travel to the resting place and petition the Torah leader on behalf of the patient.

• Kabbalah teaches us that a person's name exerts an influence on one's well-being. Therefore, in some severe cases, some have the custom to add an additional Hebrew name to the person's existing name. This is done only by a competent rabbi. Some common names that are added are *Chaim, Baruch,* or *Refael* (for a man), or *Chaya, Bracha,* or *Refaelah,* (for a woman). Chaim and Chaya mean "life" in Hebrew; Baruch and Bracha, mean "blessing," and Refael and Refaelah, mean "God will heal."

Psalms 20 and 119

The following two Psalms are particularly effective when recited in times of distress. Psalm 20 is recited for oneself or a loved one who is suffering. Psalm 119 is composed according to the Hebrew alphabet, eight verses for each letter. Each verse contains a word referring to a different aspect of Torah, thereby encompassing the entire Scriptures. It is thus customary to recite the verses that comprise the letters of the person's Hebrew name (i.e. for Dovid, recite the verses of ד, ו, and ד).

Psalm 20

Lam'na-tzay-ach mizmor l'dövid. Ya-an'chö adonöy b'yom tzörö, y'sagev'chö shaym elohay ya-akov. Yishlach ez r'chö mi-kodesh, umi-tziyon yis-ödekö. Yizkor köl min'cho-sechö, v'olös'chö y'dash'neh selöh. Yiten l'chö chil'vö-vechö, v'chöl atzös'chö y'ma-lay. N'ran'nöh bishu-ösechö, uv'shaym elo-haynu nidgol, y'malay adonöy köl mish-alo-sechö. Atöh yöda-ti, ki hoshi-a adonöy m'shi-cho, ya-anayhu mish'may köd-sho, big'vuros yay-sha y'mino. Ayleh vö-rechev, v'ayleh va-susim, va-anachnu b'shaym adonöy elo-haynu naz-kir. Hay-möh kör'u v'nöfölu, va-anachnu kam-nu vanis-ödöd. Adonöy ho-shi-öh, ha-melech ya-anaynu v'yom kör'aynu.

לַמְנַצֵּחַ מִזְמוֹר לְדָוִד: יַעַנְךָ
יְיָ בְּיוֹם צָרָה, יְשַׂגֶּבְךָ שֵׁם
אֱלֹהֵי יַעֲקֹב: יִשְׁלַח עֶזְרְךָ מִקֹּדֶשׁ,
וּמִצִּיּוֹן יִסְעָדֶךָּ: יִזְכֹּר כָּל
מִנְחֹתֶיךָ, וְעוֹלָתְךָ יְדַשְּׁנֶה סֶלָה:
יִתֶּן לְךָ כִלְבָבֶךָ, וְכָל עֲצָתְךָ
יְמַלֵּא: נְרַנְּנָה בִּישׁוּעָתֶךָ, וּבְשֵׁם
אֱלֹהֵינוּ נִדְגֹּל, יְמַלֵּא יְיָ כָּל
מִשְׁאֲלוֹתֶיךָ: עַתָּה יָדַעְתִּי, כִּי הוֹשִׁיעַ
יְיָ מְשִׁיחוֹ, יַעֲנֵהוּ מִשְּׁמֵי
קָדְשׁוֹ, בִּגְבֻרוֹת יֵשַׁע יְמִינוֹ: אֵלֶּה
בָרֶכֶב, וְאֵלֶּה בַסּוּסִים, וַאֲנַחְנוּ
בְּשֵׁם יְיָ אֱלֹהֵינוּ נַזְכִּיר:
הֵמָּה כָּרְעוּ וְנָפָלוּ, וַאֲנַחְנוּ קַמְנוּ
וַנִּתְעוֹדָד: יְיָ הוֹשִׁיעָה, הַמֶּלֶךְ
יַעֲנֵנוּ בְיוֹם קָרְאֵנוּ:

41

For the Choirmaster; a Psalm by David. May the Lord answer you on the day of distress; may the Name of the God of Jacob fortify you. May He send your help from the Sanctuary, and support you from Zion. May He remember all your offerings, and always accept favorably your sacrifices. May He grant you your heart's desire, and fulfill your every counsel. We will rejoice in your deliverance, and raise our banners in the name of our God; may the Lord fulfill all your wishes. Now I know that the Lord has delivered His anointed one, answering him from His holy heavens with the mighty saving power of His right hand. Some (rely) upon chariots and some upon horses, but we [rely upon and] invoke the Name of the Lord our God. They bend and fall, but we rise and stand firm. Lord, deliver us; may the King answer us on the day we call.

Psalm 119

א אַשְׁרֵי תְמִימֵי דָרֶךְ הַהֹלְכִים בְּתוֹרַת יְיָ: אַשְׁרֵי נֹצְרֵי עֵדֹתָיו בְּכָל לֵב יִדְרְשׁוּהוּ: אַף לֹא פָעֲלוּ עַוְלָה בִּדְרָכָיו הָלָכוּ: אַתָּה צִוִּיתָה פִקֻּדֶיךָ לִשְׁמֹר מְאֹד: אַחֲלַי יִכֹּנוּ דְרָכָי לִשְׁמֹר חֻקֶּיךָ: אָז לֹא אֵבוֹשׁ בְּהַבִּיטִי אֶל כָּל מִצְוֹתֶיךָ: אוֹדְךָ בְּיֹשֶׁר לֵבָב בְּלָמְדִי מִשְׁפְּטֵי צִדְקֶךָ: אֶת חֻקֶּיךָ אֶשְׁמֹר אַל תַּעַזְבֵנִי עַד מְאֹד:

ב בַּמֶּה יְזַכֶּה נַּעַר אֶת אָרְחוֹ לִשְׁמֹר כִּדְבָרֶךָ: בְּכָל לִבִּי דְרַשְׁתִּיךָ אַל תַּשְׁגֵּנִי מִמִּצְוֹתֶיךָ: בְּלִבִּי צָפַנְתִּי אִמְרָתֶךָ לְמַעַן לֹא אֶחֱטָא לָךְ: בָּרוּךְ אַתָּה יְיָ לַמְּדֵנִי חֻקֶּיךָ: בִּשְׂפָתַי סִפַּרְתִּי כֹּל מִשְׁפְּטֵי פִיךָ: בְּדֶרֶךְ עֵדְוֹתֶיךָ שַׂשְׂתִּי כְּעַל כָּל הוֹן: בְּפִקֻּדֶיךָ אָשִׂיחָה וְאַבִּיטָה אֹרְחֹתֶיךָ: בְּחֻקֹּתֶיךָ אֶשְׁתַּעֲשָׁע לֹא אֶשְׁכַּח דְּבָרֶךָ:

ג גְּמֹל עַל עַבְדְּךָ אֶחְיֶה וְאֶשְׁמְרָה דְבָרֶךָ: גַּל עֵינַי וְאַבִּיטָה נִפְלָאוֹת מִתּוֹרָתֶךָ: גֵּר אָנֹכִי בָאָרֶץ אַל תַּסְתֵּר מִמֶּנִּי מִצְוֹתֶיךָ: גָּרְסָה נַפְשִׁי לְתַאֲבָה אֶל מִשְׁפָּטֶיךָ בְכָל עֵת: גָּעַרְתָּ זֵדִים אֲרוּרִים הַשֹּׁגִים מִמִּצְוֹתֶיךָ: גַּל מֵעָלַי חֶרְפָּה וָבוּז כִּי עֵדֹתֶיךָ נָצָרְתִּי: גַּם יָשְׁבוּ שָׂרִים בִּי נִדְבָּרוּ עַבְדְּךָ יָשִׂיחַ בְּחֻקֶּיךָ: גַּם עֵדֹתֶיךָ שַׁעֲשֻׁעָי אַנְשֵׁי עֲצָתִי:

ד דָּבְקָה לֶעָפָר נַפְשִׁי חַיֵּנִי כִּדְבָרֶךָ: דְּרָכַי סִפַּרְתִּי וַתַּעֲנֵנִי לַמְּדֵנִי חֻקֶּיךָ: דֶּרֶךְ פִּקּוּדֶיךָ הֲבִינֵנִי וְאָשִׂיחָה בְּנִפְלְאוֹתֶיךָ: דָּלְפָה נַפְשִׁי מִתּוּגָה קַיְּמֵנִי כִּדְבָרֶךָ: דֶּרֶךְ שֶׁקֶר הָסֵר מִמֶּנִּי וְתוֹרָתְךָ חָנֵּנִי: דֶּרֶךְ אֱמוּנָה בָחָרְתִּי מִשְׁפָּטֶיךָ שִׁוִּיתִי: דָּבַקְתִּי בְעֵדְוֹתֶיךָ יְיָ אַל תְּבִישֵׁנִי: דֶּרֶךְ מִצְוֹתֶיךָ אָרוּץ כִּי תַרְחִיב לִבִּי:

ה הוֹרֵנִי יְיָ דֶּרֶךְ חֻקֶּיךָ וְאֶצְּרֶנָּה עֵקֶב: הֲבִינֵנִי וְאֶצְּרָה תוֹרָתֶךָ וְאֶשְׁמְרֶנָּה בְכָל לֵב: הַדְרִיכֵנִי בִּנְתִיב מִצְוֹתֶיךָ כִּי בוֹ חָפָצְתִּי: הַט לִבִּי אֶל עֵדְוֹתֶיךָ וְאַל אֶל בָּצַע: הַעֲבֵר עֵינַי מֵרְאוֹת שָׁוְא בִּדְרָכֶךָ חַיֵּנִי: הָקֵם לְעַבְדְּךָ אִמְרָתֶךָ אֲשֶׁר לְיִרְאָתֶךָ: הַעֲבֵר חֶרְפָּתִי אֲשֶׁר יָגֹרְתִּי כִּי מִשְׁפָּטֶיךָ טוֹבִים: הִנֵּה תָּאַבְתִּי לְפִקֻּדֶיךָ בְּצִדְקָתְךָ חַיֵּנִי:

ו וִיבֹאֻנִי חֲסָדֶךָ יְיָ תְּשׁוּעָתְךָ כְּאִמְרָתֶךָ: וְאֶעֱנֶה חֹרְפִי דָבָר כִּי בָטַחְתִּי בִּדְבָרֶךָ: וְאַל תַּצֵּל מִפִּי דְבַר אֱמֶת עַד מְאֹד כִּי לְמִשְׁפָּטֶךָ יִחָלְתִּי: וְאֶשְׁמְרָה תוֹרָתְךָ תָמִיד לְעוֹלָם וָעֶד: וְאֶתְהַלְּכָה בָרְחָבָה כִּי פִקֻּדֶיךָ דָרָשְׁתִּי: וַאֲדַבְּרָה בְעֵדֹתֶיךָ נֶגֶד מְלָכִים וְלֹא אֵבוֹשׁ: וְאֶשְׁתַּעֲשַׁע בְּמִצְוֹתֶיךָ אֲשֶׁר אָהָבְתִּי: וְאֶשָּׂא כַפַּי אֶל מִצְוֹתֶיךָ אֲשֶׁר אָהָבְתִּי וְאָשִׂיחָה בְחֻקֶּיךָ:

ז זְכֹר דָּבָר לְעַבְדֶּךָ עַל אֲשֶׁר יִחַלְתָּנִי: זֹאת נֶחָמָתִי בְעָנְיִי כִּי אִמְרָתְךָ חִיָּתְנִי: זֵדִים הֱלִיצֻנִי עַד מְאֹד מִתּוֹרָתְךָ לֹא נָטִיתִי: זָכַרְתִּי מִשְׁפָּטֶיךָ מֵעוֹלָם יְיָ וָאֶתְנֶחָם: זַלְעָפָה אֲחָזַתְנִי מֵרְשָׁעִים עֹזְבֵי תּוֹרָתֶךָ: זְמִרוֹת הָיוּ לִי חֻקֶּיךָ בְּבֵית מְגוּרָי: זָכַרְתִּי בַלַּיְלָה שִׁמְךָ יְיָ וָאֶשְׁמְרָה תּוֹרָתֶךָ: זֹאת הָיְתָה לִי כִּי פִקֻּדֶיךָ נָצָרְתִּי:

ח חֶלְקִי יְיָ אָמַרְתִּי לִשְׁמֹר דְּבָרֶיךָ: חִלִּיתִי פָנֶיךָ בְכָל לֵב חָנֵּנִי כְּאִמְרָתֶךָ: חִשַּׁבְתִּי דְרָכָי וָאָשִׁיבָה רַגְלַי אֶל עֵדֹתֶיךָ: חַשְׁתִּי וְלֹא הִתְמַהְמָהְתִּי לִשְׁמֹר מִצְוֹתֶיךָ: חֶבְלֵי רְשָׁעִים עִוְּדֻנִי תּוֹרָתְךָ לֹא שָׁכָחְתִּי: חֲצוֹת לַיְלָה אָקוּם לְהוֹדוֹת לָךְ עַל מִשְׁפְּטֵי צִדְקֶךָ: חָבֵר אָנִי לְכָל אֲשֶׁר יְרֵאוּךָ וּלְשֹׁמְרֵי פִּקּוּדֶיךָ: חַסְדְּךָ יְיָ מָלְאָה הָאָרֶץ חֻקֶּיךָ לַמְּדֵנִי:

ט טוֹב עָשִׂיתָ עִם עַבְדְּךָ יְיָ כִּדְבָרֶךָ: טוּב טַעַם וָדַעַת לַמְּדֵנִי כִּי בְמִצְוֹתֶיךָ הֶאֱמָנְתִּי: טֶרֶם אֶעֱנֶה אֲנִי שֹׁגֵג וְעַתָּה אִמְרָתְךָ שָׁמָרְתִּי: טוֹב אַתָּה וּמֵטִיב לַמְּדֵנִי חֻקֶּיךָ: טָפְלוּ עָלַי שֶׁקֶר זֵדִים אֲנִי בְּכָל לֵב אֶצֹּר פִּקּוּדֶיךָ: טָפַשׁ כַּחֵלֶב לִבָּם אֲנִי תּוֹרָתְךָ שִׁעֲשָׁעְתִּי: טוֹב לִי כִּי עֻנֵּיתִי לְמַעַן אֶלְמַד חֻקֶּיךָ: טוֹב לִי תוֹרַת פִּיךָ מֵאַלְפֵי זָהָב וָכָסֶף:

י יָדֶיךָ עָשׂוּנִי וַיְכוֹנְנוּנִי הֲבִינֵנִי וְאֶלְמְדָה מִצְוֹתֶיךָ: יְרֵאֶיךָ יִרְאוּנִי וְיִשְׂמָחוּ כִּי לִדְבָרְךָ יִחָלְתִּי: יָדַעְתִּי יְיָ כִּי צֶדֶק מִשְׁפָּטֶיךָ וֶאֱמוּנָה עִנִּיתָנִי: יְהִי נָא חַסְדְּךָ לְנַחֲמֵנִי כְּאִמְרָתְךָ לְעַבְדֶּךָ: יְבֹאוּנִי רַחֲמֶיךָ וְאֶחְיֶה כִּי תוֹרָתְךָ שַׁעֲשֻׁעָי: יֵבֹשׁוּ זֵדִים כִּי שֶׁקֶר עִוְּתוּנִי אֲנִי אָשִׂיחַ בְּפִקּוּדֶיךָ: יָשׁוּבוּ לִי יְרֵאֶיךָ וְיֹדְעֵי עֵדֹתֶיךָ: יְהִי לִבִּי תָמִים בְּחֻקֶּיךָ לְמַעַן לֹא אֵבוֹשׁ:

כ כָּלְתָה לִתְשׁוּעָתְךָ נַפְשִׁי לִדְבָרְךָ יִחָלְתִּי: כָּלוּ עֵינַי לְאִמְרָתֶךָ לֵאמֹר מָתַי תְּנַחֲמֵנִי: כִּי הָיִיתִי כְּנֹאד בְּקִיטוֹר חֻקֶּיךָ לֹא שָׁכָחְתִּי: כַּמָּה יְמֵי עַבְדֶּךָ מָתַי תַּעֲשֶׂה בְרֹדְפַי מִשְׁפָּט: כָּרוּ לִי זֵדִים שִׁיחוֹת אֲשֶׁר לֹא כְתוֹרָתֶךָ: כָּל מִצְוֹתֶיךָ אֱמוּנָה שֶׁקֶר רְדָפוּנִי עָזְרֵנִי: כִּמְעַט כִּלּוּנִי בָאָרֶץ וַאֲנִי לֹא עָזַבְתִּי פִקֻּדֶיךָ: כְּחַסְדְּךָ חַיֵּנִי וְאֶשְׁמְרָה עֵדוּת פִּיךָ:

ל לְעוֹלָם יְיָ דְּבָרְךָ נִצָּב בַּשָּׁמָיִם: לְדֹר וָדֹר אֱמוּנָתֶךָ כּוֹנַנְתָּ אֶרֶץ וַתַּעֲמֹד: לְמִשְׁפָּטֶיךָ עָמְדוּ הַיּוֹם כִּי הַכֹּל עֲבָדֶיךָ: לוּלֵי תוֹרָתְךָ שַׁעֲשֻׁעָי אָז אָבַדְתִּי בְעָנְיִי: לְעוֹלָם לֹא אֶשְׁכַּח פִּקּוּדֶיךָ כִּי בָם חִיִּיתָנִי: לְךָ אֲנִי הוֹשִׁיעֵנִי כִּי פִקּוּדֶיךָ דָרָשְׁתִּי: לִי קִוּוּ רְשָׁעִים לְאַבְּדֵנִי עֵדֹתֶיךָ אֶתְבּוֹנָן: לְכָל תִּכְלָה רָאִיתִי קֵץ רְחָבָה מִצְוָתְךָ מְאֹד:

מ מָה אָהַבְתִּי תוֹרָתֶךָ כָּל הַיּוֹם הִיא שִׂיחָתִי: מֵאֹיְבַי תְּחַכְּמֵנִי מִצְוֹתֶךָ כִּי לְעוֹלָם הִיא לִי: מִכָּל מְלַמְּדַי הִשְׂכַּלְתִּי כִּי עֵדְוֹתֶיךָ שִׂיחָה לִי: מִזְּקֵנִים אֶתְבּוֹנָן כִּי פִקּוּדֶיךָ נָצָרְתִּי: מִכָּל אֹרַח רָע כָּלִאתִי רַגְלָי לְמַעַן אֶשְׁמֹר דְּבָרֶךָ: מִמִּשְׁפָּטֶיךָ לֹא סָרְתִּי כִּי אַתָּה הוֹרֵתָנִי: מַה נִּמְלְצוּ לְחִכִּי אִמְרָתֶךָ מִדְּבַשׁ לְפִי: מִפִּקּוּדֶיךָ אֶתְבּוֹנָן עַל כֵּן שָׂנֵאתִי כָּל אֹרַח שָׁקֶר:

נ נֵר לְרַגְלִי דְבָרֶךָ וְאוֹר לִנְתִיבָתִי: נִשְׁבַּעְתִּי וָאֲקַיֵּמָה לִשְׁמֹר מִשְׁפְּטֵי צִדְקֶךָ: נַעֲנֵיתִי עַד מְאֹד יְיָ חַיֵּנִי כִדְבָרֶךָ: נִדְבוֹת פִּי רְצֵה נָא יְיָ וּמִשְׁפָּטֶיךָ לַמְּדֵנִי: נַפְשִׁי בְכַפִּי תָמִיד וְתוֹרָתְךָ לֹא שָׁכָחְתִּי: נָתְנוּ רְשָׁעִים פַּח לִי וּמִפִּקּוּדֶיךָ לֹא תָעִיתִי: נָחַלְתִּי עֵדְוֹתֶיךָ לְעוֹלָם כִּי שְׂשׂוֹן לִבִּי הֵמָּה: נָטִיתִי לִבִּי לַעֲשׂוֹת חֻקֶּיךָ לְעוֹלָם עֵקֶב:

ס סֵעֲפִים שָׂנֵאתִי וְתוֹרָתְךָ אָהָבְתִּי: סִתְרִי וּמָגִנִּי אַתָּה לִדְבָרְךָ יִחָלְתִּי: סוּרוּ מִמֶּנִּי מְרֵעִים וְאֶצְּרָה מִצְוֹת אֱלֹהָי: סָמְכֵנִי כְאִמְרָתְךָ וְאֶחְיֶה וְאַל תְּבִישֵׁנִי מִשִּׂבְרִי: סְעָדֵנִי וְאִוָּשֵׁעָה וְאֶשְׁעָה בְחֻקֶּיךָ תָמִיד: סָלִיתָ כָּל שׁוֹגִים מֵחֻקֶּיךָ כִּי שֶׁקֶר תַּרְמִיתָם: סִגִים הִשְׁבַּתָּ כָל רִשְׁעֵי אָרֶץ לָכֵן אָהַבְתִּי עֵדֹתֶיךָ: סָמַר מִפַּחְדְּךָ בְשָׂרִי וּמִמִּשְׁפָּטֶיךָ יָרֵאתִי:

ע עָשִׂיתִי מִשְׁפָּט וָצֶדֶק בַּל תַּנִּיחֵנִי לְעֹשְׁקָי: עֲרֹב עַבְדְּךָ לְטוֹב אַל יַעַשְׁקֻנִי זֵדִים: עֵינַי כָּלוּ לִישׁוּעָתֶךָ וּלְאִמְרַת צִדְקֶךָ: עֲשֵׂה עִם עַבְדְּךָ כְחַסְדֶּךָ וְחֻקֶּיךָ לַמְּדֵנִי: עַבְדְּךָ אָנִי הֲבִינֵנִי וְאֵדְעָה עֵדֹתֶיךָ: עֵת לַעֲשׂוֹת לַיְיָ הֵפֵרוּ תּוֹרָתֶךָ: עַל כֵּן אָהַבְתִּי מִצְוֹתֶיךָ מִזָּהָב וּמִפָּז: עַל כֵּן כָּל פִּקּוּדֵי כֹל יִשָּׁרְתִּי כָּל אֹרַח שֶׁקֶר שָׂנֵאתִי:

פ פְּלָאוֹת עֵדְוֹתֶיךָ עַל כֵּן נְצָרָתַם נַפְשִׁי: פֵּתַח דְּבָרֶיךָ יָאִיר מֵבִין פְּתָיִים: פִּי פָעַרְתִּי וָאֶשְׁאָפָה כִּי לְמִצְוֹתֶיךָ יָאָבְתִּי: פְּנֵה אֵלַי וְחָנֵּנִי כְּמִשְׁפָּט לְאֹהֲבֵי שְׁמֶךָ: פְּעָמַי הָכֵן בְּאִמְרָתֶךָ וְאַל תַּשְׁלֶט בִּי כָל אָוֶן: פְּדֵנִי מֵעֹשֶׁק אָדָם וְאֶשְׁמְרָה פִּקּוּדֶיךָ: פָּנֶיךָ הָאֵר בְּעַבְדֶּךָ וְלַמְּדֵנִי אֶת חֻקֶּיךָ: פַּלְגֵי מַיִם יָרְדוּ עֵינָי עַל לֹא שָׁמְרוּ תוֹרָתֶךָ:

צ צַדִּיק אַתָּה יְיָ וְיָשָׁר מִשְׁפָּטֶיךָ: צִוִּיתָ צֶדֶק עֵדֹתֶיךָ וֶאֱמוּנָה מְאֹד: צִמְּתַתְנִי קִנְאָתִי כִּי שָׁכְחוּ דְבָרֶיךָ צָרָי: צְרוּפָה אִמְרָתְךָ מְאֹד וְעַבְדְּךָ אֲהֵבָהּ: צָעִיר אָנֹכִי וְנִבְזֶה פִּקֻּדֶיךָ לֹא שָׁכָחְתִּי: צִדְקָתְךָ צֶדֶק לְעוֹלָם וְתוֹרָתְךָ אֱמֶת: צַר וּמָצוֹק מְצָאוּנִי מִצְוֹתֶיךָ שַׁעֲשֻׁעָי: צֶדֶק עֵדְוֹתֶיךָ לְעוֹלָם הֲבִינֵנִי וְאֶחְיֶה:

ק קָרָאתִי בְכָל לֵב עֲנֵנִי יְיָ חֻקֶּיךָ אֶצֹּרָה: קְרָאתִיךָ הוֹשִׁיעֵנִי וְאֶשְׁמְרָה עֵדֹתֶיךָ: קִדַּמְתִּי בַנֶּשֶׁף וָאֲשַׁוֵּעָה לִדְבָרְךָ יִחָלְתִּי: קִדְּמוּ עֵינַי אַשְׁמֻרוֹת לָשִׂיחַ בְּאִמְרָתֶךָ: קוֹלִי שִׁמְעָה כְחַסְדֶּךָ יְיָ כְּמִשְׁפָּטֶךָ חַיֵּנִי: קָרְבוּ רֹדְפֵי זִמָּה מִתּוֹרָתְךָ רָחָקוּ: קָרוֹב אַתָּה יְיָ וְכָל מִצְוֹתֶיךָ אֱמֶת: קֶדֶם יָדַעְתִּי מֵעֵדֹתֶיךָ כִּי לְעוֹלָם יְסַדְתָּם:

ר רְאֵה עָנְיִי וְחַלְּצֵנִי כִּי תוֹרָתְךָ לֹא שָׁכָחְתִּי: רִיבָה רִיבִי וּגְאָלֵנִי לְאִמְרָתְךָ חַיֵּנִי: רָחוֹק מֵרְשָׁעִים יְשׁוּעָה כִּי חֻקֶּיךָ לֹא דָרָשׁוּ: רַחֲמֶיךָ רַבִּים יְיָ כְּמִשְׁפָּטֶיךָ חַיֵּנִי: רַבִּים רֹדְפַי וְצָרָי מֵעֵדְוֹתֶיךָ לֹא נָטִיתִי: רָאִיתִי בֹגְדִים וָאֶתְקוֹטָטָה אֲשֶׁר אִמְרָתְךָ לֹא שָׁמָרוּ: רְאֵה כִּי פִקּוּדֶיךָ אָהָבְתִּי יְיָ כְּחַסְדְּךָ חַיֵּנִי: רֹאשׁ דְּבָרְךָ אֱמֶת וּלְעוֹלָם כָּל מִשְׁפַּט צִדְקֶךָ:

ש שָׂרִים רְדָפוּנִי חִנָּם וּמִדְּבָרְךָ פָּחַד לִבִּי: שָׂשׂ אָנֹכִי עַל אִמְרָתֶךָ כְּמוֹצֵא שָׁלָל רָב: שֶׁקֶר שָׂנֵאתִי וַאֲתַעֵבָה תוֹרָתְךָ אָהָבְתִּי: שֶׁבַע בַּיּוֹם הִלַּלְתִּיךָ עַל מִשְׁפְּטֵי צִדְקֶךָ: שָׁלוֹם רָב לְאֹהֲבֵי תוֹרָתֶךָ וְאֵין לָמוֹ מִכְשׁוֹל: שִׂבַּרְתִּי לִישׁוּעָתְךָ יְיָ וּמִצְוֹתֶיךָ עָשִׂיתִי: שָׁמְרָה נַפְשִׁי עֵדֹתֶיךָ וָאֹהֲבֵם מְאֹד: שָׁמַרְתִּי פִקּוּדֶיךָ וְעֵדֹתֶיךָ כִּי כָל דְּרָכַי נֶגְדֶּךָ:

ת תִּקְרַב רִנָּתִי לְפָנֶיךָ יְיָ כִּדְבָרְךָ הֲבִינֵנִי: תָּבוֹא תְּחִנָּתִי לְפָנֶיךָ כְּאִמְרָתְךָ הַצִּילֵנִי: תַּבַּעְנָה שְׂפָתַי תְּהִלָּה כִּי תְלַמְּדֵנִי חֻקֶּיךָ: תַּעַן לְשׁוֹנִי אִמְרָתֶךָ כִּי כָל מִצְוֹתֶיךָ צֶּדֶק: תְּהִי יָדְךָ לְעָזְרֵנִי כִּי פִקּוּדֶיךָ בָחָרְתִּי: תָּאַבְתִּי לִישׁוּעָתְךָ יְיָ וְתוֹרָתְךָ שַׁעֲשֻׁעָי: תְּחִי נַפְשִׁי וּתְהַלְלֶךָּ וּמִשְׁפָּטֶךָ יַעְזְרֻנִי: תָּעִיתִי כְּשֶׂה אֹבֵד בַּקֵּשׁ עַבְדֶּךָ כִּי מִצְוֹתֶיךָ לֹא שָׁכָחְתִּי:

The Final Days and Moments

Throughout the history of the Jewish people, the time when the soul departs from this world has been regarded with great awe and trepidation. Many people would typically spend their last days deep in prayer and repentance, searching their hearts, and preparing to meet their Maker.

Yet one must also recognize that the culmination of a life on earth is not the end. Rather it represents a new beginning; one that builds upon all of the good thoughts, deeds and actions done throughout one's life.

The Jewish Perspective

The following parable helps define this experience: A king sent his prince on a mission to a faraway land and gave him a scroll with instructions. The king ordered the prince to return only after accomplishing the mission. If the prince would fail and come back early, the king would be disappointed. The king would then send the prince back again to the faraway place.

After many long, hard years, the prince felt his time to return was approaching. He believed the goal was accomplished. However, he was not sure that he had done everything precisely as his father had instructed. He re-read the scroll again and again, matching its content with the reality before him. "Did I do it right? Am I ready to return home and face my father? Could I have done any better?" As the date approached, the young prince grew increasingly anxious.

Finally, the big day arrived and the prince stood before his father. Before relating his accomplishments, he begged the king to listen to his request. "Father, look favorably upon my achievements. Do not just view the result of my work; rather, look at the effort that I put into it. Please forgive me if I have fallen short in fulfilling your mission, for I want nothing but to please you."

Like the prince, we are each put in this world with a mission (see page 15), and before we return our soul to our Maker (better even, years before); we must review our life and spiritual accomplishments. We must ask, "Did I lead my life in concert with my soul's mission? Am I ready to meet my Maker? Did I fill my days with spirituality and holiness, or did I squander away my time with foolishness?"

This type of accounting can prepare one to face his Day of Judgment assured that the gates of Heaven will be opened wide upon one's arrival.

Putting Things In Order

Jewish law deals with all aspects of life, including passing on. Following are laws and traditions regarding putting one's spiritual and material affairs in order.

Material Affairs

It is important to write a will under the guidance of a competent rabbi, even while one is perfectly healthy. If one is not capable of writing such a document, he may verbally instruct others to write down his wishes.

One should indicate:

- If he owes any money, or if money is owed to him.
- If he is guarding anything that someone deposited with him.
- How to dispose of his property and belongings.
- That his funeral and burial be in accordance with Jewish law.
- That his descendants should follow Jewish ways and tradtions.

One should not bequeath all his property to strangers and leave his heirs empty-handed, even if they did not treat him properly. Additionally, one should will a portion of one's property or money to charity.

Spiritual Affairs

One should take stock of his spiritual state and commit to improve whatever he can. If his heart is full of repentance, even in the final second, he is given entrance to Heaven. As we find in the *Mishna*, "Anyone who confesses is guaranteed a place in the World to Come." Our sages have instituted a set of prayers called *Viduy*, Confession (see following chapter). This should be recited before one feels his final moments are approaching.

Notes for Caregivers

• A person in the final days or hours of life is considered alive in all respects. It is forbidden to bring or hasten his death. Doing so is considered shedding blood. Proper halachic guidance in this area is extremely important, for these are very severe matters in Jewish law. Before making any medical decisions, one should seek the advice of an experienced rabbi who specializes in this area of Jewish law.

• When death is imminent, it is forbidden to touch or move the person, except to provide life-saving medical intervention and/or to provide water to drink (see page 62).

• It is forbidden for the family to prepare for the funeral while the person is still alive. (Writing a will and arranging for a plot, may be done in advance.)

The Viduy - Confession

The returning of one's soul to God at the end of its journey in this world is probably the most profound moment in a person's life. It is for this purpose that our sages prepared a special set of prayers called *Viduy*, Confession, to be recited before one departs from this world. These prayers evoke God's mercy, and bring great atonement upon the person.

Viduy reminds us that what really matters is our relationship with God and with our fellow man, and not material possessions or accomplishments. It is a truly powerful message for everyone.

Preparing for the Viduy

One should not delay reciting Viduy out of fear that it may be a bad omen. Many people have recited the Viduy and gone on to live many long years. In fact, saying the Viduy is helpful for one's recovery, as sincere repentance brings merit to the person and can nullify a severe decree from Heaven.

It is best for Viduy to be recited with a clear mind. Therefore, one should say it before he becomes too weak. If one cannot speak, he may say the Viduy in his heart.

Below are some laws concerning the recitation of the Viduy. However, it is a good idea to seek the guidance of a competent rabbi in these final moments.

- Viduy is recited by both men and women of any age.

- It is recited on any day, even on Shabbat and Jewish holidays and on days when *Tachnun* (supplications of forgiveness) are not recited.

- Before reciting the Viduy one should endeavor to ask forgiveness from those whom he may have caused pain or hardship.

- It is advisable to clear the room of crying relatives so that one may concentrate fully on his prayers.

- It is customary to wash one's hands ritually before reciting Viduy. Take a large cup of water in the left hand, pour it over the entire right hand, covering up to the wrist. Take the cup in the right hand, and pour it over the entire left hand, covering up to the wrist. Repeat two additional times.

- Men should wear a *Kippah* or *Yarmulka*, and a pair of *Tzitzit* (four-cornered garment with ritual fringes). Some also don a *Gartel* (special prayer sash).

- If the person's children are present, he should exhort them to follow the ways of the Torah.

- Once Viduy is recited, and death seems imminent, one should not leave the person alone (see page 62). Those who remain with the person should recite Psalms for his recovery.

The Viduy Prayers

While there are various customs concerning the order of the Viduy prayers, or different additions, the underlying theme remains the same. We have presented a common format below. One may also add prayers or Psalms as one wishes.

Try to recite the entire Viduy. If it is not possible, say at least from *Adon Olam* (page 58) onwards. If one is even further pressed, one should recite the verses from *Shema Yisroel* onward (page 61). The least one should say is "*Let my death be an atonement for my sins,*" and to recite the verse of Shema.

Modeh ani l'fönechö,	מוֹדֶה אֲנִי לְפָנֶיךָ,
adonöy elohai, vay-lohay avosai,	יְיָ אֱלֹהַי, וֵאלֹהֵי אֲבוֹתַי,
she-r'fu-ösi b'yödechö umisösi	שֶׁרְפוּאָתִי בְּיָדֶךְ וּמִיתָתִי
b'yödechö. Y'hi rötzon mil'fönechö,	בְּיָדֶךְ : יְהִי רָצוֹן מִלְּפָנֶיךָ,
she-tirpö-ayni r'fu-öh sh'laymöh,	שֶׁתִּרְפָּאֵנִי רְפוּאָה שְׁלֵמָה,
v'im ömus, t'hay misösi cha-pöröh al	וְאִם אָמוּת, תְּהֵא מִיתָתִי כַּפָּרָה עַל

51

köl chatö-im va-avonos uf'shö-im
she-chötösi v'she-övisi v'shepösha-ti
l'fönechö, v'sayn chelki b'gan
ayden, v'zakayni lö-olöm habö
ha-tzöfun la-tzadikim.

כָּל חֲטָאִים וַעֲוֹנוֹת וּפְשָׁעִים
שֶׁחָטָאתִי וְשֶׁעָוִיתִי וְשֶׁפָּשַׁעְתִּי
לְפָנֶיךָ, וְתֵן חֶלְקִי בְּגַן
עֵדֶן, וְזַכֵּנִי לְעוֹלָם הַבָּא
הַצָּפוּן לַצַּדִּיקִים:

I acknowledge before You, Lord my God and the God of my fathers, that my recovery and my death are in Your hands. May it be Your will that You heal me with total recovery, but, if I die, may my death be an atonement for all the errors, iniquities, and willful sins that I have erred, sinned and transgressed before You, and may You grant my share in the Garden of Eden, and grant me the merit to abide in the World to Come which is vouchsafed for the righteous.

Elo-haynu vay-lohay avosaynu,
tövo l'fönechö t'filösaynu,
v'al tis-alam mit'chinösaynu,
she-ayn önu azay fönim uk'shay oref
lomar l'fönechö adonöy el-ohaynu
vay-lohay avosaynu, tza-dikim
anachnu v'lo chö-tönu, avöl
anach-nu va-avosaynu chötönu.

אֱלֹהֵינוּ וֵאלֹהֵי אֲבוֹתֵינוּ,
תָּבֹא לְפָנֶיךָ תְּפִלָּתֵנוּ,
וְאַל תִּתְעַלַּם מִתְּחִנָּתֵנוּ,
שֶׁאֵין אָנוּ עַזֵּי פָנִים וּקְשֵׁי עֹרֶף
לוֹמַר לְפָנֶיךָ יְיָ אֱלֹהֵינוּ
וֵאלֹהֵי אֲבוֹתֵינוּ, צַדִּיקִים
אֲנַחְנוּ וְלֹא חָטָאנוּ, אֲבָל
אֲנַחְנוּ וַאֲבוֹתֵינוּ חָטָאנוּ:

Our God and God of our fathers, may our prayers come before You, and do not turn away from our supplication, for we are not so impudent and obdurate as to declare before You, Lord our God and God of our fathers, that we are righteous and have not sinned. Indeed, we and our fathers have sinned.

Ösham-nu, bögadnu, gözalnu, אָשַׁמְנוּ, בָּגַדְנוּ, גָּזַלְנוּ,
dibarnu dofi. He-evinu, v'hirsha-nu, דִּבַּרְנוּ דֹפִי: הֶעֱוִינוּ, וְהִרְשַׁעְנוּ,
zad-nu, chömas-nu, töfal'nu sheker. זַדְנוּ, חָמַסְנוּ, טָפַלְנוּ שֶׁקֶר:
Yö-atznu rö, kizavnu, latz-nu, יָעַצְנוּ רָע, כִּזַּבְנוּ, לַצְנוּ,
mörad-nu, ni-atznu, sörarnu, övinu, מָרַדְנוּ, נִאַצְנוּ, סָרַרְנוּ, עָוִינוּ,
pösha-nu, tzörarnu, ki-shinu oref. פָּשַׁעְנוּ, צָרַרְנוּ, קִשִּׁינוּ עֹרֶף:
Rösha-nu, shichas-nu, tiavnu, tö-inu, רָשַׁעְנוּ, שִׁחַתְנוּ, תִּעַבְנוּ, תָּעִינוּ,
ti-tö-nu. Sarnu mimitz-vosechö תִּעְתָּעְנוּ: סַרְנוּ מִמִּצְוֹתֶיךָ
umi-mish-pötechö ha-tovim v'lo וּמִמִּשְׁפָּטֶיךָ הַטּוֹבִים וְלֹא
shövöh lönu. V'atöh tzadik al köl שָׁוָה לָנוּ: וְאַתָּה צַדִּיק עַל כָּל
habö ölaynu, ki emes ösiso, הַבָּא עָלֵינוּ, כִּי אֱמֶת עָשִׂיתָ,
va-anachnu hirshö-nu. וַאֲנַחְנוּ הִרְשָׁעְנוּ:

We have transgressed, we have acted perfidiously, we have robbed, we have slandered. We have acted perversely and wickedly, we have willfully sinned, we have done violence, we have imputed falsely. We have given evil counsel, we have lied, we have scoffed, we have rebelled, we have provoked, we have been disobedient, we have committed iniquity, we have wantonly transgressed, we have oppressed, we have been obstinate. We have committed evil, we have acted perniciously, we have acted abominably, we have gone astray, we have led others astray. We have strayed from Your good precepts and ordinances, and it has not profited us. Indeed, You are just in all that has come upon us, for You have acted truthfully, and it is we who have acted wickedly.

One may add the "Long Confession" found in the Yom Kippur prayer book.

Following the Confession, recite the following:

Ri-bono shel olöm,	רִבּוֹנוֹ שֶׁל עוֹלָם,
y'hi rötzon mil'fönechö	יְהִי רָצוֹן מִלְּפָנֶיךָ
she-yih-yeh shölom m'nuchösi.	שֶׁיִּהְיֶה שָׁלוֹם מְנוּחָתִי:

Master of the universe, may it be Your will that my passing be in peace.

Concentrate strongly on God and His unity, and on the event of the giving of the Torah on Mount Sinai.

Between Two Worlds

The time between life and death is considered extremely sacred in Jewish tradition. On one hand, the passage marks the conclusion of the soul's journey on earth. On the other hand, death heralds the beginning of the soul's eternal life in Heaven.

Kabbalah teaches that at the moment of passing, every positive thought, word, or deed that occurred during the person's life is concentrated into a pristine spiritual light. This light is revealed to the world and in the Heavenly spheres, where it continues to shine and have an effect on those above and below.

Prayers for the Final Moments

Shir la-ma-alos, esö aynai el	שִׁיר לַמַּעֲלוֹת, אֶשָּׂא עֵינַי אֶל
he-hörim, may-ayin yövo ez-ri.	הֶהָרִים, מֵאַיִן יָבֹא עֶזְרִי׃
Ez-ri may-im adonöy, osay	עֶזְרִי מֵעִם יְיָ, עֹשֵׂה
shöma-yim vö-öretz. Al yi-tayn	שָׁמַיִם וָאָרֶץ׃ אַל יִתֵּן
la-mot rag-lechö, al yönum	לַמּוֹט רַגְלֶךָ, אַל יָנוּם
shom'rechö. Hinay lo yönum v'lo	שֹׁמְרֶךָ׃ הִנֵּה לֹא יָנוּם וְלֹא
yishön shomayr yisrö-ayl.	יִישָׁן שׁוֹמֵר יִשְׂרָאֵל׃
Adonöy shom-rechö, adonöy	יְיָ שֹׁמְרֶךָ, יְיָ
tzil'chö al yad y'minechö.	צִלְּךָ עַל יַד יְמִינֶךָ׃
Yomöm ha-shemesh lo ya-keköh,	יוֹמָם הַשֶּׁמֶשׁ לֹא יַכֶּכָּה,
v'yöray-ach ba-löylöh. Adonöy	וְיָרֵחַ בַּלָּיְלָה׃ יְיָ
yish-mör'chö mi-köl rö, yishmor es	יִשְׁמָרְךָ מִכָּל רָע, יִשְׁמֹר אֶת
naf-shechö. Adonöy yish-mör	נַפְשֶׁךָ׃ יְיָ יִשְׁמֹר
tzays'chö uvo-echö may-atöh	צֵאתְךָ וּבוֹאֶךָ, מֵעַתָּה
v'ad olöm	וְעַד עוֹלָם׃

A Song of Ascents. I lift my eyes to the mountains — from where will my help come? My help will come from the Lord, Maker of heaven and earth. He will not let your foot falter; your guardian does not slumber. Indeed, the Guardian of Israel neither slumbers nor sleeps. The Lord is your guardian; the Lord is your protective shade at your right hand. The sun will not harm you by day, nor the moon by night. The Lord will guard you from all evil; He will guard your soul. The Lord will guard your going and your coming from now and for all time.

Shir hama-alos, mima-ama-kim
k'rösichö adonöy. Adonöy
shim-öh v'koli, tih-yenöh
öz-nechöh ka-shuvos l'kol
tacha-nunöy. Im avonos tish-mör
yöh, adonöy mi ya-amod. Ki imchö
ha-s'lichöh, l'ma-an tivöray. Kivisi
adonöy kiv-söh naf-shi, v'lidvöro
ho-chöl-ti. Naf-shi la-donöy,
mi-shom'rim la-boker, shom'rim
la-boker. Ya-chayl yis-rö-ayl el
adonöy, ki im adonöy ha-chesed
v'har-bay imo f'dus. V'hu yif-deh
es yis-röayl mi-kol avonosöv.

שִׁיר הַמַּעֲלוֹת, מִמַּעֲמַקִּים
קְרָאתִיךָ יְיָ: אֲדֹנָי
שִׁמְעָה בְקוֹלִי, תִּהְיֶינָה
אָזְנֶיךָ קַשֻּׁבוֹת לְקוֹל
תַּחֲנוּנָי: אִם עֲוֹנוֹת תִּשְׁמָר
יָהּ, אֲדֹנָי מִי יַעֲמֹד: כִּי עִמְּךָ
הַסְּלִיחָה, לְמַעַן תִּוָּרֵא: קִוִּיתִי
יְיָ קִוְּתָה נַפְשִׁי, וְלִדְבָרוֹ
הוֹחָלְתִּי: נַפְשִׁי לַאדֹנָי,
מִשֹּׁמְרִים לַבֹּקֶר, שֹׁמְרִים
לַבֹּקֶר: יַחֵל יִשְׂרָאֵל אֶל
יְיָ, כִּי עִם יְיָ הַחֶסֶד
וְהַרְבֵּה עִמּוֹ פְדוּת: וְהוּא יִפְדֶּה
אֶת יִשְׂרָאֵל מִכֹּל עֲוֹנֹתָיו:

A Song of Ascents. Out of the depths I call to You, O Lord. My Lord, hearken to my voice; let Your ears be attentive to the voice of my pleas. God, if You were to preserve iniquities, my Lord, Who could survive? But forgiveness is with You, that You may be feared. I hope in the Lord; my soul hopes, and I long for His word. My soul yearns for the Lord more than [night] watchmen [waiting] for the morning, wait for the morning. Israel, put your hope in the Lord, for with the Lord there is kindness; with Him there is abounding deliverance. And He will redeem Israel from all its iniquities.

Yo-shayv b'sayser el-yon,
b'tzayl sha-dai yis-lonön. Omar
la-donöy mach-si um'tzudösi, elohai

יֹשֵׁב בְּסֵתֶר עֶלְיוֹן,
בְּצֵל שַׁדַּי יִתְלוֹנָן: אֹמַר
לַייָ מַחְסִי וּמְצוּדָתִי, אֱלֹהַי

ev-tach bo. Ki hu ya-tzil'chö mi-pach
yökush, mi-dever havos. B'ev-röso
yösech löch v'sachas k'nöföv tech-seh,
tzinöh v'sochayröh amito. Lo sirö
mi-pachad löy-löh, may-chaytz yö-uf
yo-möm. Midever bö-ofel ya-haloch,
mi-ketev yöshud tzö-höröy-im. Yipol
mi-tzid'chö elef ur'vövö mimi-nechö,
aylechö lo yigösh. Rak b'ay-nechö
sabit, v'shilumas r'shö-im tir-eh. Ki
atöh adonöy mach-si, el-yon sam-tö
m'o-nechö. Lo s'uneh ay-lechö rö-öh,
v'negah lo yik-rav b'ö-hö-lechö. Ki
mal-öchöv y'tzaveh löch, lish-mör'chö
b'chöl d'rö-chechö. Al kapa-yim
yisö-un'chö, pen ti-gof bö-even
rag-lechö. Al sha-chal vö-fesen
tid roch, tii-mos k'fir v'sanin. Ki vi
chöshak va-afaltay-hu, asag-vayhu ki
yöda sh'mi. Yikrö-ayni v'e-enayhu,
imo ö-nochi v'tzörö, achal'tzayhu
va-achab'dayhu. Orech yömim
asbi-ayhu, v'ar-ayhu bi-shu-ösi.

אֶבְטַח בּוֹ: כִּי הוּא יַצִּילְךָ מִפַּח
יָקוּשׁ, מִדֶּבֶר הַוּוֹת: בְּאֶבְרָתוֹ
יָסֶךְ לָךְ וְתַחַת כְּנָפָיו
תֶּחְסֶה, צִנָּה וְסֹחֵרָה אֲמִתּוֹ: לֹא תִירָא
מִפַּחַד לָיְלָה, מֵחֵץ יָעוּף
יוֹמָם: מִדֶּבֶר בָּאֹפֶל יַהֲלֹךְ,
מִקֶּטֶב יָשׁוּד צָהֳרָיִם: יִפֹּל
מִצִּדְּךָ אֶלֶף וּרְבָבָה מִימִינֶךָ,
אֵלֶיךָ לֹא יִגָּשׁ: רַק בְּעֵינֶיךָ
תַבִּיט, וְשִׁלֻּמַת רְשָׁעִים תִּרְאֶה: כִּי
אַתָּה יְיָ מַחְסִי, עֶלְיוֹן שַׂמְתָּ
מְעוֹנֶךָ: לֹא תְאֻנֶּה אֵלֶיךָ רָעָה,
וְנֶגַע לֹא יִקְרַב בְּאָהֳלֶךָ: כִּי
מַלְאָכָיו יְצַוֶּה לָךְ, לִשְׁמָרְךָ
בְּכָל דְּרָכֶיךָ: עַל כַּפַּיִם
יִשָּׂאוּנְךָ, פֶּן תִּגֹּף בָּאֶבֶן
רַגְלֶךָ: עַל שַׁחַל וָפֶתֶן
תִּדְרֹךְ, תִּרְמֹס כְּפִיר וְתַנִּין: כִּי בִי
חָשַׁק וַאֲפַלְּטֵהוּ, אֲשַׂגְּבֵהוּ כִּי
יָדַע שְׁמִי: יִקְרָאֵנִי וְאֶעֱנֵהוּ,
עִמּוֹ אָנֹכִי בְצָרָה, אֲחַלְּצֵהוּ
וַאֲכַבְּדֵהוּ: אֹרֶךְ יָמִים
אַשְׂבִּיעֵהוּ, וְאַרְאֵהוּ בִּישׁוּעָתִי:

You Who dwells in the shelter of the Most High, Who abides in the shadow of the Omnipotent, I say [to you] of the Lord Who is my refuge and my stronghold, my God in Whom I trust, that He will save you from the ensnaring trap, from the destructive pestilence. He will cover you with His pinions and you will find refuge under His wings; His truth is a shield and an armor. You will not fear the terror of the night, nor the arrow that flies by day, the pestilence that prowls in the darkness, nor the destruction that ravages at noon. A thousand may fall at your [left] side, and ten thousand at your right, but it shall not reach you. You need only look with your eyes, and you will see the retribution of the wicked. Because you [have said,] "The Lord is my shelter," and you have made the Most High your haven, no evil will befall you, no plague will come near your tent. For He will instruct His angels in your behalf, to guard you in all your ways. They will carry you in their hands, lest you hurt your foot on a rock. You will tread upon the lion and the viper; you will trample upon the young lion and the serpent. Because he desires Me, I will deliver him; I will fortify him for he knows My Name. When he calls on Me, I will answer him; I am with him in distress, I will deliver him and honor him. I will satisfy him with long life, and show him My deliverance.

Adon olöm asher mö-lach,	אֲדוֹן עוֹלָם אֲשֶׁר מָלַךְ,
b'terem köl y'tzur niv-rö.	בְּטֶרֶם כָּל יְצוּר נִבְרָא :
L'ays na-aso v'chef-tzo kol,	לְעֵת נַעֲשָׂה בְחֶפְצוֹ כֹּל,
azai melech sh'mo nikrö.	אֲזַי מֶלֶךְ שְׁמוֹ נִקְרָא :
V'acharei kich-los ha-kol, l'vado	וְאַחֲרֵי כִּכְלוֹת הַכֹּל, לְבַדּוֹ
yim-loch norö. V'hu hö-yöh v'hu	יִמְלֹךְ נוֹרָא : וְהוּא הָיָה וְהוּא
ho-veh, v'hu yih-yeh b'sif-öröh.	הֹוֶה, וְהוּא יִהְיֶה בְּתִפְאָרָה :
V'hu echöd v'ayn shay-ni,	וְהוּא אֶחָד וְאֵין שֵׁנִי,
l'ham-shil lo l'hach-biröh.	לְהַמְשִׁיל לוֹ לְהַחְבִּירָה :
B'li ray-shis b'li sach-lis,	בְּלִי רֵאשִׁית בְּלִי תַכְלִית,

v'lo hö-oz v'hamis-röh. V'hu	וְלוֹ הָעֹז וְהַמִּשְׂרָה : וְהוּא
ayli v'chai go-ali, v'tzur chevli	אֵלִי וְחַי גּוֹאֲלִי, וְצוּר חֶבְלִי
b'ays tzöröh. V'hu nisi	בְּעֵת צָרָה : וְהוּא נִסִּי
umö-nos li, m'nös kosi b'yom	וּמָנוֹס לִי, מְנָת כּוֹסִי בְּיוֹם
ekrö. B'yödo af-kid ruchi,	אֶקְרָא : בְּיָדוֹ אַפְקִיד רוּחִי,
b'ays ishan v'ö-iröh. V'im ruchi	בְּעֵת אִישַׁן וְאָעִירָה : וְעִם רוּחִי
g'vi-yösi, adonöy li v'lo irö.	גְּוִיָּתִי, יְיָ לִי וְלֹא אִירָא :

Lord of the universe, Who reigned before anything was created – at the time when by His will all things were made, then was His name proclaimed King. And after all things shall cease to be, the Awesome One will reign alone. He was, He is, and He shall be in glory. He is one, and there is no other to compare to Him, to consort with Him. Without beginning, without end, power and dominion belong to Him. He is my God and my ever-living Redeemer, the strength of my lot in time of distress. He is my banner and my refuge, my portion on the day I call. Into His hand I entrust my spirit, when I sleep and when I wake. And with my soul, my body too, the Lord is with me, I shall not fear.

Önö b'cho-ach g'dulas y'min'chö,	אָנָּא בְּכֹחַ גְּדֻלַּת יְמִינְךָ,
tatir tz'ruröh. Ka-bayl ri-nas am'chö,	תַּתִּיר צְרוּרָה : קַבֵּל רִנַּת עַמְּךָ,
sag'vaynu taha-raynu, noröh.	שַׂגְּבֵנוּ טַהֲרֵנוּ, נוֹרָא :
Nö gibor, dor'shay yichud'chö,	נָא גִבּוֹר, דּוֹרְשֵׁי יִחוּדְךָ,
k'vövas shöm'raym. Bör'chaym	כְּבָבַת שָׁמְרֵם : בָּרְכֵם
taha-raym, racha-may tzid'kös'chö	טַהֲרֵם, רַחֲמֵי צִדְקָתְךָ
tömid göm'laym. Chasin ködosh,	תָּמִיד גָּמְלֵם : חֲסִין קָדוֹשׁ,
b'rov tuv'chö na-hayl adö-sechö.	בְּרוֹב טוּבְךָ נַהֵל עֲדָתֶךָ :
Yöchid, gay-eh, l'am'chö p'nay,	יָחִיד, גֵּאֶה, לְעַמְּךָ פְּנֵה,

zoch'ray k'dushö-sechö. Shav-ösaynu
kabayl, ush'ma tza-akö-saynu,
yoday-a ta-alumos. Böruch shaym
k'vod mal'chuso l'olöm vö-ed.

זוֹכְרֵי קְדֻשָּׁתֶךָ: שַׁוְעָתֵנוּ
קַבֵּל, וּשְׁמַע צַעֲקָתֵנוּ,
יוֹדֵעַ תַּעֲלוּמוֹת: בָּרוּךְ שֵׁם
כְּבוֹד מַלְכוּתוֹ לְעוֹלָם וָעֶד :

We implore you, by the great power of Your right hand, release the captive. Accept the prayer of Your people; strengthen us, purify us, Awesome One. Mighty One, we beseech You, guard as the apple of the eye those who seek Your Oneness. Bless them, cleanse them; bestow upon them forever Your merciful righteousness. Powerful, Holy One, in Your abounding goodness, guide Your congregation. Only and Exalted One, turn to Your people who are mindful of Your holiness. Accept our supplication and hear our cry, You Who knows secret thoughts. Blessed be the name of the glory of His kingdom forever and ever.

V'al kayn n'ka-veh l'chö
adonöy elo-haynu, lir-os
m'hayröh b'sif-eres uzechö, l'ha-avir
gilu-lim min hö-öretz v'hö-elilim
köros yiköray-sun, l'sakayn olöm
b'mal'chus shadai, v'chöl b'nay vösör
yik-r'u vish'mechö, l'hafnos ay-lechö
köl rish'ay öretz. Ya-kiru v'yay-d'u köl
yosh'vay say-vayl, ki l'chö tichra köl
berech, tishöva köl löshon. L'fönecho
adonöy elo-haynu yich-r'u v'yipolu,
v'lich'vod shim'chö y'kör yi-taynu,.

וְעַל כֵּן נְקַוֶּה לְךָ
יְיָ אֱלֹהֵינוּ, לִרְאוֹת
מְהֵרָה בְּתִפְאֶרֶת עֻזֶּךָ, לְהַעֲבִיר
גִּלּוּלִים מִן הָאָרֶץ וְהָאֱלִילִים
כָּרוֹת יִכָּרֵתוּן, לְתַקֵּן עוֹלָם
בְּמַלְכוּת שַׁדַּי, וְכָל בְּנֵי בָשָׂר
יִקְרְאוּ בִשְׁמֶךָ, לְהַפְנוֹת אֵלֶיךָ
כָּל רִשְׁעֵי אָרֶץ. יַכִּירוּ וְיֵדְעוּ כָּל
יוֹשְׁבֵי תֵבֵל, כִּי לְךָ תִּכְרַע כָּל
בֶּרֶךְ, תִּשָּׁבַע כָּל לָשׁוֹן. לְפָנֶיךָ
יְיָ אֱלֹהֵינוּ יִכְרְעוּ וְיִפֹּלוּ,
וְלִכְבוֹד שִׁמְךָ יְקָר יִתֵּנוּ,

60

vi-kab'lu chulöm alay-hem es ol mal'chuschö, v'simloch alay-hem m'hayröh l'olöm vö-ed, ki ha-mal'chus shel'chö hi, ul'ol'may ad tim-loch b'chövod, ka-kösuv b'sorösechö, adonöy yim-loch l'olöm vö-ed. V'ne-emar, v'hö-yöh adonöy l'melech al köl hö-öretz, ba-yom ha-hu yih-yeh adonöy echöd ush'mo echöd.

וִיקַבְּלוּ כֻלָּם עֲלֵיהֶם אֶת עוֹל מַלְכוּתֶךָ, וְתִמְלוֹךְ עֲלֵיהֶם מְהֵרָה לְעוֹלָם וָעֶד, כִּי הַמַּלְכוּת שֶׁלְּךָ הִיא, וּלְעוֹלְמֵי עַד תִּמְלוֹךְ בְּכָבוֹד, כַּכָּתוּב בְּתוֹרָתֶךָ: יְיָ יִמְלֹךְ לְעֹלָם וָעֶד. וְנֶאֱמַר: וְהָיָה יְיָ לְמֶלֶךְ עַל כָּל הָאָרֶץ, בַּיּוֹם הַהוּא יִהְיֶה יְיָ אֶחָד וּשְׁמוֹ אֶחָד:

And therefore we hope to You, Lord our God, that we may speedily behold the splendor of Your might, to banish idolatry from the earth and false gods will be utterly destroyed; to perfect the world under the sovereignty of the Almighty. All mankind shall invoke Your Name, to turn to You all the wicked of the earth. Then all the inhabitants of the world will recognize and know that every knee should bend to You, every tongue should swear [by Your Name]. Before You, Lord our God, they will bow and prostrate themselves, and give honor to the glory of Your Name; and they will all take upon themselves the yoke of Your kingdom. May You soon reign over them forever and ever, for kingship is Yours, and to all eternity You will reign in glory, as it is written in Your Torah: The Lord will reign forever and ever. And it is said: The Lord shall be King over the entire earth; on that day the Lord shall be One and His Name One.

At the very last moments, all present, including the person himself (if possible), recite the following passages aloud, and with intense concentration:

Sh'ma yisrö-ayl, adonöy elo-haynu, adonöy echöd.

שְׁמַע יִשְׂרָאֵל, יְיָ אֱלֹהֵינוּ, יְיָ אֶחָד:

Hear, O Israel, the Lord is our God, the Lord is One.

61

Recite the following verse in an undertone:

Böruch shaym k'vod mal'chuso   בָּרוּךְ שֵׁם כְּבוֹד מַלְכוּתוֹ

l'olöm vö-ed. (*Say three times.*)   לְעוֹלָם וָעֶד : (ג״פ)

Blessed be the name of the glory of His kingdom forever and ever. (Say three times.)

Recite the following aloud:

Adonöy hu hö-elohim. (*Say seven times.*)   יְיָ הוּא הָאֱלֹהִים : (ז״פ)

God is the Lord. (Say seven times.)

Adonöy melech, adonöy möloch,   יְיָ מֶלֶךְ, יְיָ מָלָךְ,

adonöy yim-loch l'olöm vö-ed.   יְיָ יִמְלוֹךְ לְעוֹלָם וָעֶד :

The Lord is King, the Lord was King, the Lord will be King forever and ever.

Following the Last Prayers

• Once death seems imminent, one should not leave the person alone, and those remaining should recite Psalms and pray for the recovery of the person.

• One should try to ensure that the person's spouse and children are present at the moment of passing. However, only those who can contain their grief should be in the room.

• If possible, there should be a *Minyan* (quorum of ten Jewish males over age thirteen) at the bedside to recite Psalms.

It is praiseworthy if the men present immersed in a *Mikvah* (ritual bath) that day. If the presence of a Minyan will frighten the person (for it may indicate to him that death is imminent), the people should stand off to the side or by the door.

• Those in the room should be careful not to wail or cry loudly. This causes the person who is leaving the world great pain and discomfort and prolongs his ordeal.

• It is customary not to stand at the foot or at the head of the bed during the person's passing.

• Before the person enters the throes of death, one should make sure that the person's limbs are not extended or hanging off of the bed. If they are, they should be moved back.

• Some kindle candles in the room, and place one candle near (but not too close to) the head of the bed.

• One may converse with the person if he expresses the desire. It is preferable to discuss Torah thoughts so that his soul departs while involved in holy matters.

• Once the person has entered the actual throes of death, it is forbidden to move or touch him, as this may hasten his death; in the eyes of Jewish law, it is considered like shedding blood. The exceptions are providing life-saving intervention or water for the person to drink.

• According to the Torah, a *Kohen* (descendants of Aaron, the high-priest) is not permitted to come in contact with a deceased body. This means that a Kohen cannot be within six feet of where a deceased person may lie; the Kohen may also not be under the same roof as the deceased.

For the Kohen, this Biblical prohibition is as serious as the laws forbidding eating unkosher food and violating the Shabbat. Thus a Kohen may not be present at the time of passing. If no one would be present otherwise, he should arrange for someone else to be there.

However, for his father, mother, wife (as long as he was permitted to marry her according to Jewish law), son, daughter, brother [including half-brother from his father's side], sister who is not married [including half-sister from the father's side], it becomes a mitzva for him to make himself ritually impure by his attendance.

Following the Passing

At the time a person passes away, God has reached down and gathered His spark, drawing the soul into His abode. Everyone present at the time of passing should recite the following (some also recite the "*Tziduk Hadin*," page 116):

Böruch da-yan hö-emes.   :בָּרוּךְ דַּיַן הָאֱמֶת
Blessed is the True Judge.

The family begins to mourn the moment the soul leaves the body. One mourns his father, mother, spouse, son, daughter, brother, and sister [including half-brother and half-sister].

The Duty of the Moment

The duty of the moment is to ensure a prompt and proper burial in accordance with Jewish law and tradition.

Kabbalah teaches that the separation of the soul and body is a very gradual process, and following passing the soul hovers near the body. The soul does not feel free to ascend to heaven until the body is prepared for burial in the traditional Jewish way and buried in the ground. We therefore must do all we can to expedite this process, enabling the soul to rest in peace to expedite this process, enabling the soul to rest in peace quickly.

Treating the Deceased with Respect

The Torah teaches that there is great holiness remaining in the body after death. This is likened to the treatment of a Torah scroll that is no longer fit for use — we do not treat it disrespectfully nor discard it, God forbid, but inter it gently in the ground. We do no less for a human body that housed a Godly soul.

One must go to great lengths to treat the deceased body with utmost awe, dignity, and respect — as if the person were still alive. Jewish tradition outlines clearly how one shows this respect, as will be explained below.

Chevra Kaddisha
The Jewish Burial Society

Caring for the deceased is one of the greatest mitzvot in the Torah and a task reserved for the pious and righteous people in each community. Many cities, especially large metropolitan areas, have dedicated teams of people who form the *Chevra Kaddisha* (lit. the holy brotherhood), also known as the Jewish

Burial Society. The members of the Chevra Kaddisha cleanse, purify and prepare the body for burial. At the same time, they ensure that the actual burial process is done in strict accordance with Jewish law and tradition.

A Prompt Burial

It is forbidden to leave the deceased unburied overnight, as it states in the Torah, "You shall bury him on that same day" (Deuteronomy 21:23). One may delay the burial for the deceased's honor (i.e. to perform the *Tahara* purification, to obtain shrouds or a burial plot, or to gather close family, etc.), but not unnecessarily or for the convenience of others.

A Moral Obligation

The deceased is utterly dependent upon his loved ones to make sure the burial process is performed according to Jewish tradition as practiced for over four thousand years. It is thus morally incumbent on those responsible for the care of the deceased to call on the services of the Chevra Kaddisha and to ensure a proper kosher burial.

When it comes to death and burial one thing is certain: we generally have only one chance to do it right.

Doing Things Right

The laws of burial and mourning in Jewish tradition are complex, and fine details may vary in some situations, therefore one must consult a competent rabbi or the Chevra Kaddisha for complete guidance.

Highlights of the Jewish laws concerning preparing the body for burial, the burial plot, proper dress for the deceased, choosing a casket, the funeral, and so on, follow in the next chapter.

Notes for Caregivers

• Do not touch or move the deceased for at least fifteen minutes from the moment of passing.

• If the passing occurred on a weekday, immediately call the local *Chevra Kaddisha* (the Jewish Burial Society) and ask for further instructions. If one contracted a Jewish funeral home, make sure that the funeral director is aware that the deceased is to receive a proper *Tahara* (purification of the body), a *Shomer* (a Jewish person to stay with the deceased until burial), *Tachrichim* (traditional shrouds), a "traditional kosher" casket, and is to be cared for by the Chevra Kaddisha.

• If the passing occurred on Shabbat or a Jewish holiday, all the laws of forbidden activities remain in effect, including preparations for burial. One should consult a competent rabbi or the Chevra Kaddisha following the conclusion of Shabbat or the holiday.

• If the passing occurred in a hospital, notify the staff that the Chevra Kaddisha will be attending to the deceased, and they should wait for instructions before doing anything on their own (including removing monitor leads, tubes, etc.). If the hospital staff insists on moving the body to the hospital mortuary, a Jewish person must accompany them and remain within viewing distance of the deceased until members of the Chevra Kaddisha arrive and take charge.

• In a case where there are tubes or I.V. lines attached to the deceased, one should not remove them; instead, wait for instructions from the Chevra Kaddisha. If for any reason they must be removed, the tubes should be cut by a Jew, and the part nearest or in the body should remain attached.

• It is also very important to ensure that any clothing, towels, linens, or similar items that may contain blood or fluids of the deceased, should be saved in a bag and given to the Chevra Kaddisha to be buried with the body.

• It is a Biblical commandment to bury the deceased as soon as possible, and no later than 24-hours from the moment of passing. If the passing occurred in the morning, one should try to ensure that the deceased is prepared for burial and buried before dusk of the same day. If this is not possible, the burial should take place on the following day. If the deceased will be buried in another country, or in other circumstances, consult the Chevra Kaddisha or a competent rabbi for guidance.

• Delaying a prompt burial for any reason other than ensuring a proper, kosher burial is considered a disgrace to the deceased. One should be aware that the soul is in turmoil and does not find rest until the body is properly buried.

• After fifteen minutes, the eyes of the deceased are closed by his children, relatives, or caregiver, and he is completely covered with a sheet. If any limbs are in an awkward position, one should return them to their normal, resting position.

• Light a candle and place it near the head of the deceased (except on Shabbat and Jewish holidays). On Jewish holidays (except on Yom Kippur), some permit kindling the candle with a flame that had been lit before the onset of the holiday.

• All mirrors and pictures of people in the room should be covered (or turned around).

• All exposed water in the room or home at the time of passing should be discarded.

• If possible, open the windows of the room.

• Relatives and friends who are nearby may enter the room to ask for forgiveness from the deceased (and to forgive) for any pain or hard feelings that might have come between them. If one was not nearby at the time of passing, he may do so later at the memorial service or at the gravesite.

• Conversations in the presence of the deceased should be restricted to discussing the funeral arrangements, describing the person's qualities, or reciting Psalms.

• The deceased must be guarded by a Jewish person until the burial. This person is called a *Shomer* (lit. guard). This role may be filled by family members, friends, or by members of the Chevra Kaddisha. The family or funeral home can also hire someone to serve as a Shomer. One may alternate with the Shomer and take turns.

• One must conduct himself in a respectful manner when in the presence of the deceased. Eating, drinking, smoking, sleeping, and frivolous talk are understandably forbidden. Instead one should recite Psalms and think about holy matters.

71

• It is forbidden to learn Torah or wear a *Tallit* or *Tefillin* within six feet of the deceased since he can no longer perform any mitzvot.

• It is permissible to recite Psalms in honor of the deceased.

• If the body is transported anywhere by car, a Jewish person should either drive, or accompany the driver.

Preparing the Deceased for the Chevra Kaddisha

• If the passing occurred on a weekday, the deceased is covered with a sheet. The covered body is then gently moved from the bed to the floor by three or four (preferably Jewish) people, and placed so that the feet are facing the door. One should put something under the deceased's head to support it.

• In a hospital or hospice environment, or where it is unfeasible to do the above, it is sufficient to leave the body in the bed until the Chevra Kaddisha arrives. The body must be completely covered out of respect for the deceased.

• On Shabbat, the body is not moved. It is covered with a sheet until the conclusion of the Shabbat.

Extremely Important!

• Embalming, pre-funeral cosmetic surgery, and cremation are all explicitly forbidden according to the Torah. These are very severe matters and should not be treated lightly.

• Autopsies are considered a pre-funeral surgical procedure and is strongly forbidden. In the case of a suspected crime, or other unusual situations, one must consult a rabbi who specializes in this area of Jewish law for guidance.

• Organ donation, in general, is a very complicated matter in Jewish law (see page 35). One must consult a rabbi who specializes in this area of Jewish law for guidance before taking any action or making any decisions in this matter.

Selected Psalms to Be Recited

The following Psalms are customarily recited when in the presence of the deceased. One can also recite additional Psalms.

Mizmor l'dövid, adonöy ro-i lo	מִזְמוֹר לְדָוִד, יְיָ רֹעִי לֹא
ech-sör. Bin'os deshe yarbi-tzayni,	אֶחְסָר: בִּנְאוֹת דֶּשֶׁא יַרְבִּיצֵנִי,
al may m'nuchos y'naha-layni.	עַל מֵי מְנֻחוֹת יְנַהֲלֵנִי:
Nafshi y'sho-vayv, yan-chayni	נַפְשִׁי יְשׁוֹבֵב, יַנְחֵנִי בְמַעְגְּלֵי
v'ma-g'lay tzedek l'ma-an sh'mo.	צֶדֶק לְמַעַן שְׁמוֹ:

73

Gam ki ay-laych b'gay tzal-mö-ves
lo irö rö, ki atöh i-modi,
shiv-t'chö umish-antechö hay-möh
y'na-chamuni. Ta-aroch l'fönai
shul-chön neged tzo-r'röy, dishan-tö
va-shemen roshi, kosi r'vö-yöh. Ach
tov vö-chesed yir-d'funi köl y'may
cha-yöy, v'shavti b'vays adonöy
l'orech yömim.

גַּם כִּי אֵלֵךְ בְּגֵיא צַלְמָוֶת
לֹא אִירָא רָע, כִּי אַתָּה עִמָּדִי,
שִׁבְטְךָ וּמִשְׁעַנְתֶּךָ הֵמָּה
יְנַחֲמֻנִי : תַּעֲרֹךְ לְפָנַי
שֻׁלְחָן נֶגֶד צֹרְרָי, דִּשַּׁנְתָּ
בַשֶּׁמֶן רֹאשִׁי, כּוֹסִי רְוָיָה : אַךְ
טוֹב וָחֶסֶד יִרְדְּפוּנִי כָּל יְמֵי
חַיָּי, וְשַׁבְתִּי בְּבֵית יְיָ
לְאֹרֶךְ יָמִים :

A Psalm by David. The Lord is my shepherd; I shall lack nothing. He makes me lie down in green pastures; He leads me beside still waters. He revives my soul; He directs me in the paths of righteousness for the sake of His Name. Even if I walk in the valley of the shadow of death, I will fear no evil, for You are with me; Your rod and Your staff – they will comfort me. You will prepare a table before my enemies; You have anointed my head with oil; my cup is full. Only goodness and kindness shall follow me all the days of my life, and I shall dwell in the House of the Lord for many long years.

Vihi no-am ado-nöy elo-haynu
ölaynu, uma-asay yö-daynu
ko-n'nöh ölaynu, uma-asay
yödaynu ko-n'nayhu.

וִיהִי נֹעַם אֲדֹנָי אֱלֹהֵינוּ
עָלֵינוּ, וּמַעֲשֵׂה יָדֵינוּ
כּוֹנְנָה עָלֵינוּ. וּמַעֲשֵׂה
יָדֵינוּ כּוֹנְנֵהוּ :

May the pleasantness of the Lord our God be upon us; establish for us the work of our hands; establish the work of our hands.

Yo-shayv b'sayser el-yon, b'tzayl sha-dai yis-lonön. Omar la-donöy mach-si um'tzudösi, elohai ev-tach bo. Ki hu ya-tzil'chö mi-pach yökush, mi-dever havos. B'ev-röso yösech löch v'sachas k'nöföv tech-seh, tzinöh v'sochayröh amito. Lo sirö mi-pachad löy-löh, may-chaytz yö-uf yo-möm. Midever bö-ofel ya-haloch, mi-ketev yöshud tzö-höröy-im. Yipol mi-tzid'chö elef ur'vövö mimi-nechö, aylechö lo yigösh. Rak b'ay-nechö sabit, v'shilumas r'shö-im tir-eh. Ki atöh adonöy mach-si, el-yon sam-tö m'o-nechö. Lo s'uneh ay-lechö rö-öh, v'negah lo yik-rav b'ö-hö-lechö. Ki mal-öchöv y'tzaveh löch, lish-mör'chö b'chöl d'rö-chechö. Al kapa-yim yisö-un'chö, pen ti-gof bö-even rag-lechö. Al sha-chal vö-fesen tid-roch, tir-mos k'fir v'sanin. Ki vi chöshak va-afaltay-hu, asag-vayhu ki yöda sh'mi. Yikrö-ayni

יֹשֵׁב בְּסֵתֶר עֶלְיוֹן,
בְּצֵל שַׁדַּי יִתְלוֹנָן : אֹמַר
לַיְיָ מַחְסִי וּמְצוּדָתִי, אֱלֹהַי
אֶבְטַח בּוֹ : כִּי הוּא יַצִּילְךָ מִפַּח
יָקוּשׁ, מִדֶּבֶר הַוּוֹת : בְּאֶבְרָתוֹ
יָסֶךְ לָךְ וְתַחַת כְּנָפָיו
תֶּחְסֶה, צִנָּה וְסֹחֵרָה אֲמִתּוֹ :
לֹא תִירָא מִפַּחַד לָיְלָה,
מֵחֵץ יָעוּף יוֹמָם : מִדֶּבֶר
בָּאֹפֶל יַהֲלֹךְ, מִקֶּטֶב יָשׁוּד
צָהֳרָיִם : יִפֹּל מִצִּדְּךָ אֶלֶף
וּרְבָבָה מִימִינֶךָ, אֵלֶיךָ לֹא
יִגָּשׁ : רַק בְּעֵינֶיךָ תַבִּיט,
וְשִׁלֻּמַת רְשָׁעִים תִּרְאֶה : כִּי אַתָּה
יְיָ מַחְסִי, עֶלְיוֹן שַׂמְתָּ
מְעוֹנֶךָ : לֹא תְאֻנֶּה אֵלֶיךָ רָעָה,
וְנֶגַע לֹא יִקְרַב בְּאָהֳלֶךָ :
כִּי מַלְאָכָיו יְצַוֶּה לָּךְ,
לִשְׁמָרְךָ בְּכָל דְּרָכֶיךָ :
עַל כַּפַּיִם יִשָּׂאוּנְךָ, פֶּן תִּגֹּף
בָּאֶבֶן רַגְלֶךָ : עַל שַׁחַל
וָפֶתֶן תִּדְרֹךְ, תִּרְמֹס
כְּפִיר וְתַנִּין : כִּי בִי חָשַׁק וַאֲפַלְּטֵהוּ,
אֲשַׂגְּבֵהוּ כִּי יָדַע שְׁמִי : יִקְרָאֵנִי

v'e-enayhu, imo ö-nochi v'tzörö,	וְאֶעֱנֵהוּ, עִמּוֹ אָנֹכִי בְצָרָה,
achal'tzayhu va-achab'dayhu.	אֲחַלְּצֵהוּ וַאֲכַבְּדֵהוּ:
Orech yömim asbi-ayhu,	אֹרֶךְ יָמִים אַשְׂבִּיעֵהוּ,
v'ar-ayhu bi-shu-ösi.	וְאַרְאֵהוּ בִּישׁוּעָתִי:

You Who dwells in the shelter of the Most High, Who abides in the shadow of the Omnipotent, I say [to you] of the Lord Who is my refuge and my stronghold, my God in Whom I trust, that He will save you from the ensnaring trap, from the destructive pestilence. He will cover you with His pinions and you will find refuge under His wings; His truth is a shield and an armor. You will not fear the terror of the night, nor the arrow that flies by day, the pestilence that prowls in the darkness, nor the destruction that ravages at noon. A thousand may fall at your [left] side, and ten thousand at your right, but it shall not reach you. You need only look with your eyes, and you will see the retribution of the wicked. Because you [have said,] "The Lord is my shelter," and you have made the Most High your haven, no evil will befall you, no plague will come near your tent. For He will instruct His angels in your behalf, to guard you in all your ways. They will carry you in their hands, lest you hurt your foot on a rock. You will tread upon the lion and the viper; you will trample upon the young lion and the serpent. Because he desires Me, I will deliver him; I will fortify him for he knows My Name. When he calls on Me, I will answer him; I am with him in distress, I will deliver him and honor him. I will satisfy him with long life, and show him My deliverance.

The State of Onain

The first stage of mourning is called *Aninut*, and the mourner is called an *Onain*. Loosely translated, the word Onain means one who is in "deep distress."

The Onain must stop what he or she is doing when he learns that a close relative has passed away, and occupy himself solely with arranging for a proper Jewish burial.

Since the Torah requires the burial to take place as quickly as possible, an Onain is exempt from all positive mitzvot requiring action (i.e. prayer, *Tefillin*, blessings before and after eating, etc.), until the burial is completed. All prohibitions (i.e. "do not...") remain in full effect.

When Others See to the Arrangements

Today, the *Chevra Kaddisha* (Jewish Burial Society) takes care of the entire burial process. Thus once the deceased is given over to their care, some authorities do not restrict the Onain from performing mitzvot. However, most authorities maintain that one is still not required to do so until after the burial. Consult a competent rabbi for guidance.

The following activities are forbidden to an Onain:

- Working and/or engaging in business

- Showering or bathing

- Using cosmetics, lotions, oils, and perfumes

- Having marital relations

- Attending joyous events (weddings, parties, etc.)

- Greeting people (i.e. "Hello," "How are you")

- Cutting hair or shaving

- Eating a regular meal at a table

- Eating meat or drinking wine, or other strong drink

- Reciting the blessings before and after eating

- Studying Torah (except the laws of mourning and works that promote repentance).

- An Onain cannot be counted for a *Minyan* (a quorum for prayer services). For exceptions, consult a competent rabbi.

- If one is not in the same city as the deceased and hears of the passing by phone, and there are others to see to the burial needs locally, he is not considered an Onain until he arrives for the funeral. Otherwise, he begins mourning once the burial is completed. In either case he is not permitted to don Tefillin until after the burial.

• Since one must close his business when he is in mourning, he may temporarily sell it to a friend (if closing the business will cause him great financial harm). Consult a competent rabbi who specializes in the area of Jewish law.

• A *Brit Milah* (circumcision of a child) is not postponed until after the burial, and an Onain may even be the *Sandek* (one who holds the baby during the circumcision). A *Pidyon Haben* (redemption of the firstborn son) is postponed until after the burial.

On Shabbat and Jewish Holidays

• On Shabbat and Jewish holidays (or if the passing occurred late Friday afternoon), one may eat meat and drink wine and fulfill all the other mitzvot of Shabbat and the holiday, since mourning is forbidden on these days. However, he must observe aspects of mourning in private (i.e. he cannot study Torah, or have marital relations). At the conclusion of Shabbat, he does not pray the *Maariv* (evening) service, not does he recite the *Havdallah* prayer. It is recited later, following the burial, over beer or another permitted beverage, and only the final blessing of *Hamavdil* is recited.

• If the passing occurred on Rosh Hashana, he does not become an Onain and must hear the blowing of the Shofar.

• If the passing occurred on the holiday of Sukkot, one may eat in the Sukkah and make *Kiddush* (if no one else can make it for him), as well as fulfill the mitzva of the Lulav and Etrog.

• If the passing occurred on the holiday of Chanuka, one appoints a messenger to kindle the *Menora* for him. If there is no one available, he may light it himself without a blessing.

• If the passing occurred on the day leading into (*Erev*) Purim, one should hear the *Megilla* that night. If it was during Purim day, one should hear the *Megilla* following the burial.

• If the passing occurred on the evening prior to Passover, one appoints a messenger to search for the *Chometz* (leaven), but he must nullify the Chometz himself.

• During the *Omer* counting (between Passover and Shavuot), one should count without a blessing and resume counting with a blessing after the burial. If possible, he should hear the blessing from another person and answer *Amen*.

• If the passing occurred on the Ninth of Av (*Tisha B'Av*), one must fast, but one is not required to attend the synagogue for the *Kinnot* (dirges).

A Jewish Funeral

A Jewish funeral is distinguished by its simplicity, humility, and solemnity. Its general format has not changed for over four thousand years. It is usually held within 24 hours of passing, but no later than three days. The mitzva of accompanying the dead to the final resting place is so great it supersedes all other mitzvot, including Torah study. However, before the funeral can take place, the body of the deceased must be prepared for burial in accordance with Jewish tradition.

It is a moral obligation for those caring for the deceased to ensure that the proper preparation is carried out. If one has contracted with a funeral home, one should make sure that the funeral director and the staff know that the family wants a traditional Jewish funeral, with all that it entails (see below).

An Historical Overview

Since Biblical times, specially trained members of the community called the *Chevra Kaddisha* (lit. the holy brotherhood), or Jewish Burial Society, prepared the body of the deceased for burial. Following this, the funeral procession proceeded from the home of the deceased to the cemetery.

Pallbearers would include close friends, and in the case of a great sage or leader, students.

The entire community stopped what they were doing and joined the funeral procession. This was especially true in the case of a *Met Mitzva*, a person who had died with no family to ensure a proper Jewish burial.

The funeral procession paused near the gravesite, Psalms were recited, and the officiating rabbi eulogized the deceased. This was followed by the performance of the *Kriah* by the mourners (the traditional rending of the outer garments). At that point the deceased was placed in the grave and men of the community covered the grave with earth. After the grave was filled in, the mourners recited the *Kaddish* (a prayer sanctifying God) and then retired to the home of the deceased, where the family would observe the *Shiva* (the first seven-day period of mourning).

The general format of the Jewish funeral as outlined above has been observed by Jewish communities in all parts of the world throughout our long history. Variations are limited to the use of a casket or not (i.e. in Israel, the deceased is buried without a casket), the recitation of certain Psalms or prayers, and the delivery of eulogies. But the main components as outlined above have remained the same.

The Components of a Jewish Funeral

1. *Tahara* (Ritual washing of the body): Before the funeral, the body of the deceased is prepared for burial by the Chevra Kaddisha in accordance with Jewish law and tradition. This includes ritually washing and dressing the deceased while certain prayers are recited, and placing the body in a kosher casket. Men attend to men, and women to women.

2. *Kriah* (Rending of one's garments): During the funeral service, the mourners recite a blessing and rend their garments in expression of grief. This includes one who lost a father, mother, spouse, son, daughter, brother, and sister.

3. *Kavod* (Paying Respects) — Accompanying the casket to its final resting place: This includes gathering at the funeral home or chapel, or at the gravesite prior to the burial, in order to recite Psalms and to speak of the merits of the deceased.

4. *Kevurah* (Burial) — Burial in a Jewish cemetery: This includes the recitation of Kaddish and other prayers by the mourners.

5. *Nechama* (Condolence): Before leaving the gravesite, all present form a pathway comprised of rows through which the mourners will walk as they leave the gravesite. As they pass, the congregated console the mourners.

A Jewish Funeral is a Jew's Right

Receiving a proper Jewish funeral is so significant and important that many Jews have mandated this in their wills, thereby ensuring that they will be buried in the ways of their ancestors. While one is still alive, one should make it clear to loved ones that his or her funeral must adhere to Jewish tradition.

If one did not leave explicit directions, family or caregivers must ensure that the funeral director will provide the services requested (i.e. traditional *Tahara* – washing and purification of the body, a *Shomer* – a Jewish person to stay with the deceased until burial, *Tachrichim* – traditional shrouds, a "kosher" casket, and to be cared for by the Chevra Kaddisha).

Some funeral homes (even those with Jewish sounding names) will not offer these services *unless specifically requested* (and insisted upon) by the family. That said, responsible funeral directors will go out of their way to accommodate the needs of the family once those needs are made known.

Scheduling the Funeral

It is a Biblical commandment to bury one's deceased immediately after passing, and it is forbidden to leave the deceased unburied overnight unless it is for his honor (i.e. to perform a proper Tahara, obtain shrouds, arrange for a burial plot, gather family, etc.).

One may not put off the burial unnecessarily, for our sages state that the soul is in turmoil until the body is properly buried in the ground. Therefore, there needs to be a great sense of urgency to complete the burial as quickly as possible.

If the passing occurred in the morning, one should try to ensure that the deceased is prepared for burial and buried before dusk of the same day. If this is not possible, the burial should take place on the following day.

If the deceased will be buried in another country, or in other circumstances, consult the Chevra Kaddisha or a competent rabbi for guidance.

Flowers, Music, Viewing

It is not the Jewish custom to send or bring flowers to a funeral or cemetery, for flowers are associated with joyous celebrations. For the same reason, music is not played or sung.

It is also forbidden to hold an "open casket" viewing. This is considered extremely disrespectful to the deceased.

When the Mourner is a Kohen

According to the Torah, a *Kohen* (descendants of Aaron, the high-priest) is not permitted to come in contact with a deceased body. This means that a Kohen cannot be within six feet of where a deceased person may lie; the Kohen may also not be under the same roof as the deceased. For the Kohen, this Biblical prohibition is as serious as the laws forbidding eating unkosher food and violating the Shabbat.

Nevertheless, the Kohen is obligated to attend the funeral of his father, mother, wife (as long as he was permitted to marry her according to Jewish law), son, daughter, brother [including half-brother from his father's side], sister who is not married [including half-sister from the father's side]. In these cases, it becomes a mitzva for him to make himself ritually impure by his attendance.

Forbidden Burial Alternatives

According to Jewish law, a Jew is to be buried as he was born — complete with all his limbs and organs. The human body is considered as sacred in death as it was in life as it contained a Godly soul. He must be buried in a traditional grave in the ground, so that the body may return to the earth.

Burial in vaults, above-ground mausoleums, crypts, and any other alternatives to a traditional ground burial are strictly forbidden according to Jewish law.

Kabbalah teaches that when a proper kosher burial is not administered, the deceased's soul is stuck in a state of turmoil and cannot find rest until the body's remains are given a proper Jewish burial and allowed to be absorbed into the earth — even after many years!

The Transgression of Cremation

Cremation is explicitly forbidden according to all authentic Jewish opinions and there are never any circumstances where it is permitted. Jewish law considers cremation as pure idol worship, and as "going in the ways of the gentiles." Any instructions to be cremated must be ignored without feelings of guilt or regret.

Aside from the permanent spiritual destruction of the link between the body and soul, if one ever witnessed the action of the "bone-crusher" that is used to pulverize the skeletal remains into the appearance of ashes after the burning of the body, no one of good heart would allow such indignity to come to someone they consider dear.

The prohibition against cremation is so severe that according to Judaism, a person is forbidden to mourn, sit Shiva, or say Kaddish for one who had himself cremated. This is because in addition to violating Torah law, the person denied God's promise of the future Resurrection of the Dead by having his body obliterated.

A proper Jewish burial affects the final peace of the soul and should never be treated lightly. Should a unique situation arise, one must consult a rabbi who specializes in this area of Jewish law for proper guidance.

The Wishes of the Deceased

If the person left specific instructions concerning his funeral and burial, we are morally obligated to do our utmost to carry them out, providing their fulfillment does not violate Jewish law. If one left instructions for actions that go against Jewish law (i.e. to be embalmed or cremated, the donation of organs for science, burial in a mixed-denomination cemetery, burial above-ground, no *Tahara* purification, the use of a metal casket, etc.), those caring for the deceased are obligated to ignore those wishes without feelings of guilt or regret. Instead one should substitute a proper Jewish burial through the local Chevra Kaddisha.

Most of the time, such requests are made out of ignorance of proper Jewish law and the severity of these matters. Judaism believes that had the person known the eternal consequences of his request, he would not have made them. In addition, now that he is in the "World of Truth," one should not cause him spiritual "pain" by deviating from the ways of the Torah.

Even if the person *knew* that what he wished went against Jewish law, we can certainly not assist him in committing a sin. On the contrary, we have an obligation to make it right for his soul, so that at least in death, he is laid to rest as a Jew. Our actions will generate merit that will advocate for him in his final judgment before God.

In a case where the requests simply deviate from local custom (i.e. the delivery of a eulogy, to be buried next to a spouse, etc.), one should seek the advice of a competent rabbi or the Chevra Kaddisha.

The *Tahara*
Preparing the Body for Burial

One of the most important elements of a proper Jewish burial is the *Tahara*, preparing the body by the Chevra Kaddisha for its final rest, until the Resurrection of the

Dead in the era of Moshiach. There is no mystery to the Tahara. It is a simple, yet dignified ritual that allows the person to meet his Maker with the utmost respect and dignity.

A proper Tahara includes cleansing, ritually washing, and dressing the deceased's body. Those who perform this *Chesed Shel Emet* (true act of kindness) recite special prayers, beseeching God to lift the soul into the Heavens and eternal rest.

It is a pity that the observance of this simple, meaningful, and vital mitzva is neither strictly observed, nor readily offered by some Jewish funeral homes unless asked for (and sometimes insisted upon) by the family.

If people only knew the merit and solace it brings to the soul of the deceased, no one would deny their loved one a kosher Tahara.

The *Tachrichim*
Shrouds and Dressing

Unlike in other religions and practices, a Jewish person is not buried in his or her usual clothing. Similarly, jewelry or other adornments are not worn.

As discussed earlier, one's soul and its spiritual rectification is far more important following death than any honor he could possibly get from his association with earthly possessions. Thus, the Jewish funeral emphasizes the spiritual and sublime over the physical and material.

According to Jewish tradition, a deceased's body is dressed in plain white *Tachrichim* (traditional shrouds). These garments are hand-made from linen or muslin and are considered fitting for someone who is about to stand before God in judgment.

Another reason given is that using simple shrouds ensures that those who cannot afford fancy clothing are not "embarrassed" that they do not have any.

In addition to Tachrichim, a man is also buried in his *Tallit* (prayer shawl). The Tallit should be given to the Chevra Kaddisha before they prepare the body for burial. In the case that a man did not have his Tallit, the funeral home will usually provide one.

Dressing the deceased in traditional Tachrichim is so important, and the meaning so profound, that Jewish law insists that the funeral be postponed until proper Tachrichim are obtained or made — even though the same *Code of Jewish Law* normally prohibits any unnecessary delays before burial.

The *Aron*
Traditional Casket

It is a Torah commandment to return the body to the earth upon passing, as it it written "Unto dust shall you return" (Genesis 3:19). Our sages teach that this means placing the body directly in the ground with no casket. In Israel, this is still the prevailing custom. In America, most, if not all, states mandate the use of caskets by law.

Nevertheless, it is not proper to bury the dead in ornate coffins. This is a gentile custom that pays honor to the person's or the relative's wealth, instead of the good deeds he performed. If one wants to truly honor the deceased, the money that could have been spent on an ornate coffin should be given to charity in the merit of the deceased.

Jewish tradition requires that the person be buried in a plain, modest, casket. The casket must be made from material that will disintegrate in the ground, allowing the body to return to the bosom of the earth as quickly as possible, and enabling the soul to attain true and final peace.

Thus, metal caskets should not be used. Some religious authorities do not even allow metal nails or bracing in a wooden casket. In their opinion, metal is the material of weapons and war, and one should not go to one's eternal peace aided by elements of war. In addition to being made of wood or other organic material, the casket interior should be plain and unadorned. It should not be lined nor filled with pillows and the like.

It is an age-old desire of Jewish people to be buried in the Land of Israel because of its sanctity, which is said to aid in the soul's atonement. When burial occurs in any other country, the Chevra Kaddisha places earth from the Land of Israel in the casket.

The *Beit Hachayim* Cemetery

According to Jewish law, a Jew should be buried among Jews. It is forbidden for a Jew to be buried in a mixed-denomination cemetery, or in a cemetery that allows the burial of questionably converted Jews.

Should a situation arise where a non-observant parent or loved one acquired a plot in such a cemetery, a rabbi who specializes in this area of Jewish law should be consulted.

The *Kever*
Grave

A kosher grave is one in which the casket is laid directly in the ground, and covered with earth until it is full and a small mound is formed on top. The grave should be at least forty inches deep, and wide and long enough for the casket.

Above-ground burial is strictly forbidden according to Jewish law, and Kabbalah adds that all alternative burial options interfere severely with the eternal rest of the soul (see page 86).

Some communities bury their loved ones in family plots, or side-by-side in the case of a spouse. Other communities will bury men and women in separate sections. Both of these approaches are permissible. One should follow the custom of his community or ask a competent rabbi for guidance.

The planting of grass or flowers on the grave is discouraged. Besides involving several transgressions, it is seen as following in the way of the gentiles.

The *Matzeivah* or *Tzion* Tombstone

Setting a tombstone at the gravesite has been a custom among Jews since Biblical times and is a fitting way to honor the deceased. The tombstone is usually placed at the head of the grave, and the plot outlined with a low lying frame.

Many erect the tombstone on the day after *Shiva* (which is eight days from burial). Others wait until the *Shloshim* (thirty days), and still others wait twelve months. One should follow the custom of his community.

The tombstone should be made from stone or granite. It should be similar to those around it, to avoid embarrassing those who cannot afford an ornate tombstone. This does not apply to erecting a special monument for a great Torah leader and sage.

It is customary to engrave the Hebrew name of the deceased and his or her father's name, as well as the Hebrew date and year of passing on the tombstone. Some also add the name of community where he lived or the name of the Tzaddik or sage whom the deceased followed.

95

On all tombstones one adds the Hebrew letters תנצב"ה, which in acrostic form means "May his (her) soul be bound in the binding of life." Others write on the heading פ"נ, which means "Here is buried."

When preparing the text for the tombstone, one should avoid embellishing the deceased's qualities and praises, since some believe that the soul will have to account for what is written there during judgment.

Carving or engraving the form of a human being on the tombstone and mounting any pictures is forbidden.

It is best to use only the Hebrew language for writing on the tombstone. It is also highly advisable to review the text with the Chevra Kaddisha or a competent rabbi before ordering the tombstone.

Kriah
Rending the Garments

According to the Torah, one of the essential elements of mourning is the performance of the *Kriah*, the rending of the outer garments by the mourners. It is designed to arouse within the mourner and all those present the ability to express their grief, and creates an "opening" for the person to release the feelings of his heart. The Kriah is performed by the mourners prior to the burial, either during the funeral service or at the gravesite (see page 104).

The following family members must tear Kriah: Father, mother, spouse, son, daughter, brother, and sister [including half-brother and half-sister].

On a more comforting note, the Kriah signifies that it is only the outer garment (representing the body) that has been torn. The soul of the deceased, and the love that the deceased and the mourners have for each other, remains, and may even grow stronger over time.

Since the proper performance of the Kriah requires one to tear, and thus quite possibly destroy one's garments, one is permitted to change into less valuable clothing prior to the Kriah.

Important note: The modern "innovation" of using a ribbon for the Kriah is insufficient. One should not mistakenly think that he fulfills the Biblical obligation this way. The mourners must still repeat the Kriah again properly.

Kavod
Paying Respects

Accompanying the deceased to his or her final resting place is a tremendous mitzva and displays great respect. One even interrupts Torah study to participate in a funeral.

A memorial service is generally held before the burial at the funeral home chapel or at the gravesite. This allows the family and community members to recite Psalms and to speak of the good qualities of the deceased.

The Funeral Service

Once the members of the *Chevra Kaddisha* (Jewish Burial Society) have completed preparing the deceased for burial, the funeral can proceed.

The family and the community gather for the funeral service either in the funeral home, synagogue, or at the cemetery. There should be at least a *Minyan* of ten Jewish males over the age of thirteen at the service and burial.

The casket is present during the service but remains closed. The Jewish custom is not to serve fancy foods, nor have flowers or music at the funeral. Those items are associated with festivity and joy, and this is a solemn occasion.

The rabbi, or designated Jewish person, begins the service by reciting Psalms, followed by the mourner's *Kriah* (ritual rending of the outer garments). Some follow this with remarks from family members or close friends. Afterwards, some close the gathering with the traditional memorial prayer *"Kel Molay Rachamim"* (O God, full of compassion).

At the conclusion of the service, the pallbearers accompany the casket to the hearse, and those who are going to be present at the burial proceed to the cemetery.

The order of prayers at a funeral may vary according to local custom. One should follow the custom of his community, or ask a competent rabbi for guidance.

The memorial service is a fitting time to give charity in memory of the deceased.

The Focus at the Funeral Service

The Jewish funeral service is more directed at honoring the deceased than comforting the mourners. Judaism does not hide from, nor try to numb, the pain of mourning.

The Torah views mourning as an important passage for mourners to experience before moving on. As a matter of fact, the Torah teaches that one should not console a mourner while his deceased lies before him. Death, as life, has its important lessons, and we must allow ourselves to hear them. Therefore, festivity, fancy foods, flowers, and music, all have no place at a Jewish funeral (or thereafter).

Thematically, the Jewish funeral emphasizes higher, more spiritual matters. True honor and respect for the deceased are achieved by recalling his or her fine character traits, special values, mitzvot he or she excelled in, and/or by telling short stories or anecdotes that will inspire the living to increase their commitment to Jewish observance and adapt the fine qualities and values of the deceased.

Sensitivity in Delivering Remarks

Our sages state that until the body is buried, the deceased hears all that is said about him. Therefore, people should be careful how they speak. Mourners and friends should also remember that the deceased is facing his final judgment in Heaven, and that the "testimony" given below is heard on High. Therefore, one should choose his words carefully, and neither praise the deceased excessively nor undeservingly, for an accounting will be demanded of him above.

Beginning the Funeral Service

The casket is present or brought in. All gathered stand. The rabbi or designated Jewish person begins with the recitation of Psalm 16 (below). Some have the custom to recite it out loud verse-by-verse, responsively.

Mich-töm l'dövid, shöm'rayni ayl ki	מִכְתָּם לְדָוִד, שָׁמְרֵנִי אֵל כִּי
chosi-si vöch. ömar-t la-donöy	חָסִיתִי בָךְ: אָמַרְתְּ לַיְיָ
adonöy ötö, tovösi bal ö-lechö.	אֲדֹנָי אָתָּה, טוֹבָתִי בַּל עָלֶיךָ:
Lik-doshim asher bö-öretz hay-möh,	לִקְדוֹשִׁים אֲשֶׁר בָּאָרֶץ הֵמָּה,

v'adiray köl chef-tzi vöm. Yir-bu
atz'vosöm achayr mö-höru, bal asich
nis-kayhem mi-döm, uval esö es
sh'mosöm al s'fösöy. Adonöy m'nös
chelki v'chosi, atöh tomich goröli.
Chavölim nöf'lu li ban'i-mim, af
nacha-lös shöf'röh ölöy. Avö-raych es
adonöy asher y'ö-tzöni, af lay-los
yis'runi chil-yosöy. Shi-visi adonöy
l'neg-di sömid, ki mimi-ni bal emot.
Löchayn sömach libi va-yögel k'vodi,
af b'söri yish-kon lö-vetach. Ki lo
sa-azov naf-shi lish'ol, lo si-tayn
chasid'chö lir-os shöchas. Todi-ayni
orach cha-yim, sova s'möchos es
pö-nechö, n'i-mos bi-min'chö netzach.

וְאַדִּירֵי כָּל חֶפְצִי בָם: יִרְבּוּ
עַצְּבוֹתָם אַחֵר מָהָרוּ, בַּל אַסִּיךְ
נִסְכֵּיהֶם מִדָּם, וּבַל אֶשָּׂא אֶת
שְׁמוֹתָם עַל שְׂפָתָי: יְיָ מְנָת
חֶלְקִי וְכוֹסִי, אַתָּה תּוֹמִיךְ גּוֹרָלִי:
חֲבָלִים נָפְלוּ לִי בַּנְּעִמִים, אַף
נַחֲלָת שָׁפְרָה עָלָי: אֲבָרֵךְ
אֶת יְיָ אֲשֶׁר יְעָצָנִי, אַף לֵילוֹת
יִסְּרוּנִי כִלְיוֹתָי: שִׁוִּיתִי יְיָ
לְנֶגְדִּי תָמִיד, כִּי מִימִינִי בַּל אֶמּוֹט:
לָכֵן שָׂמַח לִבִּי וַיָּגֶל כְּבוֹדִי,
אַף בְּשָׂרִי יִשְׁכֹּן לָבֶטַח: כִּי לֹא
תַעֲזֹב נַפְשִׁי לִשְׁאוֹל, לֹא תִתֵּן
חֲסִידְךָ לִרְאוֹת שָׁחַת: תּוֹדִיעֵנִי
אֹרַח חַיִּים, שֹׂבַע שְׂמָחוֹת אֶת
פָּנֶיךָ, נְעִמוֹת בִּימִינְךָ נֶצַח:

*A Michtam, by David. Watch over me, O God, for I have put my trust in You. You,
[my soul,] have said to God, "You are my Master; You are not obligated to benefit
me." For the sake of the holy ones who lie in the earth, and for the mighty – all my
desires are fulfilled in their merit. Those who hasten after other [gods], their sorrows
shall increase; I will not offer their libations of blood, nor take their names upon my
lips. The Lord is my allotted portion and my share; You guide my destiny. Portions
have fallen to me in pleasant places; indeed, a beautiful inheritance is mine. I bless the
Lord Who has advised me; even in the nights my intellect admonishes me. I have set
the Lord before me at all times; because He is at my right hand, I shall not falter.
Therefore my heart rejoices and my soul exults; my flesh, too, rests secure. For You will
not abandon my soul to the grave, You will not allow Your pious one to see purgatory.*

Make known to me the path of life, that I may be satiated with the joy of Your presence, with the bliss of Your right hand forever.

Some also recite Psalm 91:

Yo-shayv b'sayser el-yon,	יֹשֵׁב בְּסֵתֶר עֶלְיוֹן,
b'tzayl sha-dai yis-lonön. Omar	בְּצֵל שַׁדַּי יִתְלוֹנָן: אֹמַר
la-donöy mach-si um'tzudösi, elohai	לַיָי מַחְסִי וּמְצוּדָתִי, אֱלֹהַי
ev-tach bo. Ki hu ya-tzil'chö mi-pach	אֶבְטַח בּוֹ: כִּי הוּא יַצִּילְךָ מִפַּח
yökush, mi-dever havos. B'ev-röso	יָקוּשׁ, מִדֶּבֶר הַוּוֹת: בְּאֶבְרָתוֹ
yösech löch v'sachas k'nöföv	יָסֶךְ לָךְ וְתַחַת כְּנָפָיו
tech-seh, tzinöh v'sochayröh amito.	תֶּחְסֶה, צִנָּה וְסֹחֵרָה אֲמִתּוֹ:
Lo sirö mi-pachad löy-löh,	לֹא תִירָא מִפַּחַד לָיְלָה,
may-chaytz yö-uf yo-möm. Midever	מֵחֵץ יָעוּף יוֹמָם: מִדֶּבֶר
bö-ofel ya-haloch, mi-ketev yöshud	בָּאֹפֶל יַהֲלֹךְ, מִקֶּטֶב יָשׁוּד
tzö-höröy-im. Yipol mi-tzid'chö elef	צָהֳרָיִם: יִפֹּל מִצִּדְּךָ אֶלֶף
ur'vövö mimi-nechö, aylcchö lo	וּרְבָבָה מִימִינֶךָ, אֵלֶיךָ לֹא
yigösh. Rak b'ay-nechö sabit,	יִגָּשׁ: רַק בְּעֵינֶיךָ תַבִּיט,
v'shilumas r'shö-im tir-eh. Ki atöh	וְשִׁלֻּמַת רְשָׁעִים תִּרְאֶה: כִּי אַתָּה
adonöy mach-si, el-yon sam-tö	יְיָ מַחְסִי, עֶלְיוֹן שַׂמְתָּ
m'o-nechö. Lo s'uneh ay-lechö rö-öh,	מְעוֹנֶךָ: לֹא תְאֻנֶּה אֵלֶיךָ רָעָה,
v'negah lo yik-rav b'ö-hö-lechö.	וְנֶגַע לֹא יִקְרַב בְּאָהֳלֶךָ:
Ki mal-öchöv y'tzaveh löch,	כִּי מַלְאָכָיו יְצַוֶּה לָּךְ,
lish-mör'chö b'chöl d'rö-chechö.	לִשְׁמָרְךָ בְּכָל דְּרָכֶיךָ:

You Who dwells in the shelter of the Most High, Who abides in the shadow of the Omnipotent, I say [to you] of the Lord Who is my refuge and my stronghold, my God in Whom I trust, that He will save you from the ensnaring trap, from the destructive pestilence. He will cover you with His pinions and you will find refuge under His wings; His truth is a shield and an armor. You will not fear the terror of the night, nor the arrow that flies by day, the pestilence that prowls in the darkness, nor the destruction that ravages at noon. A thousand may fall at your [left] side, and ten thousand at your right, but it shall not reach you. You need only look with your eyes, and you will see the retribution of the wicked. Because you [have said,] "The Lord is my shelter," and you have made the Most High your haven, no evil will befall you, no plague will come near your tent. For He will instruct His angels in your behalf, to guard you in all your ways.

The *Kriah* - Rending the Garments

Following the recitation of Psalms, the mourners "tear *Kriah*." This includes one who is mourning his father, mother, spouse, son, daughter, brother, and sister [including half-brother and half-sister].

The modern "innovation" of using a ribbon for the Kriah is insufficient. One should not mistakenly think that he fulfills the Biblical obligation this way. The mourners must repeat the Kriah again properly if a ribbon was used.

When mourning a parent, one tears on the left side. For all others, one tears on the right side. If one is wearing an overcoat or raincoat, it is not necessary to tear it, only the jacket and shirt underneath. Women should wear a garment under the blouse, so that upon tearing the blouse or shirt, she is still dressed modestly.

The mourners rise and stand in a row. The officiating rabbi, or representative of the Chevra Kaddisha, makes a small starter-cut on the lapel of both the jacket and shirt with a razor or scissors, and the mourners recite the blessing below (before tearing).

Böruch atöh adonöy, בָּרוּךְ אַתָּה יְיָ,

elohay-nu melech hö-olöm, אֱלֹהֵינוּ מֶלֶךְ הָעוֹלָם,

da-yan hö-emes. דַּיַן הָאֱמֶת:

Blessed are You, Lord our God, King of the universe, the True Judge.

After the blessing is recited, tear downward from the initial cut for a length of at least four inches. (Women may use a safety-pin to maintain modesty).

One who has not performed the Kriah (or has not performed it properly), may do it within the first seven days following the burial, but without reciting the blessing. When mourning a parent, there is no time limit. The mourners wear the garments on which the Kriah was made throughout Shiva (except on Shabbat or Jewish holidays).

Forgiving and Requesting Forgiveness

Following the performance of the Kriah, it is customary for family members to forgive and request forgiveness of the deceased. This is done individually in front of the closed casket beginning with the men, followed by the women. Other relatives and friends may do the same following the service.

At this point remarks may be delivered. All may be seated.
At the conclusion of the remarks, some recite the following Memorial Prayer:

105

For a Man:

Ayl mö-lay ra-chamim, sho-chayn	אֵל מָלֵא רַחֲמִים שׁוֹכֵן
ba-m'romim, ham-tzay m'nuchö	בַּמְּרוֹמִים הַמְצֵא מְנוּחָה
n'chonöh al kan-fey hash-chinöh,	נְכוֹנָה עַל כַּנְפֵי הַשְּׁכִינָה
b'ma-alos k'doshim ut'horim	בְּמַעֲלוֹת קְדוֹשִׁים וּטְהוֹרִים
k'zohar hö-röki-a maz-hirim, es	כְּזֹהַר הָרָקִיעַ מַזְהִירִים, אֶת
nish-mas (mention his Hebrew name and	נִשְׁמַת (פלוני בן פלוני)
that of his father) she-hölach l'olömo,	שֶׁהָלַךְ לְעוֹלָמוֹ,
ba-avur she-nöd'vu tz'dököh	בַּעֲבוּר שֶׁנָּדְבוּ צְדָקָה
b'ad haz-köras nish-möso, b'gan	בְּעַד הַזְכָּרַת נִשְׁמָתוֹ, בְּגַן
ay-den t'hay m'nuchö-so, lö-chayn	עֵדֶן תְּהֵא מְנוּחָתוֹ, לָכֵן
ba-al hö-racha-mim yas-tiray-hu	בַּעַל הָרַחֲמִים יַסְתִּירֵהוּ
b'sayser k'nöföv l'olö-mim, v'yitz-ror	בְּסֵתֶר כְּנָפָיו לְעוֹלָמִים, וְיִצְרֹר
bitz'ror hacha-yim es nish-möso,	בִּצְרוֹר הַחַיִּים אֶת נִשְׁמָתוֹ,
adonöy hu nacha-löso, v'yönu-ach	יְיָ הוּא נַחֲלָתוֹ, וְיָנוּחַ
al mish-kövo b'shölom,	עַל מִשְׁכָּבוֹ בְּשָׁלוֹם,
v'no-mar ömayn.	וְנֹאמַר אָמֵן :

O God, full of compassion, Who dwells on high, grant true rest upon the wings of the Shechinah (Divine Presence), in the exalted spheres of the holy and pure, who shine as the resplendence of the firmament, to the soul of (mention his Hebrew name and that of his father) who has gone to his [supernal] world, for charity has been donated in remembrance of his soul; may his place of rest be in Gan Eden. Therefore, may the All-Merciful One shelter him with the cover of His wings forever, and bind his soul in the bond of life. The Lord is his heritage; may he rest in his resting-place in peace; and let us say: Amen.

If the gathering is held at the gravesite, proceed with the burial (page 110).
Otherwise continue on page 108.

For a Woman:

Ayl mö-lay ra-chamim, sho-chayn	אֵל מָלֵא רַחֲמִים שׁוֹכֵן
ba-m'romim, ham-tzay m'nuchö	בַּמְּרוֹמִים הַמְצֵא מְנוּחָה
n'chonöh al kan-fei hash-chinöh,	נְכוֹנָה עַל כַּנְפֵי הַשְּׁכִינָה
b'ma-alos k'doshim ut'horim	בְּמַעֲלוֹת קְדוֹשִׁים וּטְהוֹרִים
k'zohar hö-röki-a maz-hirim, es	כְּזֹהַר הָרָקִיעַ מַזְהִירִים, אֶת
nish-mas (mention her Hebrew name and	נִשְׁמַת (פלונית בן פלוני)
that of her father) she-höl-chöh l'olömöh,	שֶׁהָלְכָה לְעוֹלָמָהּ,
ba-avur she-nöd'vu tz'dököh	בַּעֲבוּר שֶׁנָּדְבוּ צְדָקָה
b'ad haz-köras nish-mösöh, b'gan	בְּעַד הַזְכָּרַת נִשְׁמָתָהּ, בְּגַן
ay-den t'hay m'nu-chösöh, lö-chayn	עֵדֶן תְּהֵא מְנוּחָתָהּ, לָכֵן
ba-al hö-racha-mim yasti-rehö b'sayser	בַּעַל הָרַחֲמִים יַסְתִּירֶהָ בְּסֵתֶר
k'nöföv l'olömim, v'yitz-ror bitz'ror	כְּנָפָיו לְעוֹלָמִים, וְיִצְרֹר בִּצְרוֹר
hacha-yim es nish-mösöh, adonöy	הַחַיִּים אֶת נִשְׁמָתָהּ, יְיָ
hu nacha lösöh, v'sönu-ach	הוּא נַחֲלָתָהּ, וְתָנוּחַ
al mish-kövöv b'shölom,	עַל מִשְׁכָּבָהּ בְּשָׁלוֹם,
v'no-mar ömayn.	וְנֹאמַר אָמֵן:

O God, full of compassion, Who dwells on high, grant true rest upon the wings of the Shechinah (Divine Presence), in the exalted spheres of the holy and pure, who shine as the resplendence of the firmament, to the soul of (mention her Hebrew name and that of her father) who has gone to her [supernal] world, for charity has been donated in remembrance of her soul; may her place of rest be in Gan Eden. Therefore, may the All-Merciful One shelter her with the cover of His wings forever, and bind her soul in the bond of life. The Lord is her heritage; may she rest in her resting-place in peace; and let us say: Amen.

If the gathering is held at the gravesite, proceed with the burial (page 110).
Otherwise continue below.

Following the Memorial Service

• The casket is carried by Jewish men (pallbearers) to the hearse. All the men walk behind it while reciting Psalms. Women follow at a small distance to maintain modesty. Since it is a great mitzva to assist in the burial, the pallbearers may let other Jewish men participate.

• It is customary that direct descendants of the deceased neither touch nor carry the casket, nor walk behind it. Instead, they proceed directly to the cemetery in their own cars.

• All males who will be within six feet of the deceased, or going to the cemetery, should tuck in their *Tzitzit* (four-cornered garment with ritual fringes). The reason for this sensitive custom is that one should not "mock" the deceased with a mitzva that he can no longer perform.

• Once the casket is placed in the hearse, the car drives slowly away, allowing everyone to follow for about half a block.

• Those continuing on to the cemetery form a line with their cars behind the hearse. Everyone else remains until the hearse and procession are out of sight.

• Sometimes the hearse may stop at another location en-route to the cemetery, such as the deceased's synagogue or yeshiva, giving the people there a chance to pay their respects. The casket usually remains in the hearse. The rear door of the hearse is opened, allowing the people to part with the deceased and to request forgiveness (and forgive). The door is closed, and the hearse begins to drive slowly away, and the people walk behind the hearse and say Psalm 91 (see page 112).

• Afterwards, everyone must wash their hands ritually: Take a large cup of water in the left hand, pour it over the entire right hand, covering up to the wrist. Take the cup in the right hand, and pour it over the entire left hand, covering up to the wrist. Repeat two additional times. It is customary to place the cup upside down after washing, and not to dry one's hands with a towel or paper, so that the memory of the deceased will linger.

• It is customary to recite Psalm 91 as one leaves a funeral. Some recite it seven times, each time sitting in a different place, to remove the spirit of impurity (see page 112).

At the Cemetery

One who has not been to a Jewish cemetery for thirty days recites the
following blessing upon arrival. Mourners do not recite it at the funeral.

Böruch atöh adonöy, elo-haynu	בָּרוּךְ אַתָּה יְיָ, אֱלֹהֵינוּ
melech hö-olöm, asher yötzar	מֶלֶךְ הָעוֹלָם, אֲשֶׁר יָצַר
es-chem ba-din, v'zön es-chem ba-din,	אֶתְכֶם בַּדִּין, וְזָן אֶתְכֶם בַּדִּין,
v'chil-kayl es-chem ba-din, v'haymis	וְכִלְכֵּל אֶתְכֶם בַּדִּין, וְהֵמִית
es-chem ba-din, v'yoday-a mis-par	אֶתְכֶם בַּדִּין, וְיוֹדֵעַ מִסְפַּר
kul'chem, v'hu ösid l'hacha-yos'chem	כֻּלְּכֶם, וְהוּא עָתִיד לְהַחֲיוֹתְכֶם
ul'ka-yaym es-chem ba-din. Böruch	וּלְקַיֵּם אֶתְכֶם בַּדִּין: בָּרוּךְ
atöh adonöy, m'cha-yeh hamay-sim.	אַתָּה יְיָ, מְחַיֵּה הַמֵּתִים:

*Blessed are You, Lord our God, King of the universe, Who created you [who lie here] in
judgment, nourished you in judgment, sustained you in judgment, and brought you to
death in judgment. He knows the number of you all and He will eventually resurrect you
and maintain you in judgment. Blessed are You, Who revives the dead.*

Atöh gi-bor l'olöm adonöy,	אַתָּה גִבּוֹר לְעוֹלָם אֲדֹנָי,
m'cha-yeh may-sim atöh, rav	מְחַיֵּה מֵתִים אַתָּה, רַב
l'hoshi-a. M'chal-kayl cha-yim	לְהוֹשִׁיעַ: מְכַלְכֵּל חַיִּים
b'chesed, m'cha-yeh may-sim	בְּחֶסֶד, מְחַיֵּה מֵתִים
b'racha-mim rabim, so-maych	בְּרַחֲמִים רַבִּים, סוֹמֵךְ
nof'lim, v'rofay cholim, umatir	נוֹפְלִים, וְרוֹפֵא חוֹלִים, וּמַתִּיר
asurim, um'ka-yaym emunöso	אֲסוּרִים, וּמְקַיֵּם אֱמוּנָתוֹ
lishay-nay öför, mi chö-mochö	לִישֵׁנֵי עָפָר, מִי כָמוֹךָ

ba-al g'vuros umi do-meh löch, בַּעַל גְּבוּרוֹת וּמִי דוֹמֶה לָּךְ,

melech may-mis um'cha-yeh מֶלֶךְ מֵמִית וּמְחַיֶּה

umatz-mi-ach y'shu-öh. וּמַצְמִיחַ יְשׁוּעָה:

You are mighty forever, my Lord; You resurrect the dead; You are powerful to save. He sustains the living with loving-kindness, resurrects the dead with great mercy, supports the falling, heals the sick, releases the bound, and fulfills His trust to those who sleep in the dust. Who is like You, mighty One! And who can be compared to You, King, Who brings death and restores life, and causes deliverance to spring forth!

V'al köl zeh anach-nu cha-yövim וְעַל כָּל זֶה אֲנַחְנוּ חַיָּבִים

l'hodos l'chö ul'yachayd es shim-chö לְהוֹדוֹת לְךָ וּלְיַחֵד אֶת שִׁמְךָ

ha-gödol ha-gibor v'ha-norö. הַגָּדוֹל הַגִּבּוֹר וְהַנּוֹרָא:

Ayn aroch l'chö adonöy elo-haynu אֵין עֲרוֹךְ לְךָ יְיָ אֱלֹהֵינוּ

bö-olöm ha-zeh, v'ayn zulös'chö בָּעוֹלָם הַזֶּה, וְאֵין זוּלָתְךָ

mal-kaynu l'cha-yay hö-olöm ha-böh. מַלְכֵּנוּ לְחַיֵּי הָעוֹלָם הַבָּא:

Efes bil-t'chö go alaynu li-mos אֶפֶס בִּלְתְּךָ גּוֹאֲלֵנוּ לִימוֹת

ha-möshi-ach, v'ayn domeh l'chö הַמָּשִׁיחַ, וְאֵין דוֹמֶה לְךָ

moshi-aynu lis-chiyas ha-maysim. מוֹשִׁיעֵנוּ לִתְחִיַּת הַמֵּתִים:

For all the above we are obligated to thankfully acknowledge You and proclaim the oneness of Your great, mighty and awesome name. There is none comparable to You, Lord our God, in this world; and none apart from You, our King, in the life of the World to Come; there is nothing without You, our Redeemer, in the days of Moshiach; and there is none like You, our Deliverer, in the era of the resurrection of the dead.

111

Carrying the Casket

The casket is carried from the hearse to the gravesite by Jewish men, usually by the Chevra Kaddisha, with the decedent's feet facing the front. It is customary that direct descendants of the deceased do not touch or carry the casket.

The Seven "Rests"

During the procession, Psalm 91 is recited seven times. Beginning from a short distance from the grave (approximately thirty feet), it is customary to halt the procession every few feet and repeat the Psalm, pausing at certain words in the final verse and reciting again from the top (see following page).

On days when *Tachnun* (supplications of forgiveness) is not recited, and when burying a woman, the stops are not made, but the Psalm is still recited seven times. According to Kabbalah, the stops serve to drive away any harmful spiritual influences. These influences are not present on days when Tachnun is not recited, nor affect women.

Yo-shayv b'sayser el-yon,	יֹשֵׁב בְּסֵתֶר עֶלְיוֹן,
b'tzayl sha-dai yis-lonön. Omar	בְּצֵל שַׁדַּי יִתְלוֹנָן : אֹמַר
la-donöy mach-si um'tzudösi, elohai	לַיָי מַחְסִי וּמְצוּדָתִי, אֱלֹהַי

ev-tach bo. Ki hu ya-tzil'chö mi-pach אֶבְטַח בּוֹ: כִּי הוּא יַצִּילְךָ מִפַּח
yökush, mi-dever havos. B'ev-röso יָקוּשׁ, מִדֶּבֶר הַוּוֹת: בְּאֶבְרָתוֹ
yösech löch v'sachas k'nöföv יָסֶךְ לָךְ וְתַחַת כְּנָפָיו
tech-seh, tzinöh v'sochayröh amito. תֶּחְסֶה, צִנָּה וְסֹחֵרָה אֲמִתּוֹ:
Lo sirö mi-pachad löy-löh, לֹא תִירָא מִפַּחַד לָיְלָה,
may-chaytz yö-uf yo-möm. Midever מֵחֵץ יָעוּף יוֹמָם: מִדֶּבֶר
bö-ofel ya-haloch, mi-ketev yöshud בָּאֹפֶל יַהֲלֹךְ, מִקֶּטֶב יָשׁוּד
tzö-höröy-im. Yipol mi-tzid'chö elef צָהֳרָיִם: יִפֹּל מִצִּדְּךָ אֶלֶף
ur'vövö mimi-nechö, aylechö lo וּרְבָבָה מִימִינֶךָ, אֵלֶיךָ לֹא
yigösh. Rak b'ay-nechö sabit, יִגָּשׁ: רַק בְּעֵינֶיךָ תַבִּיט,
v'shilumas r'shö-im tir-eh. Ki atöh וְשִׁלֻּמַת רְשָׁעִים תִּרְאֶה: כִּי אַתָּה
adonöy mach-si, el-yon sam-tö יְיָ מַחְסִי, עֶלְיוֹן שַׂמְתָּ
m'o-nechö. Lo s'uneh ay-lechö rö-öh, מְעוֹנֶךָ: לֹא תְאֻנֶּה אֵלֶיךָ רָעָה,
v'negah lo yik-rav b'ö-hö-lechö. וְנֶגַע לֹא יִקְרַב בְּאָהֳלֶךָ:
Ki (1st rest, begin from the top) כִּי (עמידה ראשונה, ומתחילים עוד הפעם
mal-öchöv (2nd rest, recite from the top) יושב בסתר וגו') מַלְאָכָיו (עמידה ב')
y'tzaveh (3rd rest, recite from the top) יְצַוֶּה (עמידה ג')
löch (4th rest, recite from the top) לָךְ (עמידה ד')
lish-mör'chö (5th rest, recite from the top) לִשְׁמָרְךָ (עמידה ה')
b'chöl (6th rest, recite from the top) בְּכָל (עמידה ו')
d'rö-chechö (7th rest, recite from the top). דְּרָכֶיךָ (עמידה אחרונה).

You who dwells in the shelter of the Most High, who abides in the shadow of the Omnipotent, I say [to you] of the Lord who is my refuge and my stronghold, my God in Whom I trust, that He will save you from the ensnaring trap, from the destructive pestilence. He will cover you with His pinions and you will find refuge under His wings; His truth is a shield and an armor. You will not fear the terror of the night, nor the arrow that flies by day, the pestilence that prowls in the darkness, nor the destruction that ravages at noon. A thousand may fall, at your [left] side, and ten thousand at your right, but it shall not reach you. You need only look with your eyes, and you will see the retribution of the wicked. Because you [have said,] "The Lord is my shelter," and you have made the Most High your haven, no evil will befall you, no plague will come near your tent. (See above for the seven rests) For He will instruct His angels in your behalf, to guard you in all your ways.

Placing the Casket into the Grave

If one has not yet performed the *Kriah* (obligatory rending of the garments by mourners), do so now (see page 104).

Before the casket is lowered into the grave, it is fitting to part with the deceased and, if one has not done so earlier at the memorial service, ask for forgiveness (and to forgive) for any pain or hard feelings that might have come between them.

Following the recitation of certain Psalms and prayers, the casket is laid in the grave by the Chevra Kaddisha. It is set in the direction so that the deceased's head rests where the tombstone will be erected, and the feet are positioned to the front of the grave. It is then covered with earth and the grave is filled until a small mound is formed on top. This is followed by the recitation of "*Tziduk Hadin*," and the Mourner's Kaddish.

In cemeteries that have an automatic casket lowering device, it is important that only a Jew operate the mechanism that allows the casket to descend into the grave.

It is imperative that the casket rest on the actual ground and not in any vault (i.e. cement, metal, etc.), some even remove the bottom board of the casket once it is laid in the grave. If one has no choice (i.e. local law), one should shovel earth into the vault before placing the casket onto it. Also, the lid of the casket (and vault) should be kept slightly ajar with a pebble or twig.

Closing the Grave

The Chevra Kaddisha sprinkles earth from the Land of Israel into the grave, as the land is holy. All the men present then fill the grave with earth, beginning by covering the upper part of the casket. The men can take turns, but the shovel must not be passed directly from one person to the next. Instead, it is placed face down on the ground, and the next person takes it, to show that this is not "regular" work.

Some have the custom that members of the Chevra Kaddisha begin the filling of the grave by scooping earth in their hands and delicately placing it on the casket until it is completely covered, followed by everyone else with shovels.

As one fills the grave with earth, recite the following verse three times:

V'hu ra-chum, y'cha-payr övon,   וְהוּא רַחוּם, יְכַפֵּר עָוֹן,

v'lo yash-chis, v'hirböh l'höshiv apo,   וְלֹא יַשְׁחִית, וְהִרְבָּה לְהָשִׁיב אַפּוֹ,

v'lo yö-ir köl cha-möso: וְלֹא יָעִיר כָּל חֲמָתוֹ :

He, being compassionate, pardons iniquity, and does not destroy; time and again He turns away His anger, and does not arouse all His wrath.

It is highly preferable for Jewish men to fill in the grave. In the case where there are not enough men for this task, the casket must be at least completely covered with earth before allowing cemetery workers to finish the job.

The "*Tziduk Hadin*" Prayer

Once the grave is completely filled with earth and the top is in the shape of a small mound, a marker is placed on the grave with the name of the deceased and date of passing. The prayer of "*Tziduk Hadin*" is then recited. With this deeply meaningful prayer the mourners declare their acceptance of God's decree and pray to God to have mercy upon those who are living.

If *Tachnun* is not recited on that day, we omit "*Tziduk Hadin,*" and proceed directly with Psalm 49 (page 120). This also applies for a burial on late Friday afternoon, or on a day leading into a Jewish holiday (*Erev Yom Tov*).

Ha-tzur tömim pö-ölo ki chöl d'röchöv mish-pöt, ayl emunöh v'ayn övel, tzadik v'yöshör hu.
Ha-tzur tömim b'chöl po-al, mi yomar lo mah tif-öl, ha-shalit b'matöh uv'ma-al, may-mis um'cha-yeh, mo-rid sh'ol va-yöal.
Ha-tzur tömim b'chöl ma-aseh, mi yomar lo mah ta-aseh, hö-omayr v'oseh, chesed chi-növ lönu ta-aseh, uviz'chus ha-ne-ekad k'seh, hak-shivöh va-asay. Tzadik b'chöl d'rö-chöv ha-tzur tömim, erech apa-yim umö-lay racha-mim, chamol nö v'chus nö al övos uvö-nim, ki l'chö hasli-chos v'höra-chamim.
Tzadik atöh adonöy l'hömis ul'ha-chayos, asher b'yöd'chö pik-don köl ruchos, chöli-löh l'chö zichro-naynu lim-chos, v'yih-yu nö ay-nechö b'racha-mim ölaynu f'kuchos, ki l'chö odon höracha-mim v'hasli-chos. Ödöm ben shönöh yih-yeh, o elef shönim yich-yeh,

הַצוּר תָּמִים פָּעֳלוֹ כִּי כָל דְּרָכָיו מִשְׁפָּט, אֵל אֱמוּנָה וְאֵין עָוֶל, צַדִּיק וְיָשָׁר הוּא :
הַצוּר תָּמִים בְּכָל פּוֹעַל, מִי יֹאמַר לוֹ מַה תִּפְעָל, הַשַׁלִּיט בְּמַטָּה וּבְמַעַל, מֵמִית וּמְחַיֶּה, מוֹרִיד שְׁאוֹל וַיָּעַל :
הַצוּר תָּמִים בְּכָל מַעֲשֶׂה, מִי יֹאמַר לוֹ מַה תַּעֲשֶׂה, הָאוֹמֵר וְעוֹשֶׂה, חֶסֶד חִנָּם לָנוּ תַּעֲשֶׂה, וּבִזְכוּת הַנֶּעֱקַד כְּשֶׂה, הַקְשִׁיבָה וַעֲשֵׂה : צַדִּיק בְּכָל דְּרָכָיו הַצוּר תָּמִים, אֶרֶךְ אַפַּיִם וּמָלֵא רַחֲמִים, חֲמוֹל נָא וְחוּס נָא עַל אָבוֹת וּבָנִים, כִּי לְךָ אֲדוֹן הַסְּלִיחוֹת וְהָרַחֲמִים :
צַדִּיק אַתָּה יְיָ לְהָמִית וּלְהַחֲיוֹת, אֲשֶׁר בְּיָדְךָ פִּקְדוֹן כָּל רוּחוֹת, חָלִילָה לְךָ זִכְרוֹנֵנוּ לִמְחוֹת, וְיִהְיוּ נָא עֵינֶיךָ בְּרַחֲמִים עָלֵינוּ פְּקוּחוֹת, כִּי לְךָ אֲדוֹן הָרַחֲמִים וְהַסְּלִיחוֹת : אָדָם בֶּן שָׁנָה יִהְיֶה, אוֹ אֶלֶף שָׁנִים יִחְיֶה,

117

mah yis-ron lo, k'lo hö-yöh yih-yeh,
böruch da-yan hö-emes may-mis
um'cha-yeh. Böruch hu ki emes dino,
um'sho-tayt hakol b'ay-no,
um'sha-laym l'ödöm chesh-bono
v'dino, v'hakol lish-mo hodö-yöh
yitaynu. Yöda-nu adonöy ki tzedek
mish-pö-techö, titz-dak b'döv-rechö,
v'sizkeh b'shöf-techö, v'ayn l'har-hayr
achar midas sh'fö-techö, tzadik
atöh adonöy, v'yöshör mish-pö-techö.
Da-yan emes, sho-fayt tzedek ve-emes,
böruch da-yan hö-emes, she-köl
mish-pötöv tzedek ve-emes. Nefesh
köl chai b'yödechö, tzedek möl-öh
y'min'chö v'yö-dechö, ra-chaym al
p'lay-tas tzon yö-dechö, v'somar
l'mal-öch heref yö-dechö. G'dol
hö-aytzöh v'rav hö-ali-liyöh, asher
ay-nechö f'ku-chos al köl dar-chay
b'nay ödöm, lösays l'ish ki-d'röchöv
v'chif-ri ma-alö-löv. L'hagid ki yöshör
adonöy, tzuri v'lo av-lösö bo. Adonöy
nösan, va-donöy lököch, y'hi shaym

מַה יִּתְרוֹן לוֹ, כְּלֹא הָיָה יִהְיֶה,
בָּרוּךְ דַּיַּן הָאֱמֶת מֵמִית
וּמְחַיֶּה: בָּרוּךְ הוּא כִּי אֱמֶת דִּינוֹ,
וּמְשׁוֹטֵט הַכֹּל בְּעֵינוֹ,
וּמְשַׁלֵּם לְאָדָם חֶשְׁבּוֹנוֹ
וְדִינוֹ, וְהַכֹּל לִשְׁמוֹ הוֹדָיָה
יִתֵּנוּ: יָדַעְנוּ יְיָ כִּי צֶדֶק
מִשְׁפָּטֶיךָ, תִּצְדַּק בְּדָבְרֶךָ,
וְתִזְכֶּה בְּשָׁפְטֶךָ, וְאֵין לְהַרְהֵר
אַחַר מִדַּת שְׁפָטֶיךָ, צַדִּיק
אַתָּה יְיָ, וְיָשָׁר מִשְׁפָּטֶיךָ:
דַּיַּן אֱמֶת, שׁוֹפֵט צֶדֶק וֶאֱמֶת,
בָּרוּךְ דַּיַּן הָאֱמֶת, שֶׁכָּל
מִשְׁפָּטָיו צֶדֶק וֶאֱמֶת: נֶפֶשׁ
כָּל חַי בְּיָדֶךָ, צֶדֶק מָלְאָה
יְמִינְךָ וְיָדֶךָ, רַחֵם עַל
פְּלֵיטַת צֹאן יָדֶיךָ, וְתֹאמַר
לַמַּלְאָךְ הֶרֶף יָדֶךָ: גְּדֹל
הָעֵצָה וְרַב הָעֲלִילִיָּה, אֲשֶׁר
עֵינֶיךָ פְקֻחוֹת עַל כָּל דַּרְכֵי
בְּנֵי אָדָם, לָתֵת לְאִישׁ כִּדְרָכָיו
וְכִפְרִי מַעֲלָלָיו: לְהַגִּיד כִּי יָשָׁר
יְיָ, צוּרִי וְלֹא עַוְלָתָה בּוֹ: יְיָ
נָתַן, וַייָ לָקָח, יְהִי שֵׁם

adonöy m'voröch. V'hu ra-chum,   יְיָ מְבֹרָךְ : וְהוּא רַחוּם,

y'cha-payr övon, v'lo yash-chis,   יְכַפֵּר עָוֹן וְלֹא יַשְׁחִית,

v'hirböh l'höshiv apo,   וְהִרְבָּה לְהָשִׁיב אַפּוֹ,

v'lo yö-ir köl chamöso.   וְלֹא יָעִיר כָּל חֲמָתוֹ :

The Rock, His work is perfect, for all His ways are justice; a God of faithfulness and without iniquity, righteous and just is He. The Rock, perfect in all His works. Who can say to Him 'What have You done?' He rules below and above, He brings death and restores life, brings down to the grave and raises up from there. The Rock, perfect in all His deeds. Who can say to Him, 'What do You do?' You Who says and fulfills, do undeserved kindness with us, and in the merit of him [Isaac] who was bound [on the altar] like a lamb, hearken and grant our request. Righteous One in all His ways, O Rock Who is perfect, slow to anger and abundant in mercy, take pity and spare both parents and children, for to You, O Lord, pertain forgiveness and mercy. Righteous are You, Lord, to bring death and to restore life, for in Your hands are entrusted all spirits. Far be it from You to erase our memory. Look towards us with mercy, for Yours, O Lord, are mercy and forgiveness. A man, whether he be a year old, or whether he lives a thousand years, what does it profit him? For is it not as if he has never been? Blessed be the True Judge, Who brings death and restores life. Blessed be He, for His judgment is true, as He scans everything with His eye, and He rewards man according to his account and his judgment. Let all give praise to His Name. We know, Lord, that Your judgment is right. You are righteous when You speak and pure when You judge, and none shall question Your judgments. Righteous are You, Lord, and Your judgments are just. You are the True Judge, Who judges with righteousness and truth. Blessed is the True Judge, for all of His judgments are righteous and true. The soul of every living creature is in Your hand, righteousness fills Your right and left hand. Have mercy on the remnant of the flock under Your hand, and say to the angel of death, 'Hold back your hand!' You are great in counsel and mighty in action, Your eyes are watching all the ways of man, to give man according to his ways and according to the fruit of his deeds. That is to say that the Lord is Just; He is my Strength, and there is no injustice in Him. The Lord has given and the Lord has taken. May the Name of the Lord be blessed. He, being compassionate, pardons iniquity, and does not destroy; time and again He turns away His anger, and does not arouse all His wrath.

Continue with Psalm 49:

Lam'natzay-ach liv-nay korach miz-mor. Shim-u zos köl hö-amim, ha-azinu köl yosh'vey chöled. Gam b'nay ödöm gam b'nay sh, yachad öshir v'ev-yon. Pi y'da-bayr chöch-mos v'högus libi s'vunos. Ateh l'möshöl öz-ni, ef-tach b'chinor chi-dösi. Lömö irö bi-may rö, avon akay-vai y'subay-ni. Habot'chim al chay-löm, uv'rov ösh-röm yis-halölu. Öch lo födo yif-deh ish, lo yi-tayn laylo-him köf-ro. V'yay-kar pid-yon naf-shöm, v'chödal l'olöm. Vi-chi od lö-netzach lo yir-eh ha-shöchas. Ki yir-eh cha-chömim yömusu, yachad k'sil vöva-ar yo-vaydu, v'öz'vu la-achayrim chay-löm. Kir-böm bötay-mo l'olöm, mish-k'nosöm l'dor

לַמְנַצֵּחַ לִבְנֵי קֹרַח מִזְמוֹר: שִׁמְעוּ זֹאת כָּל הָעַמִּים, הַאֲזִינוּ כָּל יֹשְׁבֵי חָלֶד: גַּם בְּנֵי אָדָם גַּם בְּנֵי אִישׁ, יַחַד עָשִׁיר וְאֶבְיוֹן: פִּי יְדַבֵּר חָכְמוֹת, וְהָגוּת לִבִּי תְבוּנוֹת: אַטֶּה לְמָשָׁל אָזְנִי, אֶפְתַּח בְּכִנּוֹר חִידָתִי: לָמָּה אִירָא בִּימֵי רָע עֲוֹן עֲקֵבַי יְסוּבֵּנִי: הַבֹּטְחִים עַל חֵילָם, וּבְרֹב עָשְׁרָם יִתְהַלָּלוּ: אָח לֹא פָדֹה יִפְדֶּה אִישׁ, לֹא יִתֵּן לֵאלֹהִים כָּפְרוֹ: וְיֵקַר פִּדְיוֹן נַפְשָׁם, וְחָדַל לְעוֹלָם: וִיחִי עוֹד לָנֶצַח, לֹא יִרְאֶה הַשָּׁחַת: כִּי יִרְאֶה חֲכָמִים יָמוּתוּ, יַחַד כְּסִיל וָבַעַר יֹאבֵדוּ, וְעָזְבוּ לַאֲחֵרִים חֵילָם: קִרְבָּם בָּתֵּימוֹ לְעוֹלָם, מִשְׁכְּנֹתָם לְדוֹר

vödor, kör'u vish-mosöm a-lay
adömos. V'ödöm bikör bal yölin,
nim-shal kab'haymos nid-mu. Zeh
dar-köm ke-sel lömo v'acha-rayhem
b'fi-hem yir-tzu selöh. Katzon lish-ol
shatu mö-ves yir-aym va-yir-du vöm
y'shörim la-boker, v'tzuröm l'valos
sh'ol miz'vul lo. Al elohim yif-deh
naf-shi mi-yad sh'ol, ki yikö-chayni
selöh. Al tirö ki ya-ashir ish, ki
yir-beh k'vod bayso. Ki lo v'moso
yi-kach hakol, lo yay-rayd acharöv
k'vodo. Ki naf-sho b'cha-yöv
y'vöraych, v'yoduchö ki saytiv löch.
Tövo ad dor avosöv, ad nay-tzach
lo yir-u or. Ödöm bikör v'lo yövin,
nim-shal kab'haymos nid-mu.

וָדֹר, קָרְאוּ בִשְׁמוֹתָם עֲלֵי
אֲדָמוֹת: וְאָדָם בִּיקָר בַּל יָלִין,
נִמְשַׁל כַּבְּהֵמוֹת נִדְמוּ: זֶה
דַרְכָּם כֵּסֶל לָמוֹ, וְאַחֲרֵיהֶם
בְּפִיהֶם יִרְצוּ סֶלָה: כַּצֹּאן לִשְׁאוֹל
שַׁתּוּ מָוֶת יִרְעֵם, וַיִּרְדּוּ בָם
יְשָׁרִים לַבֹּקֶר, וְצוּרָם לְבַלּוֹת
שְׁאוֹל מִזְּבֻל לוֹ: אַךְ אֱלֹהִים יִפְדֶּה
נַפְשִׁי מִיַּד שְׁאוֹל, כִּי יִקָּחֵנִי
סֶלָה: אַל תִּירָא כִּי יַעֲשִׁר אִישׁ, כִּי
יִרְבֶּה כְּבוֹד בֵּיתוֹ: כִּי לֹא בְמוֹתוֹ
יִקַּח הַכֹּל, לֹא יֵרֵד אַחֲרָיו
כְּבוֹדוֹ: כִּי נַפְשׁוֹ בְּחַיָּיו
יְבָרֵךְ, וְיוֹדֻךָ כִּי תֵיטִיב לָךְ:
תָּבוֹא עַד דּוֹר אֲבוֹתָיו, עַד נֵצַח
לֹא יִרְאוּ אוֹר: אָדָם בִּיקָר וְלֹא יָבִין,
נִמְשַׁל כַּבְּהֵמוֹת נִדְמוּ:

For the Conductor, by the sons of Korach, a Psalm. Hear this, all you peoples; listen, all you inhabitants of the world; sons of common folk and sons of nobility, rich and poor alike. My mouth speaks wisdom, and the thoughts of my heart are understanding. I incline my ear to the parable; I will unravel my riddle upon the harp. Why am I afraid in times of trouble? [Because] the sins I trod upon surround me. There are those who rely on their wealth, who boast of their great riches. Yet a man cannot redeem his brother, nor pay his ransom to God. The redemption of their soul is too costly, and forever unattainable. Can one live forever, never to see the grave? Though he sees that wise men die, that the fool and the senseless both perish, leaving their wealth to others — [nevertheless,] in their inner thoughts their houses will last forever, their dwellings for generation after generation; they have proclaimed their names throughout the lands. But man will not repose in glory; he is likened to the silenced animals. This is their way – their folly remains with them, and their descendants approve of their talk, Selah. Like sheep, they are destined for the grave; death shall be their shepherd, and the upright will dominate them at morning; their form will rot in the grave, away from its abode. But God will redeem my soul from the hands of the grave, for He will take me, Selah. Do not fear when a man grows rich, when the glory of his house is increased; for when he dies he will take nothing, his glory will not descend after him. For he [alone] praises himself in his lifetime; but [all] will praise you if you better yourself. He will come to the generation of his forefathers; they shall not see light for all eternity. Man [can live] in glory but does not understand; he is likened to the silenced animals.

The Graveside Mourner's Kaddish

The male mourners recite the specially formulated Kaddish below. It is recited in unison at the foot of the grave, facing East. If there are no male mourners, then another designated Jewish man recites the Kaddish on behalf of the family.

Kaddish can only be recited if there is a Minyan present. Bow the head while reciting the words bracketed by the following symbol: "°". While the Kaddish is recited, all present respond as indicated between the parentheses (see below).

The Graveside Kaddish is not recited on days when *Tachnun* is not recited and on days that "*Tziduk Hadin*" was omitted. Instead, recite the regular Mourner's Kaddish (page 170).

Yis-gadal v'yis-kadash °sh'may raböh°.

(Ömayn)

יִתְגַּדַּל וְיִתְקַדַּשׁ שְׁמֵהּ רַבָּא°׃

אָמֵן

B'öl'mö d'hu ösid l'is-chad-tö,
ul'ach-yö-öh maysa-yö,
ul'shach-l'löh haych'lay, ul'mifrak
cha-yö, ul'miv-nay kar-tö
di-rush'laym, ul'me-ekar pul-chönö
nuchrö-öh may-ar-ay, v'la-asövö
pul-chönö kadishö dish-mayö
l'as-ray, v'zivay viköray ush'chintay,
v'yatzmach purkönay
°vikö-rayv m'shi-chay°.

(Ömayn)

בְּעָלְמָא דְהוּא עָתִיד לְאִתְחַדָּתָא,
וּלְאַחְיָאָה מֵתַיָּא,
וּלְשַׁכְלָלָא הֵיכְלֵהּ, וּלְמִפְרַק
חַיָּא, וּלְמִבְנֵי קַרְתָּא
דִירוּשְׁלֵם, וּלְמֶעֱקַר פּוּלְחָנָא
נוּכְרָאָה מֵאַרְעָהּ. וְלַאֲתָבָא
פּוּלְחָנָא קַדִּישָׁא דִשְׁמַיָּא
לְאַתְרֵהּ, וְזִיוֵהּ וִיקָרֵהּ וּשְׁכִינְתֵּהּ,
וְיַצְמַח פּוּרְקָנֵהּ
°וִיקָרֵב מְשִׁיחֵהּ°׃

אָמֵן

B'cha-yay-chon uv'yomay-chon,
uv'chayay d'chöl bays yisrö-ayl,
tis-k'lay char-bö v'chaf-nö umos'nö
minö-nö, umi-köl amö bays yisrö-ayl,
ba-agölö uviz'man köriv
°v'im'ru ömayn°.

(Ömayn. Y'hay sh'may rabö m'vörach l'ölam
ul'öl'may öl'ma-yöh yis-böraych).

בְּחַיֵּיכוֹן וּבְיוֹמֵיכוֹן
וּבְחַיֵּי דְכָל בֵּית יִשְׂרָאֵל,
תִּתְכְּלֵא חַרְבָּא וְכַפְנָא וּמוֹתָנָא
מִנָּנָא, וּמִכָּל עַמָּא בֵּית יִשְׂרָאֵל,
בַּעֲגָלָא וּבִזְמַן קָרִיב
°וְאָמְרוּ אָמֵן°׃

אָמֵן, יְהֵא שְׁמֵהּ רַבָּא מְבָרַךְ לְעָלַם
וּלְעָלְמֵי עָלְמַיָּא יִתְבָּרַךְ׃

°Y'hay sh'may rabö m'vörach l'ölam
ul'öl'may öl'ma-yöh, yisböraych°,
°v'yishtabach, v'yispö-ayr, v'yisromöm,
v'yis-nasay, v'yis-hadör, v'yis-aleh,
v'yis-halöl°, °sh'may
d'kud-shö b'rich hu°.
(Ömayn)

°יְהֵא שְׁמֵהּ רַבָּא מְבָרַךְ לְעָלַם
וּלְעָלְמֵי עָלְמַיָּא, יִתְבָּרַךְ°,
°וְיִשְׁתַּבַּח, וְיִתְפָּאַר, וְיִתְרוֹמָם,
וְיִתְנַשֵּׂא, וְיִתְהַדָּר, וְיִתְעַלֶּה,
וְיִתְהַלָּל°, °שְׁמֵהּ דְּקֻדְשָׁא
בְּרִיךְ הוּא°:
אָמֵן

L'aylö min köl bir'chösö v'shirösö,
tush-b'chösö v'ne-che-mösö,
da-amirön b'öl'mö, °v'im'ru ömayn°.
(Ömayn)

לְעֵלָּא מִן כָּל בִּרְכָתָא וְשִׁירָתָא,
תֻּשְׁבְּחָתָא וְנֶחֱמָתָא,
דַּאֲמִירָן בְּעָלְמָא, °וְאִמְרוּ אָמֵן°:
אָמֵן

Y'hay sh'lömö rabö min sh'ma-yö,
v'cha-yim tovim ölaynu v'al köl
yisrö-ayl °v'im'ru ömayn°.
(Ömayn)

יְהֵא שְׁלָמָא רַבָּא מִן שְׁמַיָּא
וְחַיִּים טוֹבִים עָלֵינוּ וְעַל כָּל
יִשְׂרָאֵל °וְאִמְרוּ אָמֵן°:
אָמֵן

Take three steps back and say the following, while bowing the head
to the right, straight ahead, left, straight ahead, and bowing down (as indicated):

> Oseh shölom* bim'romöv, ^ hu
< ya-aseh shölom ölaynu, ^ v'al köl
yisrö-ayl, °v'im'ru ömayn°.
(Cong.: Ömayn.)

> עֹשֶׂה שָׁלוֹם* בִּמְרוֹמָיו, ^ הוּא
< יַעֲשֶׂה שָׁלוֹם עָלֵינוּ, ^ וְעַל כָּל
יִשְׂרָאֵל, °וְאִמְרוּ אָמֵן°:
אמן

Take three steps forward. (*Between Rosh Hashana and Yom Kippur, substitute with "ha-shölom.")

124

Exalted and hallowed be His great Name. (Cong: Amen.) In the world which He will create anew, where He will revive the dead, construct His temple, deliver life, and rebuild the city of Jerusalem, and uproot foreign idol worship from His land, and restore the holy service of Heaven to its place, along with His radiance, splendor and Shechinah, and may He bring forth His redemption and hasten the coming of His Moshiach. (Cong: Amen.) *In your lifetime and in your days and in the lifetime of the entire House of Israel, sword, famine and death shall cease from us and from the entire Jewish nation, speedily and soon, and say, Amen.* (Cong: Amen. May His great Name be blessed forever and to all eternity, blessed.) May His great Name be blessed forever and to all eternity. Blessed and praised, glorified, exalted and extolled, honored, adored and lauded be the Name of the Holy One, blessed be He. (Cong: Amen.) *Beyond all the blessings, hymns, praises and consolations that are uttered in the world; and say, Amen.* (Cong: Amen.) *May there be abundant peace from heaven, and a good life for us and for all Israel; and say, Amen.* (Cong: Amen.) *He Who makes peace* (Between Rosh Hashana and Yom Kippur substitute: *the peace*) *in His heavens, may He make peace for us and for all Israel; and say, Amen.* (Cong: Amen.)

Removing Leather Shoes

The mourners (both men and women) remove their leather shoes and replace them with non-leather footwear (i.e. slippers or sneakers). The mourners are now "*Aveilim*," (or "*Avel*" in the singular), which means "one who is in mourning."

Nechama - Condolence

After the Mourner's Kaddish is recited, all the Jewish men present form two rows, with at least five people in each row. The male mourners walk in the pathway between the two rows, and the people console them with the passage below. After the male mourners pass, all the men forming the rows move to one side, forming a single row. The women mourners then pass in front of them, receiving the same condolence.

As the mourners pass, those forming the rows say the following:

Hamö-kom y'na-chaym es-chem הַמָּקוֹם יְנַחֵם אֶתְכֶם

b'soch sh'ör avay-lay בְּתוֹךְ שְׁאָר אֲבֵלֵי

tzi-yon viru-shölö-yim. צִיּוֹן וִירוּשָׁלָיִם :

May the Almighty comfort you among the mourners of Zion and Jerusalem.

It is a Kaballistic custom that when leaving the gravesite, all the women should leave first, followed by the men.

Leaving the Cemetery

It is advisable that before leaving the cemetery, the mourners sit on a low stool or bench, formally initiating the Shiva mourning process. This is so that they can count this day as the first day of Shiva.

Some have the custom to place some money in a charity box, or make a pledge to do so later, in honor of the deceased.

On the way out of the cemetery, it is customary to pull out some grass, throw it back over the shoulder, and recite the passage below. This symbolizes the Resurrection of the Dead in the era of Moshiach, when the body will awaken and return from the dust of the earth, as it is written, "And may they blossom out of the city like grass of the earth" (Psalms 72:16).

As you toss the grass back over your shoulder, say the following verse three times:

וְיָצִיצוּ מֵעִיר כְּעֵשֶׂב הָאָרֶץ :   V'yötzitzu may-ir k'aysev hö-öretz.
And may they blossom out of the city like grass of the earth. (Psalms 72:16)

Some say this instead:

זָכוּר כִּי עָפָר אֲנָחְנוּ :   Zöchur ki öför anöch-nu.
He is mindful that we are but dust. (Psalms 103:14)

Washing the Hands

All those who attended the funeral must wash their hands ritually, once outside the cemetery area. Take a large cup of water in the left hand, pour it over the entire right hand, covering up to the wrist. Take the cup in the right hand, and pour it over the entire left hand, covering up to the wrist. Repeat two additional times. It is customary to place the cup upside down after washing, and not to dry one's hands with a towel or paper, so that the memory of the deceased lingers.

Mourners Retire to the Shiva Home

Following the burial, the mourners retire to the Shiva home. This is the place where the family will gather to observe the Shiva and to receive visitors (see page 137). As soon as the mourners arrive at the Shiva home, they are served a meal called the *Seudat Havra-ah*, the meal of recovery or condolence (see following chapter).

Since a mourner does not put on *Tefillin* on the day of the burial, it is advisable to consult a competent rabbi whether he should put them on and pray once the burial is complete (if it is still daytime). Some authorities permit it, but only if it is done in private.

Seudat Havra-ah - The First Meal

The first meal eaten by the mourners when they return home from the funeral is called the *Seudat Havra-ah*, the meal of recovery or condolence. It is a private meal for immediate family members and is not a public condolence event.

At this meal the mourners are not allowed to eat from their own food, instead the meal is provided by relatives and friends, or the community. This custom allows the community to show concern for the welfare of the mourners and to extend a comforting hand in the time of greatest need.

If it is not possible for friends, relatives, or the community to provide the meal, one may partake of his or her own food.

If the burial was performed during the day, the meal is served until nightfall. If the burial was completed after nightfall, the mourners do not have to partake of this special meal but may eat of their own food right away.

If one forgot and ate the first meal of his own food, he does not have to eat the special meal before eating other foods.

On a Friday or on the day leading into a Jewish holiday (*Erev Yom Tov*), one does not eat this meal after the ninth

"Halachic" hour of the day (calculated by dividing the time between sunrise and sunset into twelve parts). Mourners can skip this meal so that they will have an appetite for the evening Shabbat or holiday meal.

Foods That Are Served

In addition to bread or bagels, it customary to serve peeled hard-boiled eggs, for they are round and symbolize the cycle of life.

The bread is placed in the hands of the mourners by others. After eating the bread and an egg, one may eat other foods. At this meal, one is permitted to drink wine, but in moderation.

On the intermediate days of Sukkot and Passover (*Chol Ha-moed*) the bread and egg are replaced by cake (or matza) and coffee (or juice).

The mourners cannot be included in a *Zimun* of ten for the recitation of the Grace After Meals, but may be part of a Zimun of three. (Zimun is a special blessing added to the beginning of the Grace After Meals, when three or more men are at the meal).

The Periods of Mourning

1) *The day of passing.* The family members focus on ensuring a timely and proper Jewish burial. Many calculate the date of the annual Yartzeit from the date of passing.

2) *The day of the burial.* General mourning commences once the burial is complete and the grave is closed. The dates for *Shiva* (the first seven days) and *Shloshim* (the thirtieth day) are calculated from this day (i.e. if the burial was on Tuesday, the Shiva will end the following Monday morning — the seventh day, and the *Shloshim* will conclude in the morning, twenty-three days after Shiva). Some calculate the date of the second (and every future) Yartzeit from the date of burial. One should follow the custom of his community, or ask a competent rabbi for guidance.

3) *The first three days.* These are days in which the mourning is at its highest intensity. Activities that may be permitted during the rest of Shiva are not permitted during these days.

4) *The first seven days (Shiva).* This is the most commonly known period of mourning. The mourners gather for the entire seven days to mourn and pray, and to be consoled by visitors.

5) *From Shiva to Shloshim*. The period between the end of Shiva until the thirtieth day. Some restrictions of mourning are reduced, but mourning is still considerably intense. Many erect the tombstone on the day following Shiva.

6) *The thirtieth day (Shloshim)*. The thirtieth day from burial. Some restrictions of mourning are further reduced. Many visit the gravesite on this day. Some make a gathering for family and friends. Some erect the tombstone on this day.

7) *The first year*. From Shloshim until the Yartzeit anniversary. During this period many of the restrictions of the first thirty days are removed but many carry on for the duration of the first year. For parents, Kaddish is recited for eleven months, less one day.

8) *The anniversary (Yartzeit)*. The annual date of passing. On this day mourning is officially complete. Many visit the gravesite on this day, and the Mourner's Kaddish is recited.

The Importance of Consulting a Rabbi

Details regarding the observance of each period are provided in the following pages. However, it is very important to consult a competent rabbi for thorough guidance.

The Shiva - The First Seven Days

Shiva, in Hebrew, means seven. In our context it refers to the first seven days of mourning that are observed following the burial of one's father, mother, spouse, son, daughter, brother [including half-brother], and sister [including half-sister]. An adopted child may choose to sit Shiva, but is not obligated. One mourns a spouse only if their union was permissible according to Torah law.

The observance of Shiva is traced to the dawn of Jewish history. The Torah relates that Joseph mourned the death of Jacob his father for seven days. Moses later established the period of seven days for mourning as Jewish law. The Torah outlines specific ways in which a Jew must mourn his loss, and each period of mourning has its own rules and order.

Our sages allocate days one through three for crying, and days four through seven for eulogizing. After that, one does not mourn excessively, but follows a grieving process that gradually diminishes.

The Importance of Observing Shiva

Mourning a loved one properly is the ultimate gift that one can give to the one who has passed on. It is also a mitzva that benefits both the mourner and the one who is mourned. One should be willing and proud to follow the ways of his or her ancestors during this most sensitive and trying time.

We are taught that a person who is mourned in accordance with Jewish Law and tradition merits to enter Heaven easily, and the soul of the departed is strengthened and fortified by the process of mourning, and specifically, by the recitation of the Mourner's Kaddish and the study of Torah in its merit.

Mourning traditions are not to be treated lightly. We are taught that a Jew who does not mourn his kin as outlined in the Torah, or ignores the age-old traditions of mourning, brings disrespect and shame to the memory of the deceased. As harsh as this may sound, it indicates the seriousness of the matter and serves as a fitting call to proper observance.

As the mourning periods are time-bound, and in some way pass quickly, one should strive to observe them properly. It is important to expend effort into carrying out the traditional mourning observances and to set aside issues of personal discomfort and/or inconvenience for this short time period for the merit of the soul of the deceased.

Putting Your Best Effort

For some, the laws of Shiva, and of mourning in general, seem to deal more with what one cannot do, and less with what one can do and thus can appear as a tremendous burden. Some look for ways to avoid observing it at all and rationalize it away.

Family members who have just lost a loved one cannot simply go about their lives as if nothing happened. They need to stop what they are doing and absorb the messages of life and death, take the lessons of their loved one to heart, reaffirm their relationship with God, and ensure that the memory of the departed is honored properly.

The solace that proper mourning provides is lost if one attempts to resume one's "normal" life before one has properly mourned. After a loss, things are not as they were. A loved one has passed away! The pain is there (or should be) regardless if the person passed away at a ripe old age, or very young, God forbid. In either case, Judaism says: respect life. We demonstrate our respect for life by how we treat death.

Creating a "Space" for Yourself

Many of the laws of mourning may seem obvious (i.e. not attending parties or going to concerts). Some of the laws may not seem so obvious (taking off work for the Shiva, refraining from bathing, etc.). Yet instead of viewing these laws as restrictive, one should view them as they were intended.

The laws of mourning free the mourner from social norms and expectations, so that the mourner can focus on the memories of the deceased and begin to heal. By teaching how to mourn, the Torah balances the emotional and spiritual needs of the mourners with those of the soul of the deceased.

As one continues to observe the laws of mourning, he becomes sensitive to the cycle of life. At some point he learns to live with his loss. Eventually, he comes to accept the passing as the Will of God. This process can take years, and consolation can only occur by going through these steps. As one so aptly put it: "The only real way out is through."

The Shiva Home

For seven days following the funeral, the mourners gather in the *Shiva* home. This is the place where prayer services are held, where mourners recite Kaddish, and where family and friends come to offer comfort and solace. Ideally, mourners should not leave the Shiva home for the entire period of Shiva.

It is written in Kabbalah that the soul returns to the home where it lived and mourns there for seven days. Public worship, prayers, and Psalms console the soul and bring her satisfaction.

Location of the Shiva Home

It is a mitzva for the mourners to observe Shiva in the place where the soul departed. If this is not possible, another location (i.e. the home where he lived) is designated and publicized so that family and friends can come to pray and express their condolences.

Preparing the Shiva Home

• Cover all mirrors and pictures of people in the home (or just remove them or turn them around). Some permit leaving pictures of great Torah sages and Tzaddikim.

• A seven-day candle should be lit. Some kindle five candles representing the five mystical levels of the soul. These candles remains lit for the entire Shiva. If one cannot find a seven-day candle, one may use seven regular candles. In either case, a candle should always remain lit in the home. One reason for this custom is that the candle and light represent a metaphor for the body and soul. Another reason is that the candle helps to console the soul, which returns to the home where it lived and mourns there for seven days.

• Arrange for low stools or crates for the mourners to sit on, and regular chairs for visitors.

• Prepare *Kippot* (*Yarmulkas*), *Tallit* and *Tefillin*, prayer books for services, a charity box, and several books of Psalms.

• One may put out refreshments, but should refrain from putting out elaborate food and drink (including fancy cakes and cookies), as those are associated with festive occasions. Simple kosher cake and juice and/or coffee is enough.

• If a Torah scroll is to be kept in the Shiva home for prayer services, it should be placed in a respectable location and covered with a *Tallit* when not being used.

• Prepare a copy of the traditional "Condolence Declaration" for visitors to recite (see page 159).

Daily Prayer Services in the Shiva Home

We are taught that the soul benefits when Kaddish is said. Therefore, it is a great merit for the departed soul that the three daily prayer services be held in the Shiva home and for the mourners to recite the Kaddish. Members of the community are expected to help complete a *Minyan* (quorum of ten Jewish males over age thirteen) that is required to hold services.

• The daily prayer services at the Shiva home should begin after the funeral. If this is not possible, then at least one of the three daily prayer services should be held in the home following the funeral or the next day.

• It is customary to light candles during the services. The candles are placed in front of, or near, the prayer leader. Many people light five candles representing the five mystical levels of the soul. One may use the candles already lit in the Shiva home.

• If possible, the mourner should lead all the services throughout the entire Shiva (except on Shabbat and Jewish holidays). If there is more than one male mourner and enough people for another Minyan, the services may be scheduled at different times, or held concurrently in other rooms.

• If there are no male mourners, the family appoints a prayer leader from those gathered for the Minyan.

• If the mourner cannot lead the service, another person is designated as the prayer leader, and the mourner should recite the Mourner's Kaddish at the designated points (see page 168).

• If it is not possible to gather a Minyan for all three daily services, one should at least arrange one for the evening service, when the attributes of judgment and severity are strongest.

• On days that it is not possible to gather a Minyan in the Shiva home, the mourner may leave the Shiva home to attend services in the synagogue and to recite the Mourner's Kaddish.

Additional Notes About the Services

• *Tachnun* (supplications of forgiveness) is omitted from prayers during all services in the Shiva home.

• The *Birkat Kohanim* (Priestly Blessing) is omitted in the leader's repetition of the Shacharit (morning service) *Amidah*.

• When reciting the *Hallel* (Verses of Praise) during the morning service on *Rosh Chodesh* (beginning of the new month), the mourner must leave the room while it is said, for he is not permitted to recite it. (However, when one cannot hold services at the Shiva home and thus joins a Minyan in the synagogue, he recites it along with the congregation).

• On days when the Torah is read during the morning service, the mourner is not called upon to bless the Torah. However he may bring the Torah to the reading table and return it to the Ark. He may also raise it after the reading. (If he raises the Torah, he may sit in a regular chair while it is being wrapped and dressed with the mantle).

• Psalm 49 is recited following *Shacharit* (morning) and *Mincha* (afternoon) prayer services, except on days when *Tachnun* is not recited (Psalm 16 is substituted), see page 205. Some communities recite Psalm 49 also following the *Maariv* (evening) service.

• The mourner may recite *Kiddush Levana* (blessing recited when a new moon appears) if the opportunity will pass before the conclusion of Shiva. Some say he omits the *Sholom Aleichem* greeting found in the prayer.

Studying *Mishnayot*

It is a great honor for the departed soul when others study Torah on its behalf. For this reason, it is customary for volunteers to divide and study all the tractates of the *Mishna* (codified compilation of Jewish law), completing it by the *Shloshim* (thirty days from the burial).

The word *Mishna* (study) has the same letters as the Hebrew word *Neshama* (soul). Studying Mishna on the soul's behalf can deliver the soul from harsh judgments and elevate it to a higher level in Gan Eden (the Heavenly residence of souls).

An easy-to-use chart is provided to help divide the chapters among the volunteers (see page 279).

The Laws of Shiva

Below is a summary of laws concerning the proper observance of the *Shiva* period. Consult a competent rabbi for complete guidance and for answers to questions.

During Shiva, the mourner is prohibited from:

• Sitting on regular chairs, stools, recliners, or couches

• Working

• Bathing for pleasure

• Using cosmetics, lotions, oils, and perfumes

• Wearing leather shoes

• Engaging in marital relations

• Studying Torah (except parts dealing with mourning and repentance)

• Greeting people in the usual manner (i.e "Hello," "Hi")

• Wearing fresh clothing

• Taking a haircut

• Shaving

• Playing or listening to music

• Participating in joyful activities (i.e. reading papers or entertaining books, watching videos or shows, attending social events, concerts, or weddings, etc.)

All these activities interrupt and negate the intense mourning that should be experienced during this period.

Sitting on Regular Chairs

A mourner should not sit on a regular chair, stool, recliner, or couch during the Shiva. He may, however, sit on a low stool or crate, but it should not be higher than three *Tefachim* (approximately twelve inches) from the ground.

This restriction does not apply during meals, nor does it apply to a pregnant or nursing mother, or to the very elderly.

Greeting People

A mourner should not greet people with the usual expressions of friendship and recognition (i.e. "Shalom," "Good morning," "How are you?" etc.). Instead, he nods his head in greeting. If a person who is unaware of the passing greets the mourner, during the first three days, he should reply by saying that he is in mourning. After the first three days, he may respond in kind.

A mourner may say "Mazal Tov" or "Congratulations" upon hearing good news, and may also say to guests who leave "Go in peace," and the like. On Shabbat and Jewish holidays, the mourner may wish someone "Good Shabbos," "Shabbat Shalom," and the like. One may greet a mourner with the same expressions.

Working or Conducting Business

A mourner may neither work nor conduct business during the entire seven days of Shiva. This is to prevent him from being distracted from mourning. A store owner must close his store for the entire Shiva, even if he has a partner who is not in mourning.

If the mourner is in extreme financial need, and there is no one else who can do the work for him, and in all other situations (including one who runs a company with many employees), it is advisable to consult a competent rabbi who specializes in this area of Jewish law for guidance.

A doctor may attend a patient during Shiva, even if there are others who may see him as well.

Housework such as cooking, baking, washing dishes, and cleaning the home is permitted throughout the Shiva, although the custom is that it should be done by others (if possible).

Self-Care, Grooming

A mourner may not experience the luxury of a hot bath or shower during Shiva. However, he may wash his face, hands and feet in cool water, and rinse his mouth and brush his teeth.

This prohibition against bathing does not include a person who is ill, one whose doctor advised him to bathe, or a woman who gave birth in the past thirty days. However, even in those cases one should be strict on the first day of Shiva.

The prohibition against bathing and showering is very strict during the Shiva. However, if one became dirty or overly sweaty, he may wash those areas alone, but he may not shower.

A woman may not go to the Mikvah during the Shiva. Consult a competent rabbi for guidance in this case.

Anointing with Oils

A mourner may not use cosmetics, lotions, oils, perfumes, makeup and the like during Shiva, unless it is for medical purposes. He or she may, however, use deodorants. A bride in the first thirty days of marriage is permitted to wear makeup.

Haircutting and Shaving

A mourner may not take a haircut or shave for thirty days after the burial; nor may he cut his nails with an instrument. If one is mourning a parent, he is forbidden from cutting his hair even after thirty days. It must grow until his friends reprimand him and tell him to cut his hair (approximately three months from his last haircut).

Clothing and Dress

Mourners cannot change their outer clothing and must wear the shirt and jacket on which the *Kriah* (rending of the garments) was made for the entire Shiva period. However, at night one may change into sleeping attire, and one does not have to perform Kriah on them. One may change underwear and socks or stockings as needed.

Wearing leather shoes is forbidden, except in the case of a person who is ill or a woman who gave birth in the past thirty days. It is customary for the mourner to wear just socks or non-leather footwear (i.e. slippers or sneakers).

During Shiva, one may not wear new clothing or clothing that has been freshly laundered. One may not wash or iron his clothing, linen, sheets, and towels. This prohibition does not apply to household members who are not mourning.

If one's clothing becomes dirty with sweat or other dirt, he or she may change his clothes. If a fresh shirt/blouse or jacket is worn, it requires Kriah (without the blessing) (see page 104).

Women may not adorn themselves with jewelry (except a wedding ring) during Shiva. A bride in the first thirty days of marriage is permitted to wear her jewelry.

Intimate Relations

During Shiva, it is forbidden to have marital relations or other intimate demonstrations of affection. However, one need not follow all the *Harchokot* (customary refraining measures) during Shiva, if one's wife is not in the state of *Nidda*.

Torah Study

In general, a mourner is forbidden to study Torah, Mishna, Talmud, and Jewish Law, unless they pertain to mourning. One may also study texts that will inspire and awaken the heart to the service of God, including the esoteric parts of Torah, and/or those that arouse the person to repentance. For example, a mourner may recite Psalms if it will arouse feelings of repentance.

Reading and Entertainment

It is forbidden to read newspapers, magazines, novels, and the like if it is done simply for pleasure. The same applies to playing board games, watching videos, television, or movies. One must maximize the time of Shiva to mourn the deceased and to honor the memory through holy thoughts and matters.

Leaving the Shiva Home

Mourners may not leave the Shiva home during the entire seven days of Shiva, except on Shabbat and Jewish holidays. If one must go out, one may only do so at night, when the streets have emptied. In a case of dire need, or great financial loss, one may go out during the day, but preferably not during the first three days.

If for any reason it is difficult to have the daily prayer services in the Shiva home, he may leave to bring people to pray or to go to the synagogue to pray with a Minyan and recite the Mourner's Kaddish.

A nursing mother who has joined the mourners in the Shiva home for the week of Shiva, may leave to go to her home to feed her baby, if she cannot arrange to have the baby with her at the Shiva home. The same applies to others for sleeping (see below).

If one has to leave the city during Shiva (i.e. to sit Shiva elsewhere), he should consult a competent rabbi for guidance.

Sleeping

A mourner may sleep in his bed as usual. Some have the custom to remove a pillow (if he sleeps with two), or in some other way reduce one's accustomed comfort as a reminder that he is in mourning. If one cannot sleep in the Shiva home (i.e. there are not enough beds), he may go to another place to sleep, but only late at night.

Joyous Celebrations

A mourner is forbidden from engaging in any activity that brings joy. Thus, he may not attend a wedding, Bar Mitzva, *Brit Milah* (circumcision of a child), or other happy religious events during Shiva.

Needless to say, he also must avoid live music performances, recitals, shows, and all similar events. If one is mourning a parent, this prohibition lasts for twelve months; for all other relatives, the prohibition lasts for thirty days. In general, there are few exceptions to this prohibition, and in all circumstances, it is best to consult a competent rabbi.

If one's child is getting married during Shiva, consult a competent rabbi for guidance.

If a relative or close friend is getting married, one may not attend the wedding during Shiva, but only after the first thirty days. At the wedding, he should help serve food so that his personal honor and feeling of festivity is somewhat reduced. Also, he should not remain in the room when music is playing and/or people are dancing.

Parents may attend the *Brit Milah* (circumcision of a child), and *Pidyon Haben* (redemption of the firstborn son) of their son, after the first three days of mourning, but they may not remain for the reception meal (unless it is held in their own home).

In all of the above cases, one may wear fine clothing, including leather shoes, for the occasion. At the conclusion of the event, regular mourning observances resume.

Shabbat and Jewish Holidays

Overt mourning on Shabbat and Jewish holidays is forbidden. Thus the mourners should wear regular shoes, sit on regular chairs, and change into clothing that bears no sign of mourning.

When the Jewish holidays of Rosh Hashana, Yom Kippur, Sukkot, Passover, and Shavuot, occur in the middle of Shiva, the remaining days of Shiva mourning are annulled. (This applies as long as at least a few moments of Shiva were observed before the holiday began, i.e. one took off his leather shoes, sat on a low stool, or did any other activity related to mourning.) However, a candle should remain lit for all seven days, but should not be in the same room as the holiday meals.

If the burial took place on the morning leading into the holiday (*Erev Yom Tov*), the mourners may prepare for the holiday after midday.

Preparing for Shabbat and Holidays

• On Friday afternoon, and on the day leading into a Jewish holiday, one may bathe and change into Shabbat or holiday clothing as usual, starting two and a half hours before sunset.

• A mourner is permitted to review the Torah portion (*Maaver Sedra*) before Shabbat.

• One may spread a clean tablecloth on the table in honor of Shabbat or the holiday.

• The candle that was kindled for the Shiva should remain lit during Shabbat and Jewish holidays, but shouldn't be rekindled if it goes out on the Shabbat. Some remove the candle to another room (before Shabbat) if it was in the dining room, to avoid dampening the Shabbat atmosphere.

• Those who have the custom to bless their children on the eve of Shabbat should not do so during the mourning period.

• A mourner may go to the synagogue for services, but he may not lead the prayer services. He recites the Mourner's Kaddish at all the appropriate places throughout the service.

• The mourner does not recite the hymn *"Sholom Aleichem"* before making *Kiddush* Friday night, but he may sing the regular Shabbat and holiday songs during the meal.

• He may not engage in marital relations, study Torah, nor be called to recite the blessing over the Torah reading (*Aliyah*). If he is called to the Torah by mistake, he may accept.

• At the conclusion of Shabbat or holidays, the mourner says *"Böruch hamavdil bayn kodesh l'chol"* (short Havdallah), and removes his shoes before praying the *Maariv* (evening) service. Once he is back home, he should immediately change into the clothing on which the Kriah was done.

• The mourner should hear *Havdallah* from another person. If this is not possible, he may recite it himself, omitting the opening verses and beginning with the blessing over wine.

Rosh Hashana, Erev Yom Kippur, Sukkot, Chanuka, Purim, Passover, Fast Days

On Rosh Hashana, Shiva is annulled. The mourner goes to the synagogue and hears the blowing of the Shofar.

On Erev Yom Kippur, the mourner should do *Kaparot* in the Shiva home. If this is not possible, Kaparot is done with money.

On Sukkot, Shiva is annulled. The mourner eats in the Sukkah, and performs the mitzva of *Lulav* and *Etrog* (the four-kinds).

On Chanuka, the mourner should kindle the Chanuka *Menora* with a blessing.

On Purim, the *Megilla* is read in the Shiva home. Mourners send only the two minimum *Mishloach Manot* (food gifts) as is customary on Purim; however, one should not send items associated with joy (i.e. wine, fancy foods, etc.). One does not send the customary *Mishloach Manot* to a mourner.

On Passover, Shiva is annulled. The mourner is obligated to search for *Chametz* (leavened bread), perform all the requirements of the *Seder*, and observe all the laws of Passover.

On all public fast days, the mourner is obligated to fast. On the fast of the Ninth of Av, one may go to the synagogue.

Comforting the Mourners

A Truly Great Mitzva

Just as showing respect for the deceased is a great mitzva and an act of kindness, so too is comforting the mourners. This mitzva is fulfilled by personally visiting the house of mourning.

The mitzva of *Nichum Aveilim* (Heb. comforting mourners) lasts throughout the entire seven days of Shiva. Each visit is considered another mitzva. If one heard of the passing after Shiva, he may fulfill this mitzva until the thirtieth day.

The Needs of the Mourners

The mitzva of comforting mourners includes looking after their material needs. One should respectfully and discreetly find out what their needs may be and fulfill them.

For example, if the mourners lost their main source of financial support, it is important to help gather funds for their continued support and to help the family in any other way one can.

Visiting the Mourners

In many communities, the three daily prayer services are held in the Shiva home. This provides family and friends the opportunity to visit with the mourners during different times of the day. If services are not held in the Shiva home, it is important to arrange visits, so that there are people around to comfort the mourners and attend to their needs. One should be considerate and neither visit too early in the morning nor very late at night, and to respect the privacy of the mourners.

One does not pay a condolence visit on Shabbat and Jewish holidays, since overt mourning on those days is prohibited.

Receiving Visitors

Just as it is a mitzva to comfort the mourners, it is a mitzva for the mourners to receive those who seek to comfort them. Depending on the mourners' personal needs and abilities, they may, however, restrict visitations to a few hours during the day or evening.

When receiving those coming to comfort, it is best to focus on sharing memories of the deceased and reciting Psalms. The key is to remember that one needn't "entertain" during Shiva.

How to Comfort

Many people do not know what to say to a mourner. In reality your presence alone is comforting enough. Saying the right thing is of secondary importance. Below are some general guidelines to observe when visiting a Shiva house.

For Visitors

• Upon arriving, do not greet the mourner (or anyone else) with usual greetings (i.e. "Hello," "How are you," etc.).

• Visitors may stand or sit.

• One does not begin talking until the mourners initiate (unless the mourner does not know about this custom). If there are many people present, one does not have to wait for the mourner to initiate with each person individually.

• It is best to engage the mourners in interesting and inspirational talk to ease their pain. One should not speak or act frivolously, or joke around. It is fitting to relate stories and memories of the deceased. One should be careful not to relate anything that may increase the pain or distress of the mourners.

• When speaking of the deceased, one says "*Alav Ha-sholom*" for men ("may he rest in peace"), or "*Ale-ha Ha-sholom*" for women ("may she rest in peace"), after the person's name. Some may say "*Zichrono Livrocho*" for men, or "*Zichrona Livrocho*" for women, meaning "of blessed memory."

• Visitors should not be expected to be served any food.

• Before the visitor is about to leave, he consoles the mourners with the "Condolence Declaration" (see following page).

• When one sees that the mourners would like privacy, one should politely take leave.

For Mourners

• The mourner should sit on a low stool or crate.

• When visitors arrive, one does not rise to greet them, even if it is a rabbi or great sage.

• The mourner should refrain from excessive conversation on the phone, or engaging in frivolous banter, as it appears that he has forgotten his grief.

• The mourner does not say goodbye or the like, but simply says "*Amen*" when offered the "Condolence Declaration."

Comforting from a Distance

If for whatever reason it is not possible to come in person to comfort the mourners, one may do so by phone, fax, email, etc., or by sending a messenger.

The Condolence Declaration

After spending time with the mourners, before leaving, each visitor consoles them with the following passage.

The mourners sit on a low stool or crate when receiving the condolence and respond with *"Amen."* If this is done immediately after the morning prayer service, the male mourners remain in their *Tallit* and *Tefillin* to accommodate those who need to leave to work.

Recite the following to the mourners:

Ha-mökom y'na-chaym es-chem	הַמָּקוֹם יְנַחֵם אֶתְכֶם
b'soch sh'ör a-vaylay	בְּתוֹךְ שְׁאָר אֲבֵלֵי
tzi-yon viy'rushö-lö-yim.	צִיּוֹן וִירוּשָׁלָיִם:

May the Almighty comfort you among the mourners of Zion and Jerusalem.

The Meaning of the Declaration

The traditional wording of the above condolence declaration expresses two themes:

1) The pain of the individual is connected to the pain of the community. Just as the destruction of Zion and Jerusalem is mourned by the entire nation of Israel, so, too, does the entire

community share in the mourning of the individual's loss, since all Israel constitutes a single body. This helps to make the pain and sorrow bearable.

2) Just as the consolation over the destruction of Zion and Jerusalem is certain to come — this being a fundamental principle of our faith — so, too, will the consolation for the individual's loss. For, as Maimonides writes, the purpose of all mourning is to awaken us to *Teshuva* (repentance), which will surely bring the ultimate consolation from "The Consoler of Zion and the Builder of Jerusalem."

The Mourner's Kaddish

The *Kaddish* is a deeply meaningful prayer that expresses and reflects the values of the Jewish people. A male mourner is obligated to recite the Mourner's Kaddish during the three daily prayer services. This continues for the first eleven months (less one day) for the parent, and for thirty days for other relatives. Kaddish is then said on each Yartzeit (anniversary of passing). A step-son or an adopted son may take upon himself to recite the Kaddish, but he is not obligated to do so.

If a relative has left no sons, close male relatives have a responsibility to ensure that the Kaddish is recited for eleven months and three weeks, and on each Yartziet thereafter.

What is Kaddish?

The Kaddish is in essence a prayer of praise for God. It was written in Aramaic, the common language in Talmudic times, to ensure that everyone understood what was being said.

The title "*Kaddish*" is translated as "holy," and its recitation brings holiness to God's name and to all those who respond "*Amen*" while it is being recited.

There are five forms of Kaddish:

1. *Half-Kaddish*: Recited during services to indicate the conclusion of minor sections of the prayer service.

2. *Whole-Kaddish*: This Kaddish is the same as the half-Kaddish, but adds the section "*Titkabel*" (may the prayers be accepted) and concluding paragraphs. This is recited after the conclusion of major sections of the prayer services.

3. *Kaddish-D'Rabannan*: This Kaddish is the same as the half-Kaddish, but adds the section "*Al Yisrael*" (upon Israel, upon our sages) and concluding paragraphs. This is recited after the conclusion of studying a section from the Talmud or Mishna.

4. *Kaddish-Yatom* (the Mourner's Kaddish): This Kaddish is the same as the half-Kaddish, but adds the section "*Y'hey Shloma*" (May there be abundant peace) and concluding paragraphs. It is recited by mourners at specific points during the services.

5. *Kaddish-D'Itchad'ta*: Recited at the conclusion of a major tractate of Talmud, and at a funeral. Just as one who concludes a major tractate of the Talmud, which is a holy endeavor, recites Kaddish, so, too, one who passes from this world has completed a holy endeavor and thus, this Kaddish is recited.

Kaddish is for the Living

Remarkably, the Mourner's Kaddish does not mention death, nor make any reference to the deceased. It is directed, instead, at the living.

The Kaddish affirms God's justice and speaks of the value of life. It states that God is the Creator of the world and that He rules it. Kaddish also states that there will be an Era of Moshiach, when all illness and suffering will cease, and requests that this time be ushered in during our lifetime.

Furthur, it praises God's name and describes His glory, and petitions God to give His people "abundant peace, grace, kindness, compassion, long life, ample sustenance and deliverance, to those who occupy themselves with the Torah, and to all of Israel."

Restoring Perfection

Our sages teach that every Jewish person reveals a particular expression of Godliness in this world. Once he or she passes away, God's radiance is "diminished" somewhat in this world. When Kaddish is recited, it restores this radiance and brings additional glory to God's name in this world.

On a mystical note, there are ten words of praise in Kaddish. They correlate to the ten *Sefirot* (Divine manifestations) and relate to the ten Utterances of Creation. This indicates that we, who are still alive, have a role to play in perfecting Creation.

The Power of One's Children

According to the Talmud, parents are judged by the deeds of their children. If one's children follow in God's ways, then the lives of the parents attain additional sanctity.

Similarly, if reciting Kaddish serves as a catalyst for personal spiritual growth, this too adds sanctity to the life that the parent lived, while elevating the soul in its current state. Therefore, the message of Kaddish should permeate one's personal life. In this way, children, through their actions below, will directly benefit their parents in the world above.

Daily Recitation of Kaddish

The Mourner's Kaddish can only be recited in the presence of a *Minyan* (quorum of ten Jewish males over age thirteen) during a prayer service, or after reciting Psalms or Mishnayot. It is normally recited at specific points during each of the three daily services. Kabbalah explains that a son who recites Kaddish for his father or mother saves them from certain judgment. One should, therefore, do the utmost to recite Kaddish at every opportunity during the first eleven months from the passing, and on each Yartzeit thereafter.

Women may undertake to do a specific mitzva in honor and memory of the loved one. Our sages state that for them, this brings the same merit to the soul as the recitation of Kaddish.

Leading the Prayer Services

Many mourners make a point to lead the weekday prayer services in their synagogue for the entire eleven months (less one day), for then one can recite the different forms of Kaddish throughout the services. This adds more and more holiness to the soul of the departed. By leading the services, one also joins the merit of all those praying and praising God to the soul of their dear departed.

In the case when there are two mourners in one synagogue, there are several ways to proceed. If there are at least two Minyanim (twenty or more Jewish men over the age thirteen) present, separate services can held in different rooms or at different times, allowing each mourner the opportunity to lead the services and to recite Kaddish. Some authorities oppose the idea of making different minyanim because of the concept of "a large number of people gives greater glory to God."

If there are not enough men to form two minyanim, then those saying Kaddish can take turns leading the services. During the morning service, they can each lead for different sections of the service. One should follow the custom of his community.

If One Cannot Lead the Services

If one cannot lead the services, one must still pray with the Minyan and recite the Mourner's Kaddish at the designated points. If one cannot attend all three daily services, he should at least attend one of them to recite the Mourner's Kaddish.

If the Deceased Did Not Leave Any Sons

If one did not leave any sons, or if it is impossible for the sons to recite the Mourner's Kaddish every day with a Minyan, one must hire someone to recite the Mourner's Kaddish in the merit of the deceased. It is preferable that this person should not be reciting Kaddish for anyone else at the time, but it is not imperative.

Hiring a "Kaddish proxy" is not an ideal first choice and the option should not be misused for convenience or to discharge oneself from duty, but only in a case of genuine need.

When a person is hired to recite the Kaddish, the mourner should still study Torah and give charity (except on Shabbat and Jewish holidays) on each day that Kaddish is recited.

Reciting Kaddish for Eleven Months

The Mourner's Kaddish is recited during all prayer services for eleven months, less one day when recited by a son, and eleven months and three weeks, when recited by all others.

Why is Kaddish recited by son(s) for only eleven months, less one day? According to Kabbalah, the soul of the departed is judged by a Heavenly Court. If one's good deeds are outweighed by one's sins, the soul undergoes a painful spiritual cleansing. Depending on the sins, the cleansing period could last up to twelve months, following which the soul is allowed into its eternal spiritual resting place. Reciting Kaddish eases this judgment and any travails the soul might have to endure.

However, one does not recite Kaddish the full twelve months out of respect for the departed. Pausing a month early indicates our confidence that the person's life was sufficiently meritorious to have avoided the full twelve months of cleansing. From another perspective, a son stops reciting the Mourner's Kaddish earlier than others because he still is obligated to honor his parents — even after their passing.

The Text of the Mourner's Kaddish

Mourners recite Kaddish up to six times during the morning services, and twice during the afternoon and evening service, for a total of ten times on each day, as follows:

During Shacharit (morning services):
1) *Kaddish D'Rabbanan*, following the readings before "*Hodu.*" 2) *Kaddish Yatom*, following "*Shir Shel Yom.*" 3) *Kaddish D'Rabbanan*, following the readings before "*Olaynu.*" 4) *Kaddish Yatom*, following "*Olaynu.*" 5) *Kaddish Yatom*, following the recitation of the daily Psalms. 6) *Kaddish D'Rabbanan*, following the studying of selected Mishnayot.

During Mincha (afternoon) and Maariv (evening) services:
1) *Kaddish Yatom*, following "*Olaynu.*" 2) *Kaddish D'Rabbanan*, following the studying of selected Mishnayot.

Directions for Reciting Kaddish

• The Kaddish can only be recited in the presence of a Minyan (quorum of ten Jewish males over age thirteen) and only following the recitation of prayers, Psalms, or Torah study.

• The Kaddish is recited aloud, while standing with the feet together.

• The one saying Kaddish should pause after each paragraph to allow the congregation to respond, as indicated.

• It is customary for the one saying Kaddish to bow the head while reciting certain words. These words are bracketed by the following symbol: "°". When the symbol appears before a word, bow the head forward, and remain bowed until the word that ends with the same symbol, then raise the head.

• Before the final paragraph of "*Oseh Shalom*," one takes three steps back, and upon concluding the Kaddish, three steps forward. It is also customary to incline the head right, left, and straight ahead, while reciting certain words in this paragraph (see instructions below).

• While reciting Kaddish, have in mind that you are performing the positive mitzva of sanctifying God, based on the verse, "I [God] shall be sanctified amidst the children of Israel" (Leviticus 22:32).

Yis-gadal v'yis-kadash °sh'may rabö°.

     (Cong.: Ömayn.)

יִתְגַּדַּל וְיִתְקַדַּשׁ °שְׁמֵהּ רַבָּא°׃

אמן

B'öl'mö di v'rö chir'u-say

v'yam-lich mal'chusay, v'yatz-mach

pur-könay °vikö-rayv m'shi-chay°.

     (Cong.: Ömayn.)

בְּעָלְמָא דִּי בְרָא כִרְעוּתֵהּ

וְיַמְלִיךְ מַלְכוּתֵהּ, וְיַצְמַח

פּוּרְקָנֵהּ °וִיקָרֵב מְשִׁיחֵהּ°׃

אמן

B'cha-yay-chon uv'yomay-chon

uv'cha-yay d'chöl bays yisrö-ayl,

ba-agölö uviz'man köriv

°v'im'ru ömayn°. (Cong.: Ömayn. Y'hay

sh'may rabö m'vörach l'ölam ul'öl'may

öl'ma-yö. Yisböraych)

בְּחַיֵּיכוֹן וּבְיוֹמֵיכוֹן

וּבְחַיֵּי דְכָל בֵּית יִשְׂרָאֵל,

בַּעֲגָלָא וּבִזְמַן קָרִיב

°וְאִמְרוּ אָמֵן°׃ אמן. יְהֵא שְׁמֵהּ

רַבָּא מְבָרַךְ לְעָלַם וּלְעָלְמֵי

עָלְמַיָּא׃ יִתְבָּרַךְ׃

°Y'hay sh'may rabö m'vörach

l'ölam ul'öl'may öl'ma-yö.

Yis-böraych° °v'yish-tabach,

v'yispö-ayr, v'yis-romöm,

v'yis-nasay, v'yis-hadör,

v'yis-aleh, v'yis-halöl°, °sh'may

d'kud-shö b'rich hu°.

     (Cong.: Ömayn.)

°יְהֵא שְׁמֵהּ רַבָּא מְבָרַךְ

לְעָלַם וּלְעָלְמֵי עָלְמַיָּא׃

יִתְבָּרַךְ° °וְיִשְׁתַּבַּח,

וְיִתְפָּאַר, וְיִתְרוֹמַם,

וְיִתְנַשֵּׂא, וְיִתְהַדָּר,

וְיִתְעַלֶּה, וְיִתְהַלָּל°, °שְׁמֵהּ

דְּקֻדְשָׁא בְּרִיךְ הוּא°׃

אמן

170

L'aylö min köl bir'chösö v'shi-rösö,   לְעֵלָּא מִן כָּל בִּרְכָתָא וְשִׁירָתָא,

tush-b'chösö v'neche-mösö,   תֻּשְׁבְּחָתָא וְנֶחֱמָתָא,

da-amirön b'öl'mö,   דַּאֲמִירָן בְּעָלְמָא,

°v'im'ru ömayn°.   °וְאִמְרוּ אָמֵן°׃

(Cong.: Ömayn.)   אמן

For *Kaddish D'Rabbanan* add the following,
otherwise skip to next paragraph:

Al yisrö-ayl v'al rabö-nön,   עַל יִשְׂרָאֵל וְעַל רַבָּנָן,

v'al tal-miday-hon, v'al köl tal-miday   וְעַל תַּלְמִידֵיהוֹן וְעַל כָּל תַּלְמִידֵי

sal-miday-hon, v'al köl mön d'ös'kin   תַלְמִידֵיהוֹן, וְעַל כָּל מָאן דְּעָסְקִין

b'oray'sö, di v'asrö hö-dayn, v'di   בְּאוֹרַיְתָא, דִּי בְאַתְרָא הָדֵין וְדִי

v'chöl asar v'asar, y'hay l'hon ul'chon   בְכָל אֲתַר וַאֲתַר, יְהֵא לְהוֹן וּלְכוֹן

sh'lömö rabö, chinö v'chisdö   שְׁלָמָא רַבָּא חִנָּא וְחִסְדָּא

v'rachamin v'cha-yin ari-chin,   וְרַחֲמִין וְחַיִּין אֲרִיכִין,

um'zonö r'vichö ufur-könö, min   וּמְזוֹנָא רְוִיחָא וּפוּרְקָנָא, מִן

ködöm avu-hon d'vish'ma-yö,   קֳדָם אֲבוּהוֹן דְּבִשְׁמַיָּא,

°v'im'ru ömayn°.   °וְאִמְרוּ אָמֵן°׃

(Ömayn)   אָמֵן

Continue here:

Y'hay sh'lömö rabö min sh'ma-yö,   יְהֵא שְׁלָמָא רַבָּא מִן שְׁמַיָּא

v'cha-yim tovim ölay-nu v'al köl   וְחַיִּים טוֹבִים עָלֵינוּ וְעַל כָּל

yisrö-ayl °v'im'ru ömayn°.   יִשְׂרָאֵל °וְאִמְרוּ אָמֵן°׃

(Cong.: Ömayn.)   אמן

Take three steps back and say the following, while bowing the head
to the right, straight ahead, left, straight ahead, and bowing down (as indicated):

> Oseh shölom* bim'romöv, ^ hu   עֹשֶׂה שָׁלוֹם* בִּמְרוֹמָיו, ^ הוּא <

< ya-aseh shölom ölaynu, ^ v'al köl   יַעֲשֶׂה שָׁלוֹם עָלֵינוּ, ^ וְעַל כָּל >

yisrö-ayl, °v'im'ru ömayn°.   יִשְׂרָאֵל, °וְאִמְרוּ אָמֵן°:

(Cong.: Ömayn.)   אמן

Take three steps forward.

*Between Rosh Hashana and Yom Kippur, substitute with "ha-shölom."

Exalted and hallowed be His great Name (Cong.: Amen). Throughout the world which He has created according to His Will. May He establish His kingship, bring forth His redemption and hasten the coming of His Moshiach (Cong.: Amen). In your lifetime and in your days and in the lifetime of the entire House of Israel, speedily and soon, and say, Amen. (Cong.: Amen. May His great Name be blessed forever and to all eternity. Blessed). May His great Name be blessed forever and to all eternity. Blessed and praised, glorified, exalted and extolled, honored, adored and lauded be the Name of the Holy One, blessed be He (Cong.: Amen). Beyond all the blessings, hymns, praises and consolations that are uttered in the world; and say, Amen. (Cong.: Amen). May the prayers and supplications of the entire House of Israel be accepted before their Father in heaven; and say, Amen. (Cong.: Amen). [Add this paragraph only for Kaddish D'Rabbanan:] Upon Israel, and upon our sages, and upon their disciples, and upon all the disciples of their disciples, and upon all those who occupy themselves with the Torah, here or in any other place, upon them and upon you, may there be abundant peace, grace, kindness, compassion, long life, ample sustenance and deliverance, from their Father in heaven; and say, Amen. (Cong: Amen.) May there be abundant peace from heaven, and a good life for us and for all Israel; and say, Amen. (Cong.: Amen). He Who makes [between Rosh Hashana and Yom Kippur: the] peace in His heavens, may He make peace for us and for all Israel; and say, Amen (Cong.: Amen).

Mincha - The Afternoon Service

After reciting the *"Korbanot"* (offerings), the service begins here:

Ash-ray yosh'vay vay-sechö,	אַשְׁרֵי יוֹשְׁבֵי בֵיתֶךָ,
od y'ha-l'luchö selöh. Ash-ray hö-öm	עוֹד יְהַלְלוּךְ סֶּלָה: אַשְׁרֵי הָעָם
she-köchö lo, ash-ray hö-öm	שֶׁכָּכָה לוֹ, אַשְׁרֵי הָעָם
she-adonöy elohöv. T'hilöh l'dövid,	שֶׁיְיָ אֱלֹהָיו: תְּהִלָּה לְדָוִד,
aro-mim'chö elohai ha-melech,	אֲרוֹמִמְךָ אֱלוֹהַי הַמֶּלֶךְ,
va-avö-r'chöh shim'chö l'olöm vö-ed.	וַאֲבָרְכָה שִׁמְךָ לְעוֹלָם וָעֶד:
B'chöl yom avö-r'chekö, va-aha-l'löh	בְּכָל יוֹם אֲבָרְכֶךָ, וַאֲהַלְלָה
shim'chö l'olöm vö-ed. Gödol	שִׁמְךָ לְעוֹלָם וָעֶד: גָּדוֹל
adonöy um'hulöl m'od, v'lig'dulöso	יְיָ וּמְהֻלָל מְאֹד, וְלִגְדֻלָתוֹ
ayn chay-ker. Dor l'dor y'shabach	אֵין חֵקֶר: דּוֹר לְדוֹר יְשַׁבַּח
ma-asechö, ug'vuro-sechö yagidu.	מַעֲשֶׂיךָ, וּגְבוּרֹתֶיךָ יַגִּידוּ:
Hadar k'vod ho-dechö, v'div'ray	הֲדַר כְּבוֹד הוֹדֶךָ, וְדִבְרֵי
nif-l'osechö ö-sichöh. Ve-ezuz	נִפְלְאֹתֶיךָ אָשִׂיחָה: וֶעֱזוּז
no-r'osechö yo-mayru, ug'dulös'chö	נוֹרְאֹתֶיךָ יֹאמֵרוּ, וּגְדֻלָתְךָ
asap'renöh. Zecher rav tuv'chö	אֲסַפְּרֶנָּה: זֵכֶר רַב טוּבְךָ
yabi-u, v'tzid'kös'chö y'ra-naynu.	יַבִּיעוּ, וְצִדְקָתְךָ יְרַנֵּנוּ:
Chanun v'rachum adonöy, erech	חַנּוּן וְרַחוּם יְיָ, אֶרֶךְ
apa-yim ug'döl chösed. Tov adonöy	אַפַּיִם וּגְדָל חָסֶד: טוֹב יְיָ
lakol, v'ra-chamöv al köl ma-asöv.	לַכֹּל, וְרַחֲמָיו עַל כָּל מַעֲשָׂיו:
Yoduchö adonöy köl ma-a-sechö,	יוֹדוּךָ יְיָ כָּל מַעֲשֶׂיךָ,

va-chasi-dechö y'vö-r'chu-chöh.	וַחֲסִידֶיךָ יְבָרְכוּכָה׃
K'vod mal'chus'chö yo-mayru,	כְּבוֹד מַלְכוּתְךָ יֹאמֵרוּ,
ug'vurö-s'chö y'da-bayru. L'hodi-a	וּגְבוּרָתְךָ יְדַבֵּרוּ׃ לְהוֹדִיעַ
liv'nay hö-ödöm g'vurosöv, uch'vod	לִבְנֵי הָאָדָם גְּבוּרֹתָיו, וּכְבוֹד
hadar mal'chuso. Mal'chus'chö,	הֲדַר מַלְכוּתוֹ׃ מַלְכוּתְךָ
mal'chus köl olö-mim,	מַלְכוּת כָּל עוֹלָמִים,
umem-shal-t'chö b'chöl dor vödor.	וּמֶמְשַׁלְתְּךָ בְּכָל דּוֹר וָדֹר׃
So-maych adonöy l'chöl ha-nof'lim,	סוֹמֵךְ יְיָ לְכָל הַנֹּפְלִים,
v'zokayf l'chöl ha-k'fufim. Aynay chol	וְזוֹקֵף לְכָל הַכְּפוּפִים׃ עֵינֵי כֹל
ay-lechö y'sa-bayru, v'atöh no-sayn	אֵלֶיךָ יְשַׂבֵּרוּ, וְאַתָּה נוֹתֵן
löhem es öch-löm b'ito. Posay-ach es	לָהֶם אֶת אָכְלָם בְּעִתּוֹ׃ פּוֹתֵחַ אֶת
yödechö, umasbi-a l'chöl chai rötzon.	יָדֶךָ, וּמַשְׂבִּיעַ לְכָל חַי רָצוֹן׃
Tzadik adonöy b'chöl d'röchöv,	צַדִּיק יְיָ בְּכָל דְּרָכָיו,
v'chösid b'chöl ma-asöv. Körov	וְחָסִיד בְּכָל מַעֲשָׂיו׃ קָרוֹב
adonöy l'chöl ko-r'öv, l'chol asher	יְיָ לְכָל קֹרְאָיו, לְכֹל אֲשֶׁר
yikrö-u-hu ve-emes. R'tzon y'ray-öv	יִקְרָאֻהוּ בֶאֱמֶת׃ רְצוֹן יְרֵאָיו
ya-aseh, v'es shav-ösöm yish-ma	יַעֲשֶׂה, וְאֶת שַׁוְעָתָם יִשְׁמַע
v'yoshi-aym. Shomayr adonöy es köl	וְיוֹשִׁיעֵם׃ שׁוֹמֵר יְיָ אֶת כָּל
ohavöv, v'ays köl hö-r'shö-im	אֹהֲבָיו, וְאֵת כָּל הָרְשָׁעִים
yash-mid. T'hilas adonöy y'daber pi,	יַשְׁמִיד׃ תְּהִלַּת יְיָ יְדַבֶּר פִּי,
vi-voraych köl bösör shaym köd-sho	וִיבָרֵךְ כָּל בָּשָׂר שֵׁם קָדְשׁוֹ
l'olöm vö-ed. Va-anachnu n'vöraych	לְעוֹלָם וָעֶד׃ וַאֲנַחְנוּ נְבָרֵךְ
yöh, may-atöh v'ad olöm, ha-l'luyöh.	יָהּ, מֵעַתָּה וְעַד עוֹלָם, הַלְלוּיָהּ׃

Happy are those who dwell in Your House; they will yet praise You forever. Happy is the people whose lot is thus; happy is the people whose God is the Lord. A Psalm of

174

praise by David: I will exalt You, my God the King, and bless Your Name forever. Every day I will bless You, and extol Your Name forever. The Lord is great and exceedingly exalted, and there is no limit to His greatness. One generation to another will laud Your works, and tell of Your mighty acts. I will speak of the splendor of Your glorious majesty and of Your wondrous deeds. They will proclaim the might of Your awesome acts, and I will recount Your greatness. They will express the remembrance of Your abounding goodness, and sing of Your righteousness. The Lord is gracious and compassionate, slow to anger and of great kindness. The Lord is good to all, and His mercies extend over all His works. Lord, all Your works will give thanks to You, and Your pious ones will bless You. They will declare the glory of Your kingdom, and tell of Your strength. To make known to men His mighty acts, and the glorious majesty of His kingdom. Your kingship is a kingship over all worlds, and Your dominion is throughout all generations. The Lord supports all who fall, and makes erect all who are bent. The eyes of all look expectantly to You, and You give them their food at the proper time. You open Your hand and satisfy the desire of every living thing. The Lord is righteous in all His ways, and benevolent in all His deeds. The Lord is close to all who call upon Him, to all who call upon Him in truth. He fulfills the desire of those who fear Him, hears their cry and delivers them. The Lord watches over all who love Him, and will destroy all the wicked. My mouth will utter the praise of the Lord, and let all flesh bless His holy Name forever. And we will bless the Lord from now to eternity. Praise the Lord.

All rise. The leader recites Half-Kaddish (below).

HALF-KADDISH

It is customary for the one saying Kaddish to bow the head while reciting certain words. These words are bracketed by the following symbol: "°". When the symbol appears before a word, bow the head forward, and remain bowed until the word that ends with the same symbol, then raise the head.

Yis-gadal v'yis-kadash •sh'may rabö•.

יִתְגַּדַּל וְיִתְקַדַּשׁ •שְׁמֵהּ רַבָּא•:

(Cong.: Ōmayn.)

אמן

B'öl'mö di v'rö chir'u-say
v'yam-lich mal'chusay, v'yatz-mach
pur-könay •vikö-rayv m'shi-chay•.

בְּעָלְמָא דִּי בְרָא כִרְעוּתֵהּ
וְיַמְלִיךְ מַלְכוּתֵהּ, וְיַצְמַח
פוּרְקָנֵהּ •וִיקָרֵב מְשִׁיחֵהּ•:

(Cong.: Ōmayn.)

אמן

B'cha-yay-chon uv'yomay-chon
uv'cha-yay d'chöl bays yisrö-ayl,
ba-agölö uviz'man köriv
•v'im'ru ömayn•. (Cong.: Ōmayn. Y'hay
sh'may rabö m'vörach l'ölam ul'öl'may
öl'ma-yö. Yisböraych)

בְּחַיֵּיכוֹן וּבְיוֹמֵיכוֹן
וּבְחַיֵּי דְכָל בֵּית יִשְׂרָאֵל,
בַּעֲגָלָא וּבִזְמַן קָרִיב
•וְאִמְרוּ אָמֵן•: אמן. יְהֵא שְׁמֵהּ
רַבָּא מְבָרַךְ לְעָלַם וּלְעָלְמֵי
עָלְמַיָּא: יִתְבָּרַךְ:

•Y'hay sh'may rabö m'vörach
l'ölam ul'öl'may öl'ma-yö.
Yis-böraych• •v'yish-tabach,
v'yispö-ayr, v'yis-romöm,
v'yis-nasay, v'yis-hadör,
v'yis-aleh, v'yis-halöl•, •sh'may
d'kud-shö b'rich hu•.

•יְהֵא שְׁמֵהּ רַבָּא מְבָרַךְ
לְעָלַם וּלְעָלְמֵי עָלְמַיָּא:
יִתְבָּרַךְ• •וְיִשְׁתַּבַּח,
וְיִתְפָּאַר, וְיִתְרוֹמַם,
וְיִתְנַשֵּׂא, וְיִתְהַדָּר,
וְיִתְעַלֶּה, וְיִתְהַלָּל•, שְׁמֵהּ
דְּקֻדְשָׁא בְּרִיךְ הוּא•:

(Cong.: Ōmayn.)

אמן

176

L'aylö min köl bir'chösö v'shi-rösö, לְעֵלָּא מִן כָּל בִּרְכָתָא וְשִׁירָתָא,

tush-b'chösö v'neche-mösö, תֻּשְׁבְּחָתָא וְנֶחֱמָתָא,

da-amirön b'öl'mö, דַּאֲמִירָן בְּעָלְמָא,

°v'im'ru ömayn°. °וְאִמְרוּ אָמֵן°:

(Cong.: Ömayn.) אמן

Exalted and hallowed be His great Name (Cong.: Amen). Throughout the world which He has created according to His Will. May He establish His kingship, bring forth His redemption and hasten the coming of His Moshiach (Cong.: Amen). In your lifetime and in your days and in the lifetime of the entire House of Israel, speedily and soon, and say, Amen. (Cong.: Amen. May His great Name be blessed forever and to all eternity. Blessed). May His great Name be blessed forever and to all eternity. Blessed and praised, glorified, exalted and extolled, honored, adored and lauded be the Name of the Holy One, blessed be He (Cong.: Amen). Beyond all the blessings, hymns, praises and consolations that are uttered in the world; and say, Amen. (Cong.: Amen).

The Amidah is recited while standing, with both feet together.
Before beginning, take three steps back, then three steps forward, and say:

Adonöy, s'fösai tif-töch ufi אֲדֹנָי, שְׂפָתַי תִּפְתָּח וּפִי

yagid t'hilö-sechö. יַגִּיד תְּהִלָּתֶךָ:

My Lord, open my lips, and my mouth shall declare Your praise.

At the word *Böruch* (blessed), bend the knee; at *Atöh* (You),
bow forward; and at *Adonöy* (Lord), straighten up.

Böruch atöh adonöy elo-haynu בָּרוּךְ אַתָּה יְיָ אֱלֹהֵינוּ

vay-lohay avosaynu, elo-hay וֵאלֹהֵי אֲבוֹתֵינוּ, אֱלֹהֵי

avröhöm, elo-hay yitzchök, vay-lohay אַבְרָהָם, אֱלֹהֵי יִצְחָק, וֵאלֹהֵי

ya-akov, hö-ayl ha-gödol ha-gibor	יַעֲקֹב, הָאֵל הַגָּדוֹל הַגִּבּוֹר
v'hanorö, ayl el-yon, gomayl	וְהַנּוֹרָא, אֵל עֶלְיוֹן, גּוֹמֵל
cha-södim tovim, ko-nay ha-kol,	חֲסָדִים טוֹבִים, קוֹנֵה הַכֹּל,
v'zochayr chas'day övos, umay-vi	וְזוֹכֵר חַסְדֵי אָבוֹת, וּמֵבִיא
go-ayl liv'nay v'nayhem l'ma-an	גוֹאֵל לִבְנֵי בְנֵיהֶם לְמַעַן
sh'mo b'ahavöh.	שְׁמוֹ בְּאַהֲבָה:

Blessed are You, Lord our God and God of our fathers, God of Abraham, God of Isaac and God of Jacob, the great, mighty and awesome God, exalted God, Who bestows bountiful kindness, Who creates all things, Who remembers the piety of the Patriarchs, and Who, in love, brings a redeemer to their children's children, for the sake of His Name.

Between Rosh Hashana and Yom Kippur add:

Zöch'raynu l'cha-yim, melech chöfaytz	זָכְרֵנוּ לְחַיִּים, מֶלֶךְ חָפֵץ
ba-cha-yim, v'chös'vaynu b'sayfer ha-cha-yim,	בַּחַיִּים, וְכָתְבֵנוּ בְּסֵפֶר הַחַיִּים,
l'ma-an'chö elohim cha-yim.	לְמַעַנְךָ אֱלֹהִים חַיִּים.

Remember us for life, King Who desires life; inscribe us in the Book of Life, for Your sake, O living God.

At the word *Böruch* (blessed), bend the knee; at *Atöh* (You), bow forward; and at *Adonöy* (Lord), straighten up.

Melech ozayr umo-shi-a umö-gayn.	מֶלֶךְ עוֹזֵר וּמוֹשִׁיעַ וּמָגֵן:
Böruch atöh adonöy,	בָּרוּךְ אַתָּה יְיָ,
mö-gayn avröhöm.	מָגֵן אַבְרָהָם:

O King, [You are] a helper, a savior and a shield. Blessed are You Lord, Shield of Abraham.

Atöh gibor l'olöm adonöy,
m'cha-yeh maysim atöh, rav l'hoshi-a.

אַתָּה גִּבּוֹר לְעוֹלָם אֲדֹנָי,
מְחַיֵּה מֵתִים אַתָּה, רַב לְהוֹשִׁיעַ:

In summer say: [Morid ha-töl.]

בַּקַּיִץ: [מוֹרִיד הַטָּל:]

In winter say: [Mashiv höru-ach umo-rid
ha-geshem.] M'chal-kayl cha-yim
b'chesed, m'cha-yeh may-sim
b'racha-mim rabim, so-maych
nof'lim, v'rofay cholim, uma-tir
asu-rim, um'ka-yaym emu-nöso
li-shaynay öför, mi chö-mochö ba-al
g'vuros umi do-meh löch,
melech may-mis um'cha-yeh
umatz-mi-ach y'shu-öh.

בַּחוֹרֶף: [מַשִּׁיב הָרוּחַ וּמוֹרִיד
הַגֶּשֶׁם:] מְכַלְכֵּל חַיִּים
בְּחֶסֶד, מְחַיֵּה מֵתִים
בְּרַחֲמִים רַבִּים, סוֹמֵךְ
נוֹפְלִים, וְרוֹפֵא חוֹלִים, וּמַתִּיר
אֲסוּרִים, וּמְקַיֵּם אֱמוּנָתוֹ
לִישֵׁנֵי עָפָר, מִי כָמוֹךָ בַּעַל
גְּבוּרוֹת וּמִי דּוֹמֶה לָּךְ,
מֶלֶךְ מֵמִית וּמְחַיֵּה
וּמַצְמִיחַ יְשׁוּעָה:

*You are mighty forever, my Lord; You resurrect the dead; You are powerful to save.
(In summer say.) He causes the dew to descend. (In winter say:) He causes the wind
to blow and the rain to fall. He sustains the living with lovingkindness, resurrects the
dead with great mercy, supports the falling, heals the sick, releases the bound, and
fulfills His trust to those who sleep in the dust. Who is like You, mighty One! And who
can be compared to You, King, Who brings death and restores life, and causes
deliverance to spring forth!*

Between Rosh Hashana and Yom Kippur add:

Mi chömochö öv hörachamön zochayr
y'tzuröv l'cha-yim b'racha-mim.

מִי כָמוֹךָ אַב הָרַחֲמָן זוֹכֵר
יְצוּרָיו לְחַיִּים בְּרַחֲמִים:

Between Rosh Hashana and Yom Kippur add: *Who is like You, merciful Father, Who in
compassion remembers His creatures for life.*

179

V'ne-emön atöh l'ha-cha-yos   וְנֶאֱמָן אַתָּה לְהַחֲיוֹת
may-sim. Boruch atöh adonöy,   מֵתִים: בָּרוּךְ אַתָּה יְיָ,
m'cha-yeh ha-maysim.   מְחַיֵּה הַמֵּתִים:

You are trustworthy to revive the dead. Blessed are You Lord, Who revives the dead.

During the silent Amidah for Mincha and Marriv, continue on page 181.
During the leader's repetition of the Mincha Amidah, recite the *Kedusha* below.

During the leader's repetition of the Mincha Amidah the congregation
rises to recite *Kedusha*, standing silently in place, with feet together.
The leader recites each paragraph, and allows the congregation to respond.

Cong. then leader: Nak-dishöch v'na-ari-tzöch   קהל וחזן: נַקְדִּישָׁךְ וְנַעֲרִיצָךְ
k'no-am si-ach sod sar'fay kodesh,   כְּנֹעַם שִׂיחַ סוֹד שַׂרְפֵי קֹדֶשׁ,
ha-m'shal'shim l'chö k'dushöh, ka-kösuv al   הַמְשַׁלְּשִׁים לְךָ קְדֻשָּׁה, כַּכָּתוּב עַל
yad n'vi-echö v'körö zeh el zeh v'ömar.   יַד נְבִיאֶךָ וְקָרָא זֶה אֶל זֶה וְאָמַר:

Cong. then leader: Ködosh, ködosh, ködosh,   קהל וחזן: קָדוֹשׁ, קָדוֹשׁ, קָדוֹשׁ,
adonöy tz'vö-os, m'lo chöl hö-öretz k'vodo.   יְיָ צְבָאוֹת, מְלֹא כָל הָאָרֶץ כְּבוֹדוֹ:

Leader: L'umösöm m'shab'chim v'om'rim.   חזן: לְעֻמָּתָם מְשַׁבְּחִים וְאוֹמְרִים:

Cong. then leader: Böruch k'vod   קהל וחזן: בָּרוּךְ כְּבוֹד
adonöy mim'komo.   יְיָ מִמְּקוֹמוֹ:

Leader: Uv'div-rei köd-sh'chö kösuv lay-mor.   חזן: וּבְדִבְרֵי קָדְשְׁךָ כָּתוּב לֵאמֹר:

Cong. then leader: Yimloch adonöy l'olöm   קהל וחזן: יִמְלֹךְ יְיָ לְעוֹלָם
eloha-yich tziyon l'dor vö-dor, ha-l'luyöh.   אֱלֹהַיִךְ צִיּוֹן לְדֹר וָדֹר, הַלְלוּיָהּ:

Seraphim who thrice repeat "holy" unto You, as it is written by Your prophet: And they call one to another and say. Cong. then leader: "Holy, holy, holy is the Lord of hosts; the whole earth is full of His glory." Leader: Those facing them offer praise and say. Cong then Leader: "Blessed be the glory of the Lord from its place." Leader: And in Your holy Scriptures it is written thus: Cong. then leader: The Lord shall reign forever; your God, O Zion, throughout all generations. Praise the Lord.

Continue here:

Atöh ködosh v'shim'chö ködosh	אַתָּה קָדוֹשׁ וְשִׁמְךָ קָדוֹשׁ
uk'doshim b'chöl yom y'ha-l'luchö	וּקְדוֹשִׁים בְּכָל יוֹם
selöh. Boruch atöh adonöy*,	יְהַלְלוּךָ סֶּלָה. בָּרוּךְ אַתָּה
hö-ayl ha-kodosh.	יְיָ, הָאֵל הַקָּדוֹשׁ:

| (*Between Rosh Hashana and Yom Kippur | (בעשי״ת: |
| substitute: Ha-melech ha-ködosh.) | הַמֶּלֶךְ הַקָּדוֹשׁ) |

You are holy and Your Name is holy, and holy beings praise You daily for all eternity. Blessed are You Lord,* the holy God. (*Between Rosh Hashana and Yom Kippur substitute: the holy King.)

Atöh chonayn l'ödöm da-as,	אַתָּה חוֹנֵן לְאָדָם דַּעַת,
um'lamayd le-enosh binöh,	וּמְלַמֵּד לֶאֱנוֹשׁ בִּינָה,
chönaynu may-it-chö chöch-möh	חָנֵּנוּ מֵאִתְּךָ חָכְמָה
binöh vödö-as. Boruch atöh	בִּינָה וָדָעַת: בָּרוּךְ אַתָּה
adonöy, chonayn hadö-as.	יְיָ, חוֹנֵן הַדָּעַת:

You graciously bestow knowledge upon man and teach mortals understanding. Graciously bestow upon us from You, wisdom, understanding and knowledge. Blessed are You Lord, Who graciously bestows knowledge.

Hashi-vaynu övinu l'sorö-sechö, הֲשִׁיבֵנוּ אָבִינוּ לְתוֹרָתֶךָ,
v'körvay-nu mal-kaynu וְקָרְבֵנוּ מַלְכֵּנוּ
la-avodö-sechö, v'hacha-ziraynu לַעֲבוֹדָתֶךָ, וְהַחֲזִירֵנוּ
bis'shuvöh sh'laymöh l'fönechö. בִּתְשׁוּבָה שְׁלֵמָה לְפָנֶיךָ:
Böruch atöh adonöy, hörotzeh בָּרוּךְ אַתָּה יְיָ, הָרוֹצֶה
bis'shuvöh. בִּתְשׁוּבָה:

Cause us to return, our Father, to Your Torah; draw us near, our King, to Your service; and bring us back to You in wholehearted repentance. Blessed are You Lord, Who desires penitence.

S'lach lönu övinu, ki chötönu, סְלַח לָנוּ אָבִינוּ, כִּי חָטָאנוּ,
m'chol lönu mal-kaynu, ki föshö-nu, מְחַל לָנוּ מַלְכֵּנוּ, כִּי פָשָׁעְנוּ,
ki ayl tov v'salöch ötöh. כִּי אֵל טוֹב וְסַלָּח אָתָּה:
Böruch atöh adonöy, chanun בָּרוּךְ אַתָּה יְיָ, חַנּוּן
ha-mar-beh lislo-ach. הַמַּרְבֶּה לִסְלֹחַ:

Pardon us, our Father, for we have sinned; forgive us, our King, for we have transgressed; for You are a good and forgiving God. Blessed are You Lord, gracious One Who pardons abundantly.

R'ay nö v'ön-yaynu v'rivöh rivaynu, רְאֵה נָא בְעָנְיֵנוּ וְרִיבָה רִיבֵנוּ,
ug'ölay-nu m'hayröh l'ma-an וּגְאָלֵנוּ מְהֵרָה לְמַעַן
sh'mechö, ki ayl go-ayl chözök ötöh. שְׁמֶךָ, כִּי אֵל גּוֹאֵל חָזָק אָתָּה:
Böruch atöh adonöy, go-ayl yisrö-ayl. בָּרוּךְ אַתָּה יְיָ, גּוֹאֵל יִשְׂרָאֵל:

O behold our affliction and wage our battle; redeem us speedily for the sake of Your Name, for You God are a mighty Redeemer. Blessed are You Lord, Redeemer of Israel.

On a public fast day, the leader recites the following during the repetition:

Anay-nu adonöy anay-nu b'yom tzom	עֲנֵנוּ יְיָ עֲנֵנוּ בְּיוֹם צוֹם
ta-ani-saynu, ki v'tzörö g'dolöh anöch-nu,	תַּעֲנִיתֵנוּ, כִּי בְצָרָה גְדוֹלָה אֲנָחְנוּ,
al taychen el rish-aynu, v'al tas-tayr pöne-chö	אַל תֵּפֶן אֶל רִשְׁעֵנוּ, וְאַל תַּסְתֵּר פָּנֶיךָ
mi-menu, v'al tis-alam mit'chinö-saynu, he-yay	מִמֶּנּוּ, וְאַל תִּתְעַלַּם מִתְּחִנָּתֵנוּ, הֱיֵה
nö körov l'shav-ösaynu, y'hi nö chas-d'chö	נָא קָרוֹב לְשַׁוְעָתֵנוּ, יְהִי נָא חַסְדְּךָ
l'nacha-maynu, terem nik-rö aylechö anay-nu,	לְנַחֲמֵנוּ, טֶרֶם נִקְרָא אֵלֶיךָ עֲנֵנוּ,
kadövör she-ne-emar: v'höyö terem yik-rö-u	כַּדָּבָר שֶׁנֶּאֱמַר: וְהָיָה טֶרֶם יִקְרָאוּ
va-ani e-eneh, od haym m'dab'rim va-ani	וַאֲנִי אֶעֱנֶה, עוֹד הֵם מְדַבְּרִים וַאֲנִי
esh-mö, ki atöh adonöy hö-oneh b'ays tzörö,	אֶשְׁמָע, כִּי אַתָּה יְיָ הָעוֹנֶה בְּעֵת צָרָה,
podeh umatzil b'chöl ays tzöröh v'tzuköh.	פּוֹדֶה וּמַצִּיל בְּכָל עֵת צָרָה וְצוּקָה:
Böruch atöh adonöy, hö oneh l'amo	בָּרוּךְ אַתָּה יְיָ, הָעוֹנֶה לְעַמּוֹ
yisrö-ayl b'ays tzöröh.	יִשְׂרָאֵל בְּעֵת צָרָה:

Answer us, O Lord, answer us on our fast day, for we are in great distress. Do not turn to our wickedness, do not conceal Your countenance from us, and do not disregard our supplications. Be near to our cry; let Your lovingkindness console us; answer us even before we call to You, as it is said: And it shall be that before they call, I will answer; while they are yet speaking, I will hear. For You, Lord, are He Who answers in time of distress, Who redeems and rescues in all times of distress and tribulation. Blessed are You Lord, Who answers His people Israel in time of distress.

R'fö-aynu adonöy v'nayrö-fay,	רְפָאֵנוּ יְיָ וְנֵרָפֵא,
hoshi-aynu v'nivöshay-öh,	הוֹשִׁיעֵנוּ וְנִוָּשֵׁעָה,
ki s'hilö-saynu ötöh, v'ha-alay	כִּי תְהִלָּתֵנוּ אָתָּה, וְהַעֲלֵה
aruchöh ur'fu-öh sh'laymö l'chöl	אֲרוּכָה וּרְפוּאָה שְׁלֵמָה לְכָל
mako-saynu. Ki ayl melech rofay	מַכּוֹתֵינוּ: כִּי אֵל מֶלֶךְ רוֹפֵא
ne-emön v'rachamön ötöh.	נֶאֱמָן וְרַחֲמָן אָתָּה:

Böruch atöh adonöy, rofay   בָּרוּךְ אַתָּה יְיָ, רוֹפֵא
cho-lay amo yisrö-ayl.   חוֹלֵי עַמּוֹ יִשְׂרָאֵל :

Heal us, O Lord, and we will be healed; help us and we will be saved; for You are our praise. Grant complete cure and healing to all our wounds; for You, Almighty King, are a faithful and merciful healer. Blessed are You Lord, Who heals the sick of His people Israel.

Böraych ölaynu adonöy elo-haynu   בָּרֵךְ עָלֵינוּ יְיָ אֱלֹהֵינוּ
es hashönöh hazos, v'ays köl   אֶת הַשָּׁנָה הַזֹּאת, וְאֶת כָּל
minay s'vu-ösöh l'tovöh,   מִינֵי תְבוּאָתָהּ לְטוֹבָה,
In summer say: [v'sayn b'röchö]   בקיץ : [וְתֵן בְּרָכָה]
In winter say: [v'sayn tal umötör   בחורף : [וְתֵן טַל וּמָטָר
liv-röchö] al p'nay hö-adömö,   לִבְרָכָה] עַל פְּנֵי הָאֲדָמָה,
v'sab'aynu mituvechö, uvöraych   וְשַׂבְּעֵנוּ מִטּוּבֶךָ, וּבָרֵךְ
sh'nösaynu ka-shönim ha-tovos   שְׁנָתֵנוּ כַּשָּׁנִים הַטּוֹבוֹת
liv-röchöh, ki ayl tov umay-tiv   לִבְרָכָה, כִּי אֵל טוֹב וּמֵטִיב
atöh um'vöraych ha-shönim. Böruch   אַתָּה וּמְבָרֵךְ הַשָּׁנִים : בָּרוּךְ
atöh adonöy, m'vöraych ha-shönim.   אַתָּה יְיָ, מְבָרֵךְ הַשָּׁנִים :

Bless for us, Lord our God, this year and all the varieties of its produce for good; and bestow [in summer say: blessing] [in winter say: dew and rain for blessing] upon the face of the earth. Satisfy us from Your bounty and bless our year like other good years, for blessing; for You are a generous God Who bestows goodness and blesses the years. Blessed are You Lord, Who blesses the years.

T'ka b'shoför gödol l'chayru-saynu,   תְּקַע בְּשׁוֹפָר גָּדוֹל לְחֵרוּתֵנוּ,
v'sö nays l'kabaytz gölu-yosaynu,   וְשָׂא נֵס לְקַבֵּץ גָּלֻיּוֹתֵינוּ,

v'kab'tzaynu yachad may-arba וְקַבְּצֵנוּ יַחַד מֵאַרְבַּע
kan'fos hö-öretz l'artzaynu. כַּנְפוֹת הָאָרֶץ לְאַרְצֵנוּ :
Böruch atöh adonöy, m'ka-baytz בָּרוּךְ אַתָּה יְיָ, מְקַבֵּץ
nid-chay amo yisrö-ayl. נִדְחֵי עַמּוֹ יִשְׂרָאֵל :

Sound the great shofar for our freedom; raise a banner to gather our exiles, and bring us together from the four corners of the earth into our land. Blessed are You Lord, Who gathers the dispersed of His people Israel.

Hö-shivöh shof'taynu k'vöri-shonöh הָשִׁיבָה שׁוֹפְטֵינוּ כְּבָרִאשׁוֹנָה,
v'yo-atzay-nu k'vat'chilöh, v'hö-sayr וְיוֹעֲצֵינוּ כְּבַתְּחִלָּה, וְהָסֵר
mi-menu yögon va-anöchöh, um'loch מִמֶּנּוּ יָגוֹן וַאֲנָחָה, וּמְלֹךְ
ölaynu atöh adonöy l'vad'chö עָלֵינוּ אַתָּה יְיָ לְבַדְּךָ
b'chesed uv'ra-chamim, b'tzedek בְּחֶסֶד וּבְרַחֲמִים, בְּצֶדֶק
uv'mishpöt. Böruch atöh adonöy*, וּבְמִשְׁפָּט : בָּרוּךְ אַתָּה יְיָ,
melech ohayv tz'dököh umish-pöt. מֶלֶךְ אוֹהֵב צְדָקָה וּמִשְׁפָּט :

(*Between Rosh Hashana and Yom Kippur (בעשי״ת
substitute: Ha-melech ha-mish-pöt.) הַמֶּלֶךְ הַמִּשְׁפָּט) :

Restore our judges as in former times, and our counselors as of yore; remove from us sorrow and sighing, and reign over us, You alone, O Lord, with kindness and compassion, with righteousness and justice. Blessed are You Lord, King Who loves righteousness and justice. (*Between Rosh Hashana and Yom Kippur substitute: the King of judgment.)*

V'la-mal-shinim al t'hi sik-vöh, v'chöl וְלַמַּלְשִׁינִים אַל תְּהִי תִקְוָה, וְכָל
ha-minim v'chöl ha-zaydim k'rega הַמִּינִים וְכָל הַזֵּדִים כְּרֶגַע
yo-vaydu, v'chöl o-y'vay am'chö יֹאבֵדוּ, וְכָל אוֹיְבֵי עַמְּךָ

m'hayröh yiköray-su, umal'chus
hörish-öh m'hayröh s'akayr
us'shabayr us'magayr, v'sachni-a
bim'hayröh v'yö-maynu. Böruch
atöh adonöy, shovayr o-y'vim
umach-ni-a zaydim.

מְהֵרָה יְכָרֵתוּ, וּמַלְכוּת
הָרִשְׁעָה מְהֵרָה תְעַקֵּר
וּתְשַׁבֵּר וּתְמַגֵּר, וְתַכְנִיעַ
בִּמְהֵרָה בְיָמֵינוּ: בָּרוּךְ
אַתָּה יְיָ, שׁוֹבֵר אוֹיְבִים
וּמַכְנִיעַ זֵדִים:

Let there be no hope for informers, and may all the heretics and all the wicked instantly perish; may all the enemies of Your people be speedily extirpated; and may You swiftly uproot, break, crush and subdue the reign of wickedness speedily in our days. Blessed are You Lord, Who crushes enemies and subdues the wicked.

Al ha-tzadikim v'al ha-chasidim,
v'al zik'nay am'chö bays yisrö-ayl,
v'al p'laytas bays sof'rayhem, v'al
gay-ray ha-tzedek v'ölaynu, ye-hemu
nö racha-mechö adonöy elo-haynu,
v'sayn söchör tov l'chöl ha-bot'chim
b'shim'chö be-emes, v'sim chel-kaynu
imö-hem, ul'olöm lo nayvosh ki
v'chö bötöch-nu. Böruch atöh adonöy,
mish-ön umiv-töch la-tzadikim.

עַל הַצַּדִּיקִים וְעַל הַחֲסִידִים,
וְעַל זִקְנֵי עַמְּךָ בֵּית יִשְׂרָאֵל,
וְעַל פְּלֵיטַת בֵּית סוֹפְרֵיהֶם, וְעַל
גֵּרֵי הַצֶּדֶק וְעָלֵינוּ, יֶהֱמוּ
נָא רַחֲמֶיךָ יְיָ אֱלֹהֵינוּ,
וְתֵן שָׂכָר טוֹב לְכָל הַבּוֹטְחִים
בְּשִׁמְךָ בֶּאֱמֶת, וְשִׂים חֶלְקֵנוּ
עִמָּהֶם, וּלְעוֹלָם לֹא נֵבוֹשׁ כִּי
בְךָ בָטָחְנוּ: בָּרוּךְ אַתָּה יְיָ,
מִשְׁעָן וּמִבְטָח לַצַּדִּיקִים:

May Your mercies be aroused, Lord our God, upon the righteous, upon the pious, upon the elders of Your people, the House of Israel, upon the remnant of their sages, upon the righteous proselytes and upon us. Grant ample reward to all who truly trust in Your Name, and place our lot among them; may we never be disgraced, for we have put our trust in You. Blessed are You Lord, the support and security of the righteous.

186

V'li-rushöla-yim ir'chö b'racha-mim
töshuv, v'sish-kon b'so-chöh ka-asher
dibar-tö, v'chisay dövid av-d'chö
m'hay-röh b'sochöh töchin, uv'nay
osöh b'körov b'yömay-nu bin-yan
olöm. Böruch atöh adonöy,
bonay y'rushölö-yim.

וְלִירוּשָׁלַיִם עִירְךָ בְּרַחֲמִים
תָּשׁוּב, וְתִשְׁכֹּן בְּתוֹכָהּ כַּאֲשֶׁר
דִּבַּרְתָּ, וְכִסֵּא דָוִד עַבְדְּךָ
מְהֵרָה בְּתוֹכָהּ תָּכִין, וּבְנֵה
אוֹתָהּ בְּקָרוֹב בְּיָמֵינוּ בִּנְיַן
עוֹלָם : בָּרוּךְ אַתָּה יְיָ,
בּוֹנֵה יְרוּשָׁלָיִם :

Return in mercy to Jerusalem Your city and dwell therein as You have promised;
speedily establish therein the throne of David Your servant, and rebuild it, soon in our
days, as an everlasting edifice. Blessed are You Lord, Who rebuilds Jerusalem.

Es tzemach dövid av-d'chö m'hay-röh
satz-mi-ach, v'kar-no törum
bishu-ösechö, ki l'shu-ös'chö kivi-nu
köl ha-yom. Böruch atöh adonöy,
matz-mi-ach keren y'shu öh.

אֶת צֶמַח דָּוִד עַבְדְּךָ מְהֵרָה
תַצְמִיחַ, וְקַרְנוֹ תָּרוּם
בִּישׁוּעָתֶךָ, כִּי לִישׁוּעָתְךָ קִוִּינוּ
כָּל הַיּוֹם : בָּרוּךְ אַתָּה יְיָ,
מַצְמִיחַ קֶרֶן יְשׁוּעָה :

Speedily cause the scion of David Your servant to flourish, and increase his power by
Your salvation, for we hope for Your salvation all day. Blessed are You Lord, Who
causes the power of salvation to flourish.

Sh'ma kolaynu adonöy elo-haynu,
öv hö-racha-mön, ra-chaym ölaynu,
v'kabayl b'racha-mim uv'rötzon es
t'filösaynu, ki ayl shomay-a t'filos
v'sacha-nunim ötöh, umil'fö-nechö
mal-kaynu rayköm al tishi-vaynu.

שְׁמַע קוֹלֵנוּ יְיָ אֱלֹהֵינוּ,
אָב הָרַחֲמָן, רַחֵם עָלֵינוּ,
וְקַבֵּל בְּרַחֲמִים וּבְרָצוֹן אֶת
תְּפִלָּתֵנוּ, כִּי אֵל שׁוֹמֵעַ תְּפִלּוֹת
וְתַחֲנוּנִים אָתָּה, וּמִלְּפָנֶיךָ
מַלְכֵּנוּ רֵיקָם אַל תְּשִׁיבֵנוּ :

187

Hear our voice, Lord our God; merciful Father, have compassion upon us and accept our prayers in mercy and favor, for You are God Who hears prayers and supplications; do not turn us away empty-handed from You, our King.

On a public fast day, during the silent Amidah for Mincha, add the following:

Anay-nu adonöy anay-nu b'yom tzom ta-ani-saynu, ki v'tzörö g'dolöh anöch-nu, al tayfen el rish-aynu, v'al tas-tayr pöne-chö mi-menu, v'al tis-alam mit'chinö-saynu, he-yay nö körov l'sha-avösaynu, y'hi nö chas-d'chö l'nacha-maynu, terem nik-rö aylechö anay-nu, kadövör she-ne-emar: v'höyö terem yik-röu va-ani e-eneh, od haym m'dab'rim va-ani esh-mö, ki atöh adonöy hö-oneh b'ays tzörö, podeh uma-tzil b'chöl ays tzöröh v'tzuköh.

עֲנֵנוּ יְיָ עֲנֵנוּ בְּיוֹם צוֹם
תַּעֲנִיתֵנוּ, כִּי בְצָרָה גְדוֹלָה אֲנָחְנוּ,
אַל תֵּפֶן אֶל רִשְׁעֵנוּ, וְאַל תַּסְתֵּר פָּנֶיךָ
מִמֶּנוּ, וְאַל תִּתְעַלַּם מִתְּחִנָּתֵנוּ, הֱיֵה
נָא קָרוֹב לְשַׁוְעָתֵנוּ, יְהִי נָא חַסְדְּךָ
לְנַחֲמֵנוּ, טֶרֶם נִקְרָא אֵלֶיךָ עֲנֵנוּ,
כַּדָּבָר שֶׁנֶּאֱמַר : וְהָיָה טֶרֶם יִקְרָאוּ
וַאֲנִי אֶעֱנֶה, עוֹד הֵם מְדַבְּרִים וַאֲנִי
אֶשְׁמָע, כִּי אַתָּה יְיָ הָעוֹנֶה בְּעֵת צָרָה,
פּוֹדֶה וּמַצִּיל בְּכָל עֵת צָרָה וְצוּקָה :

Answer us, O Lord, answer us on our fast day, for we are in great distress. Do not turn to our wickedness, do not conceal Your countenance from us, and do not disregard our supplications. Be near to our cry; let Your lovingkindness console us; answer us even before we call to You, as it is said: And it shall be that before they call, I will answer; while they are yet speaking, I will hear. For You, Lord, are He Who answers in time of distress, Who redeems and rescues in all times of distress and tribulation.

Ki atöh shomay-a t'filas köl peh.

Böruch atöh adonöy, shomay-a t'filöh.

כִּי אַתָּה שׁוֹמֵעַ תְּפִלַּת כָּל פֶּה :

בָּרוּךְ אַתָּה יְיָ, שׁוֹמֵעַ תְּפִלָּה :

For You hear the prayer of everyone. Blessed are You Lord, Who hears prayer.

R'tzay adonöy elo-haynu b'am'chö yisrö-ayl v'lis'filösöm sh'ay, v'hö-shayv hö-avodöh lid'vir

רְצֵה יְיָ אֱלֹהֵינוּ בְּעַמְּךָ
יִשְׂרָאֵל וְלִתְפִלָּתָם שְׁעֵה,
וְהָשֵׁב הָעֲבוֹדָה לִדְבִיר

bay-sechö, v'ishay yisrö-ayl   בֵּיתֶךָ, וְאִשֵׁי יִשְׂרָאֵל

us'fi-lösöm b'aha-vöh s'kabayl   וּתְפִלָּתָם בְּאַהֲבָה תְקַבֵּל

b'rö-tzon, us'hi l'rö-tzon tömid   בְּרָצוֹן, וּתְהִי לְרָצוֹן תָּמִיד

avodas yisrö-ayl a-mechö.   עֲבוֹדַת יִשְׂרָאֵל עַמֶּךָ:

Look with favor, Lord our God, on Your people Israel and pay heed to their prayer; restore the service to Your Sanctuary and accept with love and favor Israel's fire-offerings and prayer; and may the service of Your people Israel always find favor.

On Rosh Chodesh, add the following:

Elo-haynu vay-lohay avo-saynu   אֱלֹהֵינוּ וֵאלֹהֵי אֲבוֹתֵינוּ

ya-aleh v'yövo, v'yagi-a v'yayrö-eh   יַעֲלֶה וְיָבֹא, וְיַגִּיעַ וְיֵרָאֶה

v'yay-rö-tzeh, v'yishöma v'yipökayd   וְיֵרָצֶה, וְיִשָּׁמַע וְיִפָּקֵד

v'yizöchayr, zichro-naynu ufik'do-naynu,   וְיִזָּכֵר, זִכְרוֹנֵנוּ וּפִקְדוֹנֵנוּ,

v'zichron avo-saynu, v'zichron möshi-ach   וְזִכְרוֹן אֲבוֹתֵינוּ, וְזִכְרוֹן מָשִׁיחַ

ben dövid av-dechö, v'zichron y'rushöla-yim   בֶּן דָּוִד עַבְדֶּךָ, וְזִכְרוֹן יְרוּשָׁלַיִם

ir köd-shechö, v'zichron köl am'chö bays   עִיר קָדְשֶׁךָ, וְזִכְרוֹן כָּל עַמְּךָ בֵּית

yisrö-ayl l'fönecho lif'laytöh l'tovöh, l'chayn   יִשְׂרָאֵל לְפָנֶיךָ לִפְלֵיטָה לְטוֹבָה, לְחֵן

ul'chesed ul'racha-mim ul'cha-yim tovim   וּלְחֶסֶד וּלְרַחֲמִים וּלְחַיִּים טוֹבִים

ul'shölom b'yom rosh ha-chodesh ha-zeh.   וּלְשָׁלוֹם, בְּיוֹם רֹאשׁ הַחֹדֶשׁ הַזֶּה:

Zöch'raynu adonöy elo-haynu bo l'tovöh,   זָכְרֵנוּ יְיָ אֱלֹהֵינוּ בּוֹ לְטוֹבָה,

ufök'daynu vo liv'röchöh, v'hoshi-aynu   וּפָקְדֵנוּ בוֹ לִבְרָכָה, וְהוֹשִׁיעֵנוּ

vo l'cha-yim tovim. Uvid'var y'shu-öh   בוֹ לְחַיִּים טוֹבִים: וּבִדְבַר יְשׁוּעָה

v'rachamim chus v'chö-naynu v'ra-chayin   וְרַחֲמִים חוּס וְחָנֵּנוּ וְרַחֵם

ölaynu v'hoshi-aynu ki ay-lechö ay-naynu,   עָלֵינוּ וְהוֹשִׁיעֵנוּ כִּי אֵלֶיךָ עֵינֵינוּ,

ki ayl melech cha-nun v'rachum ötöh.   כִּי אֵל מֶלֶךְ חַנּוּן וְרַחוּם אָתָּה:

Our God and God of our fathers, may there ascend, come and reach, be seen, accepted, and heard, recalled and remembered before You, the remembrance and recollection of us, the remembrance of our fathers, the remembrance of Moshiach the son of David Your servant, the remembrance of Jerusalem Your holy city, and the remembrance of

189

all Your people the House of Israel, for deliverance, well-being, grace, kindness, mercy, good life and peace, on this day of Rosh Chodesh. Remember us on this [day], Lord our God, for good; be mindful of us on this [day] for blessing; help us on this [day] for good life. With the promise of deliverance and compassion, spare us and be gracious to us; have mercy upon us and deliver us; for our eyes are directed to You, for You, God, are a gracious and merciful King.

Continue here:

V'se-chezenöh ay-naynu	וְתֶחֱזֶינָה עֵינֵינוּ
b'shuv'chö l'tziyon b'racha-mim.	בְּשׁוּבְךָ לְצִיּוֹן בְּרַחֲמִים:
Böruch atöh adonöy, ha-machazir	בָּרוּךְ אַתָּה יְיָ, הַמַּחֲזִיר
sh'chinöso l'tziyon.	שְׁכִינָתוֹ לְצִיּוֹן:

May our eyes behold Your return to Zion in mercy. Blessed are You Lord, Who restores His Divine Presence to Zion.

Bow forward while reciting the first five words:

Modim anachnu löch, shö-atöh hu	מוֹדִים אֲנַחְנוּ לָךְ, שָׁאַתָּה הוּא
adonöy elo-haynu vay-lohay avo-saynu	יְיָ אֱלֹהֵינוּ וֵאלֹהֵי אֲבוֹתֵינוּ
l'olöm vö-ed, tzur cha-yaynu mö-gayn	לְעוֹלָם וָעֶד, צוּר חַיֵּינוּ מָגֵן
yish-aynu, atöh hu l'dor vödor,	יִשְׁעֵנוּ, אַתָּה הוּא לְדוֹר וָדוֹר,
no-deh l'chö un'sapayr t'hilö-sechö,	נוֹדֶה לְךָ וּנְסַפֵּר תְּהִלָּתֶךָ,
al cha-yaynu ha-m'surim b'yödechö,	עַל חַיֵּינוּ הַמְּסוּרִים בְּיָדֶךָ,
v'al nish'mosaynu ha-p'kudos löch,	וְעַל נִשְׁמוֹתֵינוּ הַפְּקוּדוֹת לָךְ,
v'al ni-sechö sheb'chöl yom imönu,	וְעַל נִסֶּיךָ שֶׁבְּכָל יוֹם עִמָּנוּ,
v'al nif-l'ösechö v'tovosechö sheb'chöl	וְעַל נִפְלְאוֹתֶיךָ וְטוֹבוֹתֶיךָ שֶׁבְּכָל
ays, erev vö-voker v'tzöhö-rö-yim,	עֵת, עֶרֶב וָבֹקֶר וְצָהֳרָיִם,

190

ha-tov, ki lo chölu racha-mechö,   **הַטּוֹב, כִּי לֹא כָלוּ רַחֲמֶיךָ,**

ham'rachaym, ki lo samu   **הַמְרַחֵם, כִּי לֹא תַמּוּ**

chasö-dechö, ki may-olöm   **חֲסָדֶיךָ, כִּי מֵעוֹלָם**

kivinu löch.   **קִוִּינוּ לָךְ:**

We thankfully acknowledge that You are the Lord our God and God of our fathers forever. You are the strength of our life, the shield of our salvation in every generation. We will give thanks to You and recount Your praise, evening, morning and noon, for our lives which are committed into Your hand, for our souls which are entrusted to You, for Your miracles which are with us daily, and for Your continual wonders and beneficence. You are the Beneficent One, for Your mercies never cease; and the Merciful One, for Your kindnesses never end; for we always place our hope in You.

On Chanuka and Purim, add the portions on the following page.
Otherwise continue on page 194.

Modim, for during the repetition of the Mincha Amidah.
Recited standing. Bow your head while reciting the first five words.

Modim anach nu löch, shö-atöh hu adonöy   **מוֹדִים אֲנַחְנוּ לָךְ, שָׁאַתָּה הוּא יְיָ**

elo-haynu vay-lohay avo-saynu, elohay köl   **אֱלֹהֵינוּ וֵאלֹהֵי אֲבוֹתֵינוּ, אֱלֹהֵי כָל בָּשָׂר,**

bösör, yo-tz'raynu, yo-tzayr b'rayshis. B'röchos   **יוֹצְרֵנוּ, יוֹצֵר בְּרֵאשִׁית, בְּרָכוֹת**

v'hodö-os l'shim'chö ha-gödol v'haködosh,   **וְהוֹדָאוֹת לְשִׁמְךָ הַגָּדוֹל וְהַקָּדוֹשׁ,**

al she-hcche-yisönu v'kiyam-tonu, kayn   **עַל שֶׁהֶחֱיִיתָנוּ וְקִיַּמְתָּנוּ, כֵּן**

t'cha-yaynu us'ka-y'maynu v'se-esof   **תְּחַיֵּנוּ וּתְקַיְּמֵנוּ, וְתֶאֱסוֹף**

gölu-yosay-nu l'chatz'ros köd-shechö,   **גָּלֻיּוֹתֵינוּ לְחַצְרוֹת קָדְשֶׁךָ,**

v'nö-shuv ay-lechö lishmor chukechö, v'la-asos   **וְנָשׁוּב אֵלֶיךָ לִשְׁמוֹר חֻקֶּיךָ, וְלַעֲשׂוֹת**

r'tzonechö, ul'öv-d'chö b'layvöv shölaym, al   **רְצוֹנֶךָ, וּלְעָבְדְּךָ בְּלֵבָב שָׁלֵם, עַל**

she-önu modim löch. Böruch ayl ha-hodö-os.   **שֶׁאָנוּ מוֹדִים לָךְ, בָּרוּךְ אֵל הַהוֹדָאוֹת:**

We thankfully acknowledge that You are the Lord our God and God of our fathers, the God of all flesh, our Creator and the Creator of all existence. We offer blessings and thanks to Your great and holy Name, for You have given us life and sustained us; so may You continue to grant us life and sustain us—gather our dispersed to the courtyards of Your Sanctuary and we shall return to You to keep Your laws, to do Your will, and to serve You with a perfect heart—for we thankfully acknowledge You. Blessed is God, Who is worthy of thanks.

On Chanuka and Purim, add the following:

V'al ha-nisim v'al ha-purkön v'al ha-g'vuros	וְעַל הַנִּסִּים וְעַל הַפֻּרְקָן וְעַל הַגְּבוּרוֹת
v'al ha-t'shu-os v'al ha-niflö-os she-ösisö	וְעַל הַתְּשׁוּעוֹת וְעַל הַנִּפְלָאוֹת שֶׁעָשִׂיתָ
la-avosaynu ba-yömim hö-haym	לַאֲבוֹתֵינוּ בַּיָּמִים הָהֵם
biz'man ha-zeh.	בִּזְמַן הַזֶּה :

And [we thank You] for the miracles, for the redemption, for the mighty deeds, for the saving acts, and for the wonders which You have wrought for our ancestors in those days, at this time.

On Chanuka, add the following. On Purim, continue on page 193.

Bi-may matis-yöhu ben yochö-nön ko-hayn	בִּימֵי מַתִּתְיָהוּ בֶּן יוֹחָנָן כֹּהֵן
gödol chash-monö-i uvönöv, k'she-öm'döh	גָּדוֹל, חַשְׁמוֹנָאִי וּבָנָיו, כְּשֶׁעָמְדָה
mal'chus yövön hö-r'shö-öh al am'chö	מַלְכוּת יָוָן הָרְשָׁעָה, עַל עַמְּךָ
yisrö-ayl, l'hash-kichöm torö-sechö	יִשְׂרָאֵל, לְהַשְׁכִּיחָם תּוֹרָתֶךָ
ul'ha-aviröm may-chukay r'tzo-nechö, v'atöh	וּלְהַעֲבִירָם מֵחֻקֵּי רְצוֹנֶךָ, וְאַתָּה
b'racha-mechö hö-rabim ömad-tö löhem b'ays	בְּרַחֲמֶיךָ הָרַבִּים עָמַדְתָּ לָהֶם בְּעֵת
tzörösöm. Ravtö es rivöm, dantö es dinöm,	צָרָתָם. רַבְתָּ אֶת רִיבָם, דַּנְתָּ אֶת דִּינָם,
nökam-tö es nik'mösöm. Mösartö gi-borim	נָקַמְתָּ אֶת נִקְמָתָם. מָסַרְתָּ גִבּוֹרִים
b'yad chalöshim, v'rabim b'yad m'atim,	בְּיַד חַלָּשִׁים, וְרַבִּים בְּיַד מְעַטִּים,
ut'may-im b'yad t'horim, ur'shö-im b'yad	וּטְמֵאִים בְּיַד טְהוֹרִים, וּרְשָׁעִים בְּיַד
tzadikim, v'zaydim b'yad os'kay sorö-sechö.	צַדִּיקִים, וְזֵדִים בְּיַד עוֹסְקֵי תוֹרָתֶךָ.
Ul'chö ösisö shaym gödol v'ködosh	וּלְךָ עָשִׂיתָ שֵׁם גָּדוֹל וְקָדוֹשׁ
bö-olömechö, ul'am'chö yisrö-ayl ösisö	בְּעוֹלָמֶךָ, וּלְעַמְּךָ יִשְׂרָאֵל עָשִׂיתָ
t'shu-öh g'dolöh ufurkön k'ha-yom ha-zeh.	תְּשׁוּעָה גְדוֹלָה וּפֻרְקָן כְּהַיּוֹם הַזֶּה.
V'achar kach bö-u vö-nechö lid'vir bay-sechö,	וְאַחַר כַּךְ בָּאוּ בָנֶיךָ לִדְבִיר בֵּיתֶךָ,
ufinu es hay-chölechö, v'tiharu es	וּפִנּוּ אֶת הֵיכָלֶךָ, וְטִהֲרוּ אֶת

192

mik-döshechö, v'hid-liku nayros b'chatz'ros מִקְדָשֶׁךָ, וְהִדְלִיקוּ נֵרוֹת בְּחַצְרוֹת
köd-shechö, v'köv'u sh'monas y'may קָדְשֶׁךָ, וְקָבְעוּ שְׁמוֹנַת יְמֵי
chanuköh aylu l'hodos ul'halyl חֲנֻכָּה אֵלּוּ לְהוֹדוֹת וּלְהַלֵּל
l'shim'chö hagödol. לְשִׁמְךָ הַגָּדוֹל:

In the days of Matityohu, the son of Yochonon the High Priest, the Hasmonean and his sons, when the wicked Hellenic government rose up against Your people Israel to make them forget Your Torah and violate the decrees of Your Will. But You, in Your abounding mercies, stood by them in the time of their distress. You waged their battles, defended their rights and avenged the wrong done to them. You delivered the mighty into the hands of the weak, the many into the hands of the few, the impure into the hands of the pure, the wicked into the hands of the righteous, and the wanton sinners into the hands of those who occupy themselves with Your Torah. You made a great and holy name for Yourself in Your world, and effected a great deliverance and redemption for Your people to this very day. Then Your children entered the shrine of Your House, cleansed Your Temple, purified Your Sanctuary, kindled lights in Your holy courtyards, and instituted these eight days of Chanuka to give thanks and praise to Your great Name.

Continue on page 194.

On Purim, add the following:

Bi-may mör-d'chai v'estayr b'shushan ha-biroh, בִּימֵי מָרְדְּכַי וְאֶסְתֵּר בְּשׁוּשַׁן הַבִּירָה,
k'she-ömad alay-hem hömön hö-röshö, כְּשֶׁעָמַד עֲלֵיהֶם הָמָן הָרָשָׁע,
bikaysh l'hash-mid la-harog ul'abayd es köl בִּקֵּשׁ לְהַשְׁמִיד לַהֲרֹג וּלְאַבֵּד אֶת כָּל
ha-y'hudim mi-na-ar v'ad zökayn taf v'nöshim הַיְּהוּדִים מִנַּעַר וְעַד זָקֵן טַף וְנָשִׁים
b'yom echöd bish'loshöh ösör l'chodesh בְּיוֹם אֶחָד בִּשְׁלֹשָׁה עָשָׂר לְחֹדֶשׁ
sh'naym ösör hu chodesh adör ush'lölöm שְׁנֵים עָשָׂר הוּא חֹדֶשׁ אֲדָר וּשְׁלָלָם לָבוֹז,
lövoz, v'atöh b'racha-mecho hö-rabim hay-fartö וְאַתָּה בְּרַחֲמֶיךָ הָרַבִּים הֵפַרְתָּ
es atzöso, v'kil-kaltö es ma-chashavto, אֶת עֲצָתוֹ, וְקִלְקַלְתָּ אֶת מַחֲשַׁבְתּוֹ,
va-hashay-vosö lo g'mulo b'rosho, v'sölu וַהֲשֵׁבוֹתָ לוֹ גְּמוּלוֹ בְּרֹאשׁוֹ, וְתָלוּ
oso v'es bönöv al hö-aytz. אוֹתוֹ וְאֶת בָּנָיו עַל הָעֵץ:

In the days of Mordechai and Esther, in Shushan the capital, when the wicked Haman rose up against them, and sought to destroy, slaughter and annihilate all the Jews, young and old, infants and women, in one day, on the thirteenth day of the twelfth month, the month of Adar, and to take their spoil for plunder. But You, in Your abounding mercies, foiled his counsel and frustrated his intention, and caused the evil he planned to recoil on his own head, and they hanged him and his sons upon the gallows.

Continue here:

V'al kulöm yis-böraych v'yisromöm
v'yisnasay shim'chö malkaynu
tömid l'olöm vö-ed.

וְעַל כֻּלָם יִתְבָּרֵךְ וְיִתְרוֹמָם
וְיִתְנַשֵׂא שִׁמְךָ מַלְכֵּנוּ
תָּמִיד לְעוֹלָם וָעֶד:

And for all these, may Your Name, our King, be continually blessed, exalted and extolled forever and all time.

Between Rosh Hashana and Yom Kippur add:

Uch'sov l'cha-yim tovim köl b'nay v'risechö.   וּכְתוֹב לְחַיִּים טוֹבִים כָּל בְּנֵי בְרִיתֶךָ:

Inscribe all the children of Your Covenant for a good life.

At the word *Böruch* (blessed), bend the knee; at *Atöh* (You), bow forward; and at *Adonöy* (Lord), straighten up.

V'chöl ha-cha-yim yo-duchö selöh
viha-l'lu shim'chö ha-gödol l'olöm ki
tov, hö-ayl y'shu-ösaynu v'ezrö-saynu
selöh, hö-ayl ha-tov. Boruch atöh
adonöy, ha-tov shim'chö ul'chö
nö-eh l'hodos.

וְכָל הַחַיִּים יוֹדוּךָ סֶּלָה
וִיהַלְלוּ שִׁמְךָ הַגָּדוֹל לְעוֹלָם כִּי
טוֹב, הָאֵל יְשׁוּעָתֵנוּ וְעֶזְרָתֵנוּ
סֶלָה, הָאֵל הַטּוֹב: בָּרוּךְ אַתָּה
יְיָ, הַטּוֹב שִׁמְךָ וּלְךָ
נָאֶה לְהוֹדוֹת:

And all living things shall forever thank You, and praise Your great Name eternally, for You are good. God, You are our everlasting salvation and help, O benevolent God. Blessed are You Lord, Beneficent is Your Name, and to You it is fitting to offer thanks.

Sim sholom tovöh uv'röchöh, שִׂים שָׁלוֹם, טוֹבָה וּבְרָכָה,

cha-yim chayn vöchesed v'rachamim, חַיִּים חֵן וָחֶסֶד וְרַחֲמִים,

ölaynu v'al köl yisrö-ayl amechö. עָלֵינוּ וְעַל כָּל יִשְׂרָאֵל עַמֶּךָ:

Bö-r'chaynu övinu kulönu k'echöd בָּרְכֵנוּ אָבִינוּ כֻּלָּנוּ כְּאֶחָד,

b'or pönechö, ki v'or pönechö, בְּאוֹר פָּנֶיךָ, כִּי בְאוֹר פָּנֶיךָ, נָתַתָּ

nösatö lönu, adonöy el-ohaynu, toras לָנוּ יְיָ אֱלֹהֵינוּ תּוֹרַת חַיִּים,

cha-yim v'ahavas chesed utz'dököh וְאַהֲבַת חֶסֶד, וּצְדָקָה וּבְרָכָה

uv'röchöh v'rachamim v'cha-yim וְרַחֲמִים וְחַיִּים וְשָׁלוֹם:

v'shölom. V'tov b'aynechö l'vöraych וְטוֹב בְּעֵינֶיךָ לְבָרֵךְ אֶת

es am'chö yisrö-ayl b'chöl ays עַמְּךָ יִשְׂרָאֵל בְּכָל עֵת

uv'chöl shö-öh bish'lomechö. וּבְכָל שָׁעָה בִּשְׁלוֹמֶךָ:

Bestow peace, goodness and blessing, life, graciousness, kindness and mercy, upon us and upon all Your people Israel. Bless us, our Father, all of us as one, with the light of Your countenance. For by the light of Your countenance You gave us, Lord our God, the Torah of life and lovingkindness, righteousness, blessing, mercy, life and peace. May it be favorable in Your eyes to bless Your people Israel, at all times and at every moment, with Your peace.

Between Rosh Hashana and Yom Kippur add:

Uv'sayfer cha-yim b'röchöh v'shölom וּבְסֵפֶר חַיִּים בְּרָכָה וְשָׁלוֹם

ufar-nösöh tovöh, y'shu-öh v'nechömöh, וּפַרְנָסָה טוֹבָה יְשׁוּעָה וְנֶחָמָה,

ug'zayros tovos, ni-zöchayr v'nikösayv וּגְזֵרוֹת טוֹבוֹת נִזָּכֵר וְנִכָּתֵב

l'fönechö, anachnu v'chöl am'chö bays לְפָנֶיךָ, אֲנַחְנוּ וְכָל עַמְּךָ בֵּית

yisrö-ayl, l'cha-yim tovim ul'shölom. יִשְׂרָאֵל, לְחַיִּים טוֹבִים וּלְשָׁלוֹם:

And in the Book of Life, blessing, peace and prosperity, deliverance, consolation and favorable decrees, may we and all Your people the House of Israel be remembered and inscribed before You for a happy life and for peace.

Böruch atöh adonöy, ha-m'voraych
es amo yisrö-ayl ba-shölom.

בָּרוּךְ אַתָּה יְיָ, הַמְבָרֵךְ
אֶת עַמּוֹ יִשְׂרָאֵל בַּשָּׁלוֹם:

Blessed are You Lord, Who blesses His people Israel with peace.

During the repetition of the Amidah, the leader recites the following verse silently.

Yih-yu l'rö-tzon im'ray fi, v'heg-yon
libi l'fönechö, adonöy tzuri v'go-ali.

יִהְיוּ לְרָצוֹן אִמְרֵי פִי, וְהֶגְיוֹן
לִבִּי לְפָנֶיךָ, יְיָ צוּרִי וְגוֹאֲלִי:

May the words of my mouth and the meditation of my heart be acceptable before You,
Lord, my Strength and my Redeemer.

The leader's repetition of the Amidah concludes here.

Elohai, n'tzor l'shoni may-rö, us'fösai
midabayr mirmöh. V'lim'kal'lai,
nafshi sidom, v'nafshi ke-öför la-kol
tih-yeh. P'sach libi b'sorösechö,
uv'mitzvosechö tirdof nafshi, v'chöl
ha-chosh'vim ölai rö-öh, m'hayröh
hö-fayr atzösöm v'kalkayl
ma-chashavtöm. Yih-yu k'motz lif'nay
ru-ach umal-ach adonöy do-cheh.
L'ma-an yay-chöl'tzun y'didechö,
hoshi-öh y'min'chö va-anayni.
Asay l'ma-an sh'mechö, asay l'ma-an
y'minechö, asay l'ma-an torösechö,
asay l'ma-an k'dusho-sechö. Yih-yu

אֱלֹהַי, נְצוֹר לְשׁוֹנִי מֵרָע, וּשְׂפָתַי
מִדַּבֵּר מִרְמָה: וְלִמְקַלְלַי,
נַפְשִׁי תִדּוֹם, וְנַפְשִׁי כֶּעָפָר לַכֹּל
תִּהְיֶה: פְּתַח לִבִּי בְּתוֹרָתֶךָ,
וּבְמִצְוֹתֶיךָ תִּרְדּוֹף נַפְשִׁי, וְכָל
הַחוֹשְׁבִים עָלַי רָעָה, מְהֵרָה
הָפֵר עֲצָתָם וְקַלְקֵל
מַחֲשַׁבְתָּם: יִהְיוּ כְּמוֹץ לִפְנֵי
רוּחַ וּמַלְאַךְ יְיָ דּוֹחֶה:
לְמַעַן יֵחָלְצוּן יְדִידֶיךָ,
הוֹשִׁיעָה יְמִינְךָ וַעֲנֵנִי:
עֲשֵׂה לְמַעַן שְׁמֶךָ, עֲשֵׂה לְמַעַן
יְמִינֶךָ, עֲשֵׂה לְמַעַן תּוֹרָתֶךָ,
עֲשֵׂה לְמַעַן קְדֻשָּׁתֶךָ: יִהְיוּ

l'rö-tzon im'ray fi, v'heg-yon libi   לְרָצוֹן אִמְרֵי פִי, וְהֶגְיוֹן לִבִּי

l'fönechö, adonöy tzuri v'go-ali.   לְפָנֶיךָ, יְיָ צוּרִי וְגוֹאֲלִי:

My God, guard my tongue from evil and my lips from speaking deceitfully. Let my soul be silent to those who curse me; let my soul be as dust to all. Open my heart to Your Torah, and let my soul eagerly pursue Your commandments. As for all those who plot evil against me, hasten to annul their counsel and frustrate their design. Let them be as chaff before the wind; let the angel of the Lord thrust them away. That Your beloved ones may be delivered, help with Your right hand and answer me. Do it for the sake of Your Name; do it for the sake of Your right hand; do it for the sake of Your Torah; do it for the sake of Your holiness. May the words of my mouth and the meditation of my heart be acceptable before You, Lord, my Strength and my Redeemer.

**Take three steps back and say the following, while bowing the head
to the right, straight ahead, left, straight ahead, and bow down (as indicated):**

< O-seh* shölom (*Between Rosh Hashana   <עֹשֶׂה שָׁלוֹם (בעשי״ת

and Yom Kippur: ha-shölom) bim'romöv,   הַשָּׁלוֹם) בִּמְרוֹמָיו,

^ hu > ya-aseh shölom   הוּא > יַעֲשֶׂה שָׁלוֹם ^

ölaynu ^ v'al köl yisrö-ayl,   עָלֵינוּ ^ וְעַל כָּל יִשְׂרָאֵל,

°v'im'ru ömayn.°   וְאִמְרוּ אָמֵן: °

He Who makes peace (Between Rosh Hashana and Yom Kippur substitute: the peace) in His heavens, may He make peace for us and for all Israel; and say: Amen.

Y'hi rö-tzon mil'fö-nechö, adonöy   יְהִי רָצוֹן מִלְפָנֶיךָ, יְיָ

elo-haynu vay-lohay avo-saynu,   אֱלֹהֵינוּ וֵאלֹהֵי אֲבוֹתֵינוּ,

she-yibö-neh bays ha-mikdös   שֶׁיִּבָּנֶה בֵּית הַמִּקְדָּשׁ

bim'hayröh v'yö-maynu,   בִּמְהֵרָה בְיָמֵינוּ,

v'sayn chel-kaynu b'sorö-sechö.   וְתֵן חֶלְקֵנוּ בְּתוֹרָתֶךָ:

May it be Your will, Lord our God and God of our fathers, that the Beit Hamikdash (Holy Temple) be speedily rebuilt in our days, and grant us our portion in Your Torah.

The Jewish Mourner's Companion

During Mincha, the leader repeats the Amidah aloud, including all the additions marked for the leader's repetition, followed by a "Full-Kaddish."

During Maariv, the leader recites a "Full-Kaddish" immediately following the silent Amidah (no repetition is recited).

Full-Kaddish

It is customary for the one saying Kaddish to bow the head while reciting certain words. These words are bracketed by the following symbol: "°". When the symbol appears before a word, bow the head forward, and remain bowed until the word that ends with the same symbol, then raise the head.

יִתְגַּדַּל וְיִתְקַדַּשׁ °שְׁמֵהּ רַבָּא°. Yis-gadal v'yis-kadash °sh'may rabö°.

אמן (Cong.: Ömayn.)

בְּעָלְמָא דִּי בְרָא כִרְעוּתֵהּ B'öl'mö di v'rö chir'u-say
וְיַמְלִיךְ מַלְכוּתֵהּ, וְיַצְמַח v'yam-lich mal'chusay, v'yatz-mach
פּוּרְקָנֵהּ °וִיקָרֵב מְשִׁיחֵהּ°: pur-könay °vikö-rayv m'shi-chay°.

אמן (Cong.: Ömayn.)

בְּחַיֵּיכוֹן וּבְיוֹמֵיכוֹן B'cha-yay-chon uv'yomay-chon
וּבְחַיֵּי דְכָל בֵּית יִשְׂרָאֵל, uv'cha-yay d'chöl bays yisrö-ayl,
בַּעֲגָלָא וּבִזְמַן קָרִיב ba-agölö uviz'man köriv
°וְאִמְרוּ אָמֵן°: אמן. יְהֵא °v'im'ru ömayn°. (Cong.: Ömayn. Y'hay
שְׁמֵהּ רַבָּא מְבָרַךְ לְעָלַם sh'may rabö m'vörach l'ölam
וּלְעָלְמֵי עָלְמַיָּא: יִתְבָּרַךְ: ul'öl'may öl'ma-yö. Yisböraych)

Yis-böraych° °v'yish-tabach,   יִתְבָּרַךְ° °וְיִשְׁתַּבַּח,
v'yispö-ayr, v'yis-romöm,   וְיִתְפָּאַר, וְיִתְרוֹמָם,
v'yis-nasay, v'yis-hadör,   וְיִתְנַשֵּׂא, וְיִתְהַדָּר,
v'yis-aleh, v'yis-halöl°, °sh'may   וְיִתְעַלֶּה, וְיִתְהַלָּל°, שְׁמֵהּ
d'kud-shö b'rich hu°.   דְּקֻדְשָׁא בְּרִיךְ הוּא°:
(Cong.: Ömayn.)   אמן

L'aylö min köl bir'chösö v'shi-rösö,   לְעֵלָּא מִן כָּל בִּרְכָתָא וְשִׁירָתָא,
tush-b'chösö v'neche-mösö,   תֻּשְׁבְּחָתָא וְנֶחֱמָתָא,
da-amirön b'öl'mö,   דַּאֲמִירָן בְּעָלְמָא,
°v'im'ru ömayn°.   °וְאִמְרוּ אָמֵן°:
(Cong.: Ömayn.)   אמן

Tiskabayl tz'los-hon uvö-us-hon   תִּתְקַבֵּל צְלוֹתְהוֹן וּבָעוּתְהוֹן
d'chöl bays yisrö-ayl, ködöm avu-hon   דְּכָל בֵּית יִשְׂרָאֵל, קֳדָם אֲבוּהוֹן
di vish'ma-yö, °v'im'ru ömayn.°   דִּי בִשְׁמַיָּא, °וְאִמְרוּ אָמֵן°:
(Cong: Ömayn)   אמן

Y'hay sh'lömö rabö min sh'ma-yö,   יְהֵא שְׁלָמָא רַבָּא מִן שְׁמַיָּא,
v'cha-yim tovim ölaynu v'al köl   וְחַיִּים טוֹבִים עָלֵינוּ וְעַל כָּל
yisrö-ayl °v'im'ru ömayn.°   יִשְׂרָאֵל °וְאִמְרוּ אָמֵן°:
(Cong: Ömayn)   אמן

**Take three steps back and say the following, while bowing the head
to the right, straight ahead, left, straight ahead, and bow down (as indicated):**

> Oseh shölom* bim'romöv, ^ hu 　　　> עֹשֶׂה שָׁלוֹם* בִּמְרוֹמָיו, ^ הוּא
< ya-aseh shölom ölaynu, ^ v'al köl 　> יַעֲשֶׂה שָׁלוֹם עָלֵינוּ, ^ וְעַל כָּל
yisrö-ayl, °v'im'ru ömayn°. 　　　　יִשְׂרָאֵל, °וְאִמְרוּ אָמֵן°:

(Cong.: Ömayn.) 　　　　　　　　　אמן

Take three steps forward.

*Between Rosh Hashana and Yom Kippur, substitute with "Ha-shölom."

Exalted and hallowed be His great Name (Cong: Amen.) *throughout the world which He has created according to His Will. May He establish His kingship, bring forth His redemption and hasten the coming of His Moshiach* (Cong: Amen.) *in your lifetime and in your days and in the lifetime of the entire House of Israel, speedily and soon, and say, Amen.* (Cong: Amen. May His great Name be blessed forever and to all eternity. Blessed.) *May His great Name be blessed forever and to all eternity. Blessed and praised, glorified, exalted and extolled, honored, adored and lauded be the Name of the Holy One, blessed be He,* (Cong: Amen.) *beyond all the blessings, hymns, praises and consolations that are uttered in the world; and say, Amen.* (Cong: Amen.) *May the prayers and supplications of the entire House of Israel be accepted before their Father in heaven; and say, Amen.* (Cong: Amen.) *May there be abundant peace from heaven, and a good life for us and for all Israel; and say, Amen.* (Cong: Amen.) *He Who makes peace* (Between Rosh Hashana and Yom Kippur say: *the peace*) *in His heavens, may He make peace for us and for all Israel; and say, Amen.* (Cong: Amen.)

For regular Mincha and Maariv:
Continue with "*Ölaynu*," (page 202).

**For Mincha from the first day of *Rosh Chodesh* Elul,
through *Hoshana Rabbah*:**
Recite Psalm 27 before "Ölaynu" (following page).

For Maariv between Passover and Shavuot:
Count the Omer before "Ölaynu" (page 222).

From *Rosh Chodesh Elul* through *Hoshana Rabbah*, during
Mincha, recite the following Psalm before "*Ôlaynu.*"

לְדָוִד, יְיָ אוֹרִי וְיִשְׁעִי מִמִּי אִירָא, יְיָ מָעוֹז חַיַּי מִמִּי אֶפְחָד: בִּקְרֹב עָלַי מְרֵעִים לֶאֱכֹל אֶת בְּשָׂרִי,
צָרַי וְאֹיְבַי לִי, הֵמָּה כָשְׁלוּ וְנָפָלוּ: אִם תַּחֲנֶה עָלַי מַחֲנֶה לֹא יִירָא לִבִּי, אִם תָּקוּם עָלַי מִלְחָמָה,
בְּזֹאת אֲנִי בוֹטֵחַ: אַחַת שָׁאַלְתִּי מֵאֵת יְיָ, אוֹתָהּ אֲבַקֵּשׁ, שִׁבְתִּי בְּבֵית יְיָ כָּל יְמֵי חַיַּי, לַחֲזוֹת בְּנֹעַם
יְיָ וּלְבַקֵּר בְּהֵיכָלוֹ: כִּי יִצְפְּנֵנִי בְּסֻכֹּה בְּיוֹם רָעָה, יַסְתִּירֵנִי בְּסֵתֶר אָהֳלוֹ, בְּצוּר יְרוֹמְמֵנִי: וְעַתָּה יָרוּם
רֹאשִׁי עַל אֹיְבַי סְבִיבוֹתַי, וְאֶזְבְּחָה בְאָהֳלוֹ זִבְחֵי תְרוּעָה, אָשִׁירָה וַאֲזַמְּרָה לַייָ: שְׁמַע יְיָ קוֹלִי
אֶקְרָא, וְחָנֵּנִי וַעֲנֵנִי: לְךָ אָמַר לִבִּי בַּקְּשׁוּ פָנָי, אֶת פָּנֶיךָ יְיָ אֲבַקֵּשׁ: אַל תַּסְתֵּר פָּנֶיךָ מִמֶּנִּי, אַל תַּט
בְּאַף עַבְדֶּךָ, עֶזְרָתִי הָיִיתָ, אַל תִּטְּשֵׁנִי וְאַל תַּעַזְבֵנִי אֱלֹהֵי יִשְׁעִי: כִּי אָבִי וְאִמִּי עֲזָבוּנִי, וַיְיָ יַאַסְפֵנִי:
הוֹרֵנִי יְיָ דַּרְכֶּךָ, וּנְחֵנִי בְּאֹרַח מִישׁוֹר, לְמַעַן שׁוֹרְרָי: אַל תִּתְּנֵנִי בְּנֶפֶשׁ צָרָי, כִּי קָמוּ בִי עֵדֵי שֶׁקֶר
וִיפֵחַ חָמָס: לוּלֵא הֶאֱמַנְתִּי לִרְאוֹת בְּטוּב יְיָ בְּאֶרֶץ חַיִּים: קַוֵּה אֶל יְיָ, חֲזַק וְיַאֲמֵץ לִבֶּךָ, וְקַוֵּה
אֶל יְיָ:

*By David. The Lord is my light and my salvation — whom shall I fear? The Lord is the strength
of my life — whom shall I dread? When evildoers approached me to devour my flesh, my
oppressors and my foes, they stumbled and fell. If an army were to beleaguer me, my heart
would not fear; if war were to arise against me, in this I trust [ed. that the Lord is my light and
salvation]. One thing I have asked of the Lord, this I seek, that I may dwell in the House of the
Lord all the days of my life, to behold the pleasantness of the Lord, and to visit in His Sanctuary.
For He will hide me in His tabernacle on a day of adversity; He will conceal me in the hidden
places of His tent; He will lift me upon a rock. And then my head will be raised above my
enemies around me, and I will offer in His tabernacle sacrifices of jubilation; I will sing and
chant to the Lord. Lord, hear my voice as I call; be gracious to me and answer me. In Your
behalf my heart says, "Seek My countenance;" Your countenance, Lord, I seek. Do not conceal
Your countenance from me; do not cast aside Your servant in wrath; You have been my help; do
not abandon me nor forsake me, God of my deliverance. Though my father and mother have
forsaken me, the Lord has taken me in. Lord, teach me Your way and lead me in the path of
righteousness because of my watchful enemies. Do not give me over to the will of my oppressors,
for there have risen against me false witnesses and they speak evil. [They would have crushed
me] had I not believed that I would see the goodness of the Lord in the land of the living. Hope
in the Lord, be strong and let your heart be valiant, and hope in the Lord.*

Ölaynu l'shabay-ach la-adon ha-kol, עָלֵינוּ לְשַׁבֵּחַ לַאֲדוֹן הַכֹּל,

lösays g'dulöh l'yo-tzayr b'rayshis, לָתֵת גְּדֻלָּה לְיוֹצֵר בְּרֵאשִׁית,

shelo ösönu k'go-yay hö-arö-tzos, v'lo שֶׁלֹּא עָשָׂנוּ כְּגוֹיֵי הָאֲרָצוֹת, וְלֹא

sömönu k'mish-p'chos hö-adömöh, שָׂמָנוּ כְּמִשְׁפְּחוֹת הָאֲדָמָה,

shelo söm chel-kaynu köhem, שֶׁלֹּא שָׂם חֶלְקֵנוּ כָּהֶם,

v'gorö-laynu k'chöl ha-monöm וְגוֹרָלֵנוּ כְּכָל הֲמוֹנָם

she-haym mish-tachavim l'hevel שֶׁהֵם מִשְׁתַּחֲוִים לְהֶבֶל

v'lörik. Va-anachnu kor'im וָרִיק. וַאֲנַחְנוּ כּוֹרְעִים

umish-tachavim umodim, lif'nay וּמִשְׁתַּחֲוִים וּמוֹדִים, לִפְנֵי

melech, mal'chay ha-m'löchim, מֶלֶךְ, מַלְכֵי הַמְּלָכִים,

ha-ködosh böruch hu. She-hu noteh הַקָּדוֹשׁ בָּרוּךְ הוּא. שֶׁהוּא נוֹטֶה

shöma-yim v'yosayd ö-retz, שָׁמַיִם וְיוֹסֵד אָרֶץ,

umo-shav y'köro ba-shöma-yim וּמוֹשַׁב יְקָרוֹ בַּשָּׁמַיִם

mima-al, ush'chinas uzo b'göv'hay מִמַּעַל, וּשְׁכִינַת עֻזּוֹ בְּגָבְהֵי

m'romim, hu elo-haynu ayn od. מְרוֹמִים, הוּא אֱלֹהֵינוּ אֵין עוֹד:

Emes mal-kaynu, efes zulöso, אֱמֶת מַלְכֵּנוּ, אֶפֶס זוּלָתוֹ, כַּכָּתוּב

kakösuv b'soröso: V'yöda-tö ha-yom בְּתוֹרָתוֹ: וְיָדַעְתָּ הַיּוֹם

va-hashay-vosö el l'vövechö, ki וַהֲשֵׁבֹתָ אֶל לְבָבֶךָ, כִּי

adonöy hu hö-elohim ba-shöma-yim יְיָ הוּא הָאֱלֹהִים בַּשָּׁמַיִם

mima-al, v'al hö-öretz מִמַּעַל, וְעַל הָאָרֶץ

mi-töchas, ayn od. מִתָּחַת, אֵין עוֹד:

It is incumbent upon us to praise the Master of all things, to exalt the Creator of all existence, that He has not made us like the nations of the world, nor caused us to be like the families of the earth; that He has not assigned us a portion like theirs, nor a lot like that of all their multitudes, for they bow to vanity and nothingness. But we bend the knee, bow down, and offer praise before the supreme King of kings, the Holy One, blessed be He, Who stretches forth the heavens and establishes the earth, the seat of Whose glory is in the heavens above and the abode of Whose majesty is in the loftiest heights. He is our God; there is none else. Truly, He is our King; there is nothing besides Him, as it is written in His Torah: Know this day and take unto your heart that the Lord is God; in the heavens above and upon the earth below there is nothing else.

V'al kayn n'ka-veh l'chö adonöy	וְעַל כֵּן נְקַוֶּה לְךָ יְיָ
elo-haynu, lir-os m'hayröh b'sif-eres	אֱלֹהֵינוּ, לִרְאוֹת מְהֵרָה בְּתִפְאֶרֶת
uzechö, l'ha-avir gilulim min hö-öretz	עֻזֶּךָ, לְהַעֲבִיר גִּלּוּלִים מִן הָאָרֶץ
v'hö-elilim köros yiköray-sun,	וְהָאֱלִילִים כָּרוֹת יִכָּרֵתוּן,
l'sakayn olöm b'mal'chus shadai,	לְתַקֵּן עוֹלָם בְּמַלְכוּת שַׁדַּי,
v'chöl b'nay vösör yik-r'u vish'mechö,	וְכָל בְּנֵי בָשָׂר יִקְרְאוּ בִשְׁמֶךָ,
l'hafnos ay-lechö köl rish'ay öretz.	לְהַפְנוֹת אֵלֶיךָ כָּל רִשְׁעֵי אָרֶץ :
Yakiru v'yay-d'u köl yosh'vay sayvayl	יַכִּירוּ וְיֵדְעוּ כָּל יוֹשְׁבֵי תֵבֵל,
ki l'chö tichra köl berech, ti-shöva köl	כִּי לְךָ תִּכְרַע כָּל בֶּרֶךְ, תִּשָּׁבַע כָּל
löshon. L'fönechö adonöy elo-haynu	לָשׁוֹן. לְפָנֶיךָ יְיָ אֱלֹהֵינוּ
yich-r'u v'yipolu, v'lich'vod shim'chö	יִכְרְעוּ וְיִפּוֹלוּ, וְלִכְבוֹד שִׁמְךָ
y'kör yi-taynu, vi-kab'lu chulöm	יְקָר יִתֵּנוּ, וִיקַבְּלוּ כֻלָּם
alay-hem es ol mal'chu-sechö,	עֲלֵיהֶם אֶת עוֹל מַלְכוּתֶךָ,
v'simloch alay-hem m'hayröh l'olöm	וְתִמְלוֹךְ עֲלֵיהֶם מְהֵרָה לְעוֹלָם
vö-ed, ki ha-mal'chus shel'chö hi,	וָעֶד, כִּי הַמַּלְכוּת שֶׁלְּךָ הִיא,
ul'ol'may ad tim-loch b'chövod,	וּלְעוֹלְמֵי עַד תִּמְלוֹךְ בְּכָבוֹד,
ka-kösuv b'sorö-sechö, adonöy	כַּכָּתוּב בְּתוֹרָתֶךָ : יְיָ
yim-loch l'olöm vö-ed. V'ne-emar:	יִמְלֹךְ לְעֹלָם וָעֶד. וְנֶאֱמַר :
v'hö-yöh adonöy l'melech al köl	וְהָיָה יְיָ לְמֶלֶךְ עַל כָּל

hö-öretz, ba-yom hahu yih-yeh   הָאָרֶץ, בַּיּוֹם הַהוּא יִהְיֶה

adonöy echöd ush'mo echöd.   יְיָ אֶחָד וּשְׁמוֹ אֶחָד :

And therefore we hope to You, Lord our God, that we may speedily behold the splendor of Your might, to banish idolatry from the earth — and false gods will be utterly destroyed; to perfect the world under the sovereignty of the Almighty. All mankind shall invoke Your Name, to turn to You all the wicked of the earth. Then all the inhabitants of the world will recognize and know that every knee should bend to You, every tongue should swear [by Your Name]. Before You, Lord our God, they will bow and prostrate themselves, and give honor to the glory of Your Name; and they will all take upon themselves the yoke of Your kingdom. May You soon reign over them forever and ever, for kingship is Yours, and to all eternity You will reign in glory, as it is written in Your Torah: The Lord will reign forever and ever. And it is said: The Lord shall be King over the entire earth; on that day the Lord shall be One and His Name One.

Mourners recite the Mourner's Kaddish (page 170), then continue below.

Al tirö mipachad pis-om, umisho-as   אַל תִּירָא מִפַּחַד פִּתְאֹם, וּמִשֹּׁאַת

r'shö-im ki sövo. Utzu ay-tzöh   רְשָׁעִים כִּי תָבֹא : עֻצוּ עֵצָה

v'suför, dab'ru dövör v'lo yökum,   וְתֻפָר, דַּבְּרוּ דָבָר וְלֹא יָקוּם,

ki imönu ayl. V'ad zik-nöh ani hu,   כִּי עִמָּנוּ אֵל : וְעַד זִקְנָה אֲנִי הוּא,

v'ad sayvöh ani esbol, ani ösisi va-ani   וְעַד שֵׂיבָה אֲנִי אֶסְבֹּל, אֲנִי עָשִׂיתִי

esö, va-ani esbol va-amalayt.   וַאֲנִי אֶשָּׂא, וַאֲנִי אֶסְבֹּל וַאֲמַלֵּט :

Ach tzadikim yodu lish'mechö   אַךְ צַדִּיקִים יוֹדוּ לִשְׁמֶךָ

yay-sh'vu y'shörim es pö-nechö.   יֵשְׁבוּ יְשָׁרִים אֶת פָּנֶיךָ :

Do not fear sudden terror, nor the destruction of the wicked when it comes. Contrive a scheme, but it will be foiled; conspire a plot, but it will not materialize, for God is with us. To your old age I am [with you]; to your hoary years I will sustain you; I have made you, and I will carry you; I will sustain you and deliver you. Indeed, the righteous will extol Your Name; the upright will dwell in Your presence.

Following *"Al Tirö"* (above), the final verse of *Mishnayot "Mikvaot"* (chapter 7) is recited aloud by a designated person, followed by *Kaddish D'Rabannan* by the mourner (page 170). (During the week of Shiva, the mourners do not say *Mishnayot*.)

Psalm 49

This Psalm is recited after *Shacharit* (morning) and *Mincha* (afternoon) services, followed by the Mourner's Kaddish. On days when *Tachnun* is not recited, Psalm 16 is substituted (page 207).

Lam'natzay-ach liv-nay korach	לַמְנַצֵּחַ לִבְנֵי קֹרַח
miz-mor. Shim-u zos köl	מִזְמוֹר: שִׁמְעוּ זֹאת כָּל
hö-amim, ha-azinu köl yosh'vey	הָעַמִּים, הַאֲזִינוּ כָּל יֹשְׁבֵי
chöled. Gam b'nay ödöm gam b'nay	חָלֶד: גַּם בְּנֵי אָדָם גַּם בְּנֵי
sh, yachad öshir v'ev-yon. Pi y'da-bayr	אִישׁ, יַחַד עָשִׁיר וְאֶבְיוֹן: פִּי יְדַבֵּר
chöch-mos v'högus libi s'vunos.	חָכְמוֹת, וְהָגוּת לִבִּי תְבוּנוֹת:
Ateh l'möshöl öz-ni, ef-tach b'chinor	אַטֶּה לְמָשָׁל אָזְנִי, אֶפְתַּח בְּכִנּוֹר
chi-dösi. Lömö irö bi-may rö, avon	חִידָתִי: לָמָּה אִירָא בִּימֵי רָע עֲוֹן
akay-vai y'subay-ni. Habot'chim al	עֲקֵבַי יְסוּבֵּנִי: הַבֹּטְחִים עַל
chay-löm, uv'rov ösh-röm yis-halölu.	חֵילָם, וּבְרֹב עָשְׁרָם יִתְהַלָּלוּ:
Öch lo födo yif-deh ish, lo yi-tayn	אָח לֹא פָדֹה יִפְדֶּה אִישׁ, לֹא יִתֵּן
laylo-him köf-ro. V'yay-kar pid-yon	לֵאלֹהִים כָּפְרוֹ: וְיֵקַר פִּדְיוֹן
naf-shöm, v'chödal l'olöm. Vi-chi od	נַפְשָׁם, וְחָדַל לְעוֹלָם: וִיחִי עוֹד
lö-netzach lo yir-eh ha-shöchas. Ki	לָנֶצַח, לֹא יִרְאֶה הַשָּׁחַת: כִּי
yir-eh cha-chömim yömusu, yachad	יִרְאֶה חֲכָמִים יָמוּתוּ, יַחַד
k'sil vöva-ar yo-vaydu, v'öz'vu	כְּסִיל וָבַעַר יֹאבֵדוּ, וְעָזְבוּ

205

la-achayrim chay-löm. Kir-böm
bötay-mo l'olöm, mish-k'nosöm l'dor
vödor, kör'u vish-mosöm a-lay
adömos. V'ödöm bikör bal yölin,
nim-shal kab'haymos nid-mu. Zeh
dar-köm ke-sel lömo v'acha-rayhem
b'fi-hem yir-tzu selöh. Katzon lish-ol
shatu mö-ves yir-aym va-yir-du vöm
y'shörim la-boker, v'tzuröm l'valos
sh'ol miz'vul lo. Al elohim yif-deh
naf-shi mi-yad sh'ol, ki yikö-chayni
selöh. Al tirö ki ya-ashir ish, ki
yir-beh k'vod bayso. Ki lo v'moso
yi-kach hakol, lo yay-rayd acharöv
k'vodo. Ki naf-sho b'cha-yöv
y'vöraych, v'yoduchö ki saytiv löch.
Tövo ad dor avosöv, ad nay-tzach
lo yir-u or. Ödöm bikör v'lo yövin,
nim-shal kab'haymos nid-mu.

לַאֲחֵרִים חֵילָם: קִרְבָּם
בָּתֵּימוֹ לְעוֹלָם, מִשְׁכְּנֹתָם לְדוֹר
וָדֹר, קָרְאוּ בִשְׁמוֹתָם עֲלֵי
אֲדָמוֹת: וְאָדָם בִּיקָר בַּל יָלִין:
נִמְשַׁל כַּבְּהֵמוֹת נִדְמוּ: זֶה
דַרְכָּם כֵּסֶל לָמוֹ, וְאַחֲרֵיהֶם
בְּפִיהֶם יִרְצוּ סֶלָה: כַּצֹּאן לִשְׁאוֹל
שַׁתּוּ מָוֶת יִרְעֵם, וַיִּרְדּוּ בָם
יְשָׁרִים לַבֹּקֶר, וְצוּרָם לְבַלּוֹת
שְׁאוֹל מִזְּבֻל לוֹ: אַךְ אֱלֹהִים יִפְדֶּה
נַפְשִׁי מִיַּד שְׁאוֹל, כִּי יִקָּחֵנִי
סֶלָה: אַל תִּירָא כִּי יַעֲשִׁר אִישׁ, כִּי
יִרְבֶּה כְּבוֹד בֵּיתוֹ: כִּי לֹא בְמוֹתוֹ
יִקַּח הַכֹּל, לֹא יֵרֵד אַחֲרָיו
כְּבוֹדוֹ: כִּי נַפְשׁוֹ בְּחַיָּיו
יְבָרֵךְ, וְיוֹדֻךָ כִּי תֵיטִיב לָךְ:
תָּבוֹא עַד דּוֹר אֲבוֹתָיו, עַד נֵצַח
לֹא יִרְאוּ אוֹר: אָדָם בִּיקָר וְלֹא יָבִין,
נִמְשַׁל כַּבְּהֵמוֹת נִדְמוּ:

For the Conductor, by the sons of Korach, a Psalm. Hear this, all you peoples; listen, all you inhabitants of the world; sons of common folk and sons of nobility, rich and poor alike. My mouth speaks wisdom, and the thoughts of my heart are understanding. I incline my ear to the parable; I will unravel my riddle upon the harp. Why am I afraid in times of trouble? [Because] the sins I trod upon surround me. There are those who rely on their wealth, who boast of their great riches. Yet a man cannot redeem his brother, nor pay his ransom to God. The redemption of their soul is too costly, and forever unattainable. Can one live forever, never to see the grave? Though he sees that wise men die, that the fool and the senseless both perish, leaving their wealth to others – [nevertheless,] in their inner thoughts their houses will last forever, their dwellings for generation after generation; they have proclaimed their names throughout the lands. But man will not repose in glory; he is likened to the silenced animals. This is their way – their folly remains with them, and their descendants approve of their talk, Selah. Like sheep, they are destined for the grave; death shall be their shepherd, and the upright will dominate them at morning; their form will rot in the grave, away from its abode. But God will redeem my soul from the hands of the grave, for He will take me, Selah. Do not fear when a man grows rich, when the glory of his house is increased; for when he dies he will take nothing, his glory will not descend after him. For he [alone] praises himself in his lifetime; but [all] will praise you if you better yourself. He will come to the generation of his forefathers; they shall not see light for all eternity. Man [can live] in glory but does not understand; he is likened to the silenced animals.

Recite the Mourner's Kaddish (page 170).

Psalm 16

This Psalm is recited after *Shacharit* (morning) and *Mincha* (afternoon) services on days when *Tachnun* is not recited, followed by the Mourner's Kaddish.

Mich-töm l'dövid, shöm'rayni ayl ki	מִכְתָּם לְדָוִד, שָׁמְרֵנִי אֵל כִּי
chösi-si vöch. ömar-t la-donöy	חָסִיתִי בָךְ : אָמַרְתְּ לַיְיָ
adonöy ötö, tovösi bal ö-lechö.	אֲדֹנָי אָתָּה, טוֹבָתִי בַּל עָלֶיךָ :
Lik-doshim asher bö-öretz hay-möh,	לִקְדוֹשִׁים אֲשֶׁר בָּאָרֶץ הֵמָּה,
v'adiray köl chef-tzi vöm. Yir-bu	וְאַדִּירֵי כָּל חֶפְצִי בָם : יִרְבּוּ
atz'vosöm achayr mö-höru, bal asich	עַצְּבוֹתָם אַחֵר מָהָרוּ, בַּל אַסִיךְ
nis-kayhem mi-döm, uval esö es	נִסְכֵּיהֶם מִדָּם, וּבַל אֶשָּׂא אֶת

sh'mosöm al s'fösöy. Adonöy m'nös chelki v'chosi, atöh tomich goröli. Chavölim nöf'lu li ban'i-mim, af nacha-lös shöf'röh ölöy. Avö-raych es adonöy asher y'ö-tzöni, af laylos yis'runi chil-yosöy. Shi-visi adonöy l'neg-di sömid, ki mimi-ni bal emot. Löchayn sömach libi va-yögel k'vodi, af b'söri yish-kon lö-vetach. Ki lo sa-azov naf-shi lish'ol, lo si-tayn chasid'chö lir-os shöchas. Todi-ayni orach cha-yim, sova s'möchos es pö-nechö, n'i-mos bi-min'chö netzach.

שְׁמוֹתָם עַל שְׂפָתָי: יְיָ מְנָת חֶלְקִי וְכוֹסִי, אַתָּה תּוֹמִיךְ גּוֹרָלִי: חֲבָלִים נָפְלוּ לִי בַּנְּעִמִים, אַף נַחֲלַת שָׁפְרָה עָלָי: אֲבָרֵךְ אֶת יְיָ אֲשֶׁר יְעָצָנִי, אַף לֵילוֹת יִסְּרוּנִי כִלְיוֹתָי: שִׁוִּיתִי יְיָ לְנֶגְדִּי תָמִיד, כִּי מִימִינִי בַּל אֶמּוֹט: לָכֵן שָׂמַח לִבִּי וַיָּגֶל כְּבוֹדִי, אַף בְּשָׂרִי יִשְׁכֹּן לָבֶטַח: כִּי לֹא תַעֲזֹב נַפְשִׁי לִשְׁאוֹל, לֹא תִתֵּן חֲסִידְךָ לִרְאוֹת שָׁחַת: תּוֹדִיעֵנִי אֹרַח חַיִּים, שֹׂבַע שְׂמָחוֹת אֶת פָּנֶיךָ, נְעִמוֹת בִּימִינְךָ נֶצַח:

A Michtam, by David. Watch over me, O God, for I have put my trust in You. You, [my soul,] have said to God, "You are my Master; You are not obligated to benefit me." For the sake of the holy ones who lie in the earth, and for the mighty – all my desires are fulfilled in their merit. Those who hasten after other [gods], their sorrows shall increase; I will not offer their libations of blood, nor take their names upon my lips. The Lord is my allotted portion and my share; You guide my destiny. Portions have fallen to me in pleasant places; indeed, a beautiful inheritance is mine. I bless the Lord Who has advised me; even in the nights my intellect admonishes me. I have set the Lord before me at all times; because He is at my right hand, I shall not falter. Therefore my heart rejoices and my soul exults; my flesh, too, rests secure. For You will not abandon my soul to the grave, You will not allow Your pious one to see purgatory. Make known to me the path of life, that I may be satiated with the joy of Your presence, with the bliss of Your right hand forever.

Recite the Mourner's Kaddish (page 170).

Maariv - The Evening Service

V'hu ra-chum, y'cha-payr övon,	וְהוּא רַחוּם, יְכַפֵּר עָוֹן,
v'lo yash-chis, v'hirböh l'höshiv	וְלֹא יַשְׁחִית, וְהִרְבָּה לְהָשִׁיב
apo, v'lo yö-ir köl cha-möso.	אַפּוֹ, וְלֹא יָעִיר כָּל חֲמָתוֹ:
Adonöy ho-shi-öh, ha-melech	יְיָ הוֹשִׁיעָה, הַמֶּלֶךְ
ya-anay-nu v'yom kör'aynu.	יַעֲנֵנוּ בְיוֹם קָרְאֵנוּ:

He, being compassionate, pardons iniquity, and does not destroy; time and again He turns away His anger, and does not arouse all His wrath. Lord, deliver us; may the King answer us on the day we call.

Shir hama-alos, hi-nay bör'chu	שִׁיר הַמַּעֲלוֹת, הִנֵּה בָּרְכוּ
es adonöy köl av'day adonöy,	אֶת יְיָ כָּל עַבְדֵי יְיָ,
hö-om'dim b'vays adonöy ba-laylos.	הָעֹמְדִים בְּבֵית יְיָ בַּלֵּילוֹת:
S'u y'day-chem kodesh, uvör'chu	שְׂאוּ יְדֶכֶם קֹדֶשׁ, וּבָרְכוּ
es adonöy. Y'vö-rech'chö adonöy	אֶת יְיָ: יְבָרֶכְךָ יְיָ
mitzi-yon, osay shöma-yim vö-öretz.	מִצִּיּוֹן, עֹשֵׂה שָׁמַיִם וָאָרֶץ:
Yomöm y'tzaveh adonöy chas-do,	יוֹמָם יְצַוֶּה יְיָ חַסְדּוֹ,
uva-lai-löh shiro imi, t'filöh l'ayl	וּבַלַּיְלָה שִׁירֹה עִמִּי, תְּפִלָּה לְאֵל
cha-yöy. Us'shu-as tzadikim	חַיָּי: וּתְשׁוּעַת צַדִּיקִם
may-adonöy, mö-uzöm b'ays tzöröh.	מֵיְיָ, מָעוּזָּם בְּעֵת צָרָה:
Vaya-z'raym adonöy va-y'fal'taym,	וַיַּעְזְרֵם יְיָ וַיְפַלְּטֵם,
y'fal'taym may-r'shö-im	יְפַלְּטֵם מֵרְשָׁעִים
v'yoshi-aym ki chösu vo.	וְיוֹשִׁיעֵם כִּי חָסוּ בוֹ:

209

Say three times: Adonöy tz'vö-os imönu, יְיָ צְבָאוֹת עִמָּנוּ,

misgöv lönu elo-hay ya-akov selöh. מִשְׂגָּב לָנוּ אֱלֹהֵי יַעֲקֹב סֶלָה: ג״פ

Say three times: Adonöy tz'vö-os, יְיָ צְבָאוֹת,

ash-ray ödöm botay-ach böch. אַשְׁרֵי אָדָם בֹּטֵחַ בָּךְ: ג״פ

Say three times: Adonöy ho-shi-öh, יְיָ הוֹשִׁיעָה,

ha-melech ya-anay-nu הַמֶּלֶךְ יַעֲנֵנוּ

v'yom kör'aynu. בְיוֹם קָרְאֵנוּ: ג״פ

A Song of Ascents. Bless the Lord all servants of the Lord who stand in the house of the Lord at night. Raise your hands in holiness and bless the Lord. May the Lord, Maker of heaven and earth, bless you from Zion. By day the Lord ordains His kindness, and at night His song is with me, a prayer to the God of my life. The deliverance of the righteous is from the Lord; He is their strength in time of distress. The Lord helps them and delivers them; He delivers them from the wicked and saves them, because they have put their trust in Him. Say three times: The Lord of hosts is with us; the God of Jacob is our stronghold forever. Say three times: Lord of hosts, happy is the man who trusts in You. Say three times: Lord, deliver us; may the King answer us on the day we call.

All rise. The leader recites Half-Kaddish (below), followed by Bör'chu.

HALF-KADDISH

It is customary for the one saying Kaddish to bow the head while reciting certain words. These words are bracketed by the following symbol: "°". When the symbol appears before a word, bow the head forward, and remain bowed until the word that ends with the same symbol, then raise the head.

Yis-gadal v'yis-kadash °sh'may rabö°. יִתְגַּדַּל וְיִתְקַדַּשׁ °שְׁמֵהּ רַבָּא°:

(Cong.: Ömayn.) אמן

B'öl'mö di v'rö chir'u-say בְּעָלְמָא דִּי בְרָא כִרְעוּתֵהּ

210

v'yam-lich mal'chusay, v'yatz-mach   וְיַמְלִיךְ מַלְכוּתֵהּ, וְיַצְמַח
pur-könay °vikö-rayv m'shi-chay°.   פּוּרְקָנֵהּ °וִיקָרֵב מְשִׁיחֵהּ°:
(Cong.: Ömayn.)   אמן

B'cha-yay-chon uv'yomay-chon   בְּחַיֵּיכוֹן וּבְיוֹמֵיכוֹן
uv'cha-yay d'chöl bays yisrö-ayl,   וּבְחַיֵּי דְכָל בֵּית יִשְׂרָאֵל,
ba-agölö uviz'man köriv   בַּעֲגָלָא וּבִזְמַן קָרִיב
°v'im'ru ömayn°. (Cong.: Ömayn. Y'hay   °וְאִמְרוּ אָמֵן°: אמן. יְהֵא שְׁמֵהּ
sh'may rabö m'vörach l'ölam ul'öl'may   רַבָּא מְבָרַךְ לְעָלַם וּלְעָלְמֵי
öl'ma-yö. Yisböraych)   עָלְמַיָּא: יִתְבָּרַךְ)

°Y'hay sh'may rabö m'vörach   °יְהֵא שְׁמֵהּ רַבָּא מְבָרַךְ
l'ölam ul'öl'may öl'ma-yö.   לְעָלַם וּלְעָלְמֵי עָלְמַיָּא:
Yis-böraych° °v'yish-tabach,   יִתְבָּרַךְ° °וְיִשְׁתַּבַּח,
v'yispö-ayr, v'yis-romöm,   וְיִתְפָּאַר, וְיִתְרוֹמַם,
v'yis-nasay, v'yis-hadör,   וְיִתְנַשֵּׂא, וְיִתְהַדָּר,
v'yis-aleh, v'yis-halöl°, °sh'may   וְיִתְעַלֶּה, וְיִתְהַלָּל°, °שְׁמֵהּ
d'kud-shö b'rich hu°.   דְּקֻדְשָׁא בְּרִיךְ הוּא°:
(Cong.: Ömayn.)   אמן

L'aylö min köl bir'chösö v'shi-rösö,   לְעֵלָּא מִן כָּל בִּרְכָתָא וְשִׁירָתָא,
tush-b'chösö v'neche-mösö,   תֻּשְׁבְּחָתָא וְנֶחֱמָתָא,
da-amirön b'öl'mö,   דַּאֲמִירָן בְּעָלְמָא,
°v'im'ru ömayn°.   °וְאִמְרוּ אָמֵן°:
(Cong.: Ömayn.)   אמן

211

Exalted and hallowed be His great Name (Cong.: Amen). *Throughout the world which He has created according to His Will. May He establish His kingship, bring forth His redemption and hasten the coming of His Moshiach* (Cong.: Amen). *In your lifetime and in your days and in the lifetime of the entire House of Israel, speedily and soon, and say, Amen.* (Cong.: Amen. May His great Name be blessed forever and to all eternity. Blessed). *May His great Name be blessed forever and to all eternity. Blessed and praised, glorified, exalted and extolled, honored, adored and lauded be the Name of the Holy One, blessed be He* (Cong.: Amen). *Beyond all the blessings, hymns, praises and consolations that are uttered in the world; and say, Amen.* (Cong.: Amen).

The leader continues below:

The Leader bows and says: חזן :

Bör'chu es adonöy ha-m'voröch. בָּרְכוּ אֶת יְיָ הַמְבֹרָךְ :

Congregation bows and says, then leader: קהל וחזן :

Böruch adonöy ha-m'voröch בָּרוּךְ יְיָ הַמְבֹרָךְ

l'olöm vö-ed. לְעוֹלָם וָעֶד :

The Leader bows and says: *Bless the Lord Who is blessed.* Congregation bows and says, then leader: *Blessed be the Lord Who is blessed for all eternity.*

The congregation may be seated, and continues below:

Böruch atöh adonöy elo-haynu בָּרוּךְ אַתָּה יְיָ אֱלֹהֵינוּ

melech hö-olöm, asher bid'vöro מֶלֶךְ הָעוֹלָם, אֲשֶׁר בִּדְבָרוֹ

ma-ariv arövim, b'chöch-möh מַעֲרִיב עֲרָבִים, בְּחָכְמָה

posay-ach sh'örim, uvis'vunöh פּוֹתֵחַ שְׁעָרִים, וּבִתְבוּנָה

m'sha-neh itim, uma-chalif מְשַׁנֶּה עִתִּים, וּמַחֲלִיף

es ha-z'manim, um'sa-dayr es אֶת הַזְּמַנִּים, וּמְסַדֵּר אֶת
ha-kochö-vim, b'mish-m'rosay-hem הַכּוֹכָבִים, בְּמִשְׁמְרוֹתֵיהֶם
börö-ki-a kir'tzono. Boray yom בָּרָקִיעַ, כִּרְצוֹנוֹ. בּוֹרֵא יוֹם
völöy-löh, go-layl or mip'nay וָלָיְלָה, גּוֹלֵל אוֹר מִפְּנֵי
cho-shech, v'cho-shech mip'nay or, חֹשֶׁךְ, וְחֹשֶׁךְ מִפְּנֵי אוֹר,
uma-avir yom umay-vi löy-löh, וּמַעֲבִיר יוֹם וּמֵבִיא לָיְלָה,
umavdil bayn yom uvayn löy-löh, וּמַבְדִּיל בֵּין יוֹם וּבֵין לָיְלָה,
adonöy tzvö-os sh'mo. Böruch atöh יְיָ צְבָאוֹת שְׁמוֹ: בָּרוּךְ אַתָּה
adonöy, ha-ma-ariv arövim. יְיָ, הַמַּעֲרִיב עֲרָבִים:

Blessed are You, Lord our God, King of the universe, Who by His word causes the evenings to become dark. With wisdom He opens the [heavenly] gates; with understanding He changes the periods [of the day], varies the times, and arranges the stars in their positions in the sky according to His Will. He creates day and night; He rolls away light before darkness and darkness before light; He causes the day to pass and brings on the night, and separates between day and night; the Lord of hosts is His Name. Blessed are You Lord, Who causes the evenings to become dark.

Ahavas olöm bays yisrö-ayl am'chö אַהֲבַת עוֹלָם בֵּית יִשְׂרָאֵל עַמְּךָ
öhöv-tö, toröh umitzvos, chukim אָהָבְתָּ, תּוֹרָה וּמִצְוֹת, חֻקִּים
umish-pörim osönu li-mad-tö. וּמִשְׁפָּטִים אוֹתָנוּ לִמַּדְתָּ:
Al kayn adonöy elo-haynu, עַל כֵּן יְיָ אֱלֹהֵינוּ,
b'shöch'vaynu uv'kumaynu nösi-ach בְּשָׁכְבֵנוּ וּבְקוּמֵנוּ נָשִׂיחַ
b'chu-kechö, v'nismach b'div'ray בְּחֻקֶּיךָ, וְנִשְׂמַח בְּדִבְרֵי
so-rös'chö uv'mitzvo-sechö l'olöm תוֹרָתֶךָ וּבְמִצְוֹתֶיךָ לְעוֹלָם
vö-ed. Ki haym cha-yaynu v'orech וָעֶד: כִּי הֵם חַיֵּינוּ וְאֹרֶךְ
yö-maynu, uvöhem neh-ge yomöm יָמֵינוּ, וּבָהֶם נֶהְגֶּה יוֹמָם

213

vö-löy-löh. V'a-havös'chö lo sösur   וְלַיְלָה, וְאַהֲבָתְךָ לֹא תָסוּר

mimenu l'olömim. Böruch atöh   מִמֶּנּוּ לְעוֹלָמִים. בָּרוּךְ אַתָּה

adonoy, ohayv amo yisrö-ayl.   יְיָ, אוֹהֵב עַמּוֹ יִשְׂרָאֵל :

With everlasting love have You loved the House of Israel Your people. You have taught us Torah and mitzvot, decrees and laws. Therefore, Lord our God, when we lie down and when we rise, we will speak of Your statutes and rejoice in the words of Your Torah and in Your mitzvot forever. For they are our life and the length of our days, and we will meditate on them day and night. May Your love never depart from us. Blessed are You Lord, Who loves His people Israel.

It is customary to cover the eyes with the right hand while reciting the first verse of the Shema, to increase concentration.

Sh'ma yisrö-ayl, adonöy   שְׁמַע יִשְׂרָאֵל, יְיָ

elo-haynu, adonöy echöd.   אֱלֹהֵינוּ, יְיָ אֶחָד :

Hear, O Israel, the Lord is our God, the Lord is One.

Remove your hand from your eyes, and say the following in an undertone:

Böruch shaym k'vod   בָּרוּךְ שֵׁם כְּבוֹד

mal'chuso l'olöm vö-ed.   מַלְכוּתוֹ לְעוֹלָם וָעֶד :

Blessed be the name of the glory of His kingdom forever and ever.

Continue in a regular tone below:

V'öhavtö ays adonöy elo-hechö,   וְאָהַבְתָּ אֵת יְיָ אֱלֹהֶיךָ,

b'chöl l'vöv'chö, uv'chöl naf-sh'chö,   בְּכָל לְבָבְךָ, וּבְכָל נַפְשְׁךָ,

uv'chöl m'odechö. V'hö-yu   וּבְכָל מְאֹדֶךָ : וְהָיוּ

ha-d'vörim hö-ay-leh asher önochi	הַדְּבָרִים הָאֵלֶּה אֲשֶׁר אָנֹכִי
m'tzav'chö ha-yom, al l'vö-vechö.	מְצַוְּךָ הַיּוֹם, עַל לְבָבֶךָ:
V'shinan-töm l'vö-nechö v'dibartö	וְשִׁנַּנְתָּם לְבָנֶיךָ וְדִבַּרְתָּ
böm, b'shiv-t'chö b'vay-sechö,	בָּם, בְּשִׁבְתְּךָ בְּבֵיתֶךָ,
uv'lech-t'chö va-derech,	וּבְלֶכְתְּךָ בַדֶּרֶךְ, וּבְשָׁכְבְּךָ,
uv'shöch-b'chö, uv'ku-mechö.	וּבְקוּמֶךָ: וּקְשַׁרְתָּם
Uk'shar-töm l'os al yö-dechö, v'hö-yu	לְאוֹת עַל יָדֶךָ, וְהָיוּ
l'totöfos bayn ay-nechö. Uch'savtöm	לְטֹטָפֹת בֵּין עֵינֶיךָ: וּכְתַבְתָּם
al m'zuzos bay-sechö, uvish'örechö.	עַל מְזֻזוֹת בֵּיתֶךָ, וּבִשְׁעָרֶיךָ:

You shall love the Lord your God with all your heart, with all your soul, and with all your might. And these words which I command you today shall be upon your heart. You shall teach them thoroughly to your children, and you shall speak of them when you sit in your house and when you walk on the road, when you lie down and when you rise. You shall bind them as a sign upon your hand, and they shall be for a reminder between your eyes. And you shall write them upon the doorposts of your house and upon your gates.

V'hö-yöh im shömo-a tish-m'u	וְהָיָה אִם שָׁמֹעַ תִּשְׁמְעוּ
el mitzvo-sai asher önochi m'tza-veh	אֶל מִצְוֹתַי אֲשֶׁר אָנֹכִי מְצַוֶּה
es'chem ha-yom, l'ahavöh es adonöy	אֶתְכֶם הַיּוֹם, לְאַהֲבָה אֶת יְיָ
elohay-chem ul'öv'do, b'chöl	אֱלֹהֵיכֶם וּלְעָבְדוֹ, בְּכָל
l'vav'chem uv'chöl naf-sh'chem.	לְבַבְכֶם וּבְכָל נַפְשְׁכֶם:
V'nösati m'tar ar-tz'chem b'ito yo-reh	וְנָתַתִּי מְטַר אַרְצְכֶם בְּעִתּוֹ יוֹרֶה
umal-kosh, v'ösaftö d'gönechö	וּמַלְקוֹשׁ, וְאָסַפְתָּ דְגָנֶךָ
v'si-rosh'chö v'yitz-hörechö. V'nösati	וְתִירֹשְׁךָ וְיִצְהָרֶךָ: וְנָתַתִּי
aysev b'söd'chö liv'hem-techö,	עֵשֶׂב בְּשָׂדְךָ לִבְהֶמְתֶּךָ,

v'öchaltö v'sövö-tö. Hi-shöm'ru öchem pen yifteh l'vav'chem, v'sartem va-avad-tem elohim achay-rim v'hish-tacha-visem löhem. V'chöröh af adonöy bö-chem v'ötzar es ha-shöma-yim v'lo yih-yeh mötör v'hö-adömöh lo si-tayn es y'vulöh, va-avad-tem m'hayröh may-al hö-öretz ha-tovöh asher adonöy no-sayn löchem. V'sam-tem es d'vörai ayleh al l'vav'chem v'al naf-sh'chem, uk'shar-tem osöm l'os al yed'chem v'hö-yu l'to-töfos bayn ay-nay-chem. V'limad-tem osöm es b'nay-chem l'da-bayr böm, b'shiv-t'chö b'vay-sechö uv'lech-t'chö va-derech uv'shöch-b'chö uv'ku-mechö. Uch'savtöm al m'zuzos bay-sechö uvish'örechö. L'ma-an yirbu y'may-chem vimay v'naychem al hö-adömöh asher nishba adonöy la-avo-saychem lösays löhem, kimay ha-shöma-yim al hö-öretz.

וְאָכַלְתָּ וְשָׂבָעְתָּ: הִשָּׁמְרוּ לָכֶם פֶּן יִפְתֶּה לְבַבְכֶם, וְסַרְתֶּם וַעֲבַדְתֶּם אֱלֹהִים אֲחֵרִים וְהִשְׁתַּחֲוִיתֶם לָהֶם: וְחָרָה אַף יְיָ בָּכֶם וְעָצַר אֶת הַשָּׁמַיִם וְלֹא יִהְיֶה מָטָר וְהָאֲדָמָה לֹא תִתֵּן אֶת יְבוּלָהּ, וַאֲבַדְתֶּם מְהֵרָה מֵעַל הָאָרֶץ הַטֹּבָה אֲשֶׁר יְיָ נֹתֵן לָכֶם: וְשַׂמְתֶּם אֶת דְּבָרַי אֵלֶּה עַל לְבַבְכֶם וְעַל נַפְשְׁכֶם, וּקְשַׁרְתֶּם אֹתָם לְאוֹת עַל יֶדְכֶם וְהָיוּ לְטוֹטָפֹת בֵּין עֵינֵיכֶם: וְלִמַּדְתֶּם אֹתָם אֶת בְּנֵיכֶם לְדַבֵּר בָּם, בְּשִׁבְתְּךָ בְּבֵיתֶךָ וּבְלֶכְתְּךָ בַדֶּרֶךְ וּבְשָׁכְבְּךָ וּבְקוּמֶךָ: וּכְתַבְתָּם עַל מְזוּזוֹת בֵּיתֶךָ וּבִשְׁעָרֶיךָ: לְמַעַן יִרְבּוּ יְמֵיכֶם וִימֵי בְנֵיכֶם עַל הָאֲדָמָה אֲשֶׁר נִשְׁבַּע יְיָ לַאֲבֹתֵיכֶם לָתֵת לָהֶם, כִּימֵי הַשָּׁמַיִם עַל הָאָרֶץ:

And it will be, if you will diligently obey My commandments which I enjoin upon you this day, to love the Lord your God and to serve Him with all your heart and with all your soul, I will give rain for your land at the proper time, the early rain and the late rain, and you will gather in your grain, your wine and your oil. And I will give grass in your fields for your cattle, and you will eat and be sated. Take care lest your heart be lured away, and you turn astray and worship alien gods and bow down to them. For then the Lord's wrath will flare up against you, and He will close the heavens so that there will be no rain and the earth will not yield its produce, and you will swiftly perish from the good land which the Lord gives you. Therefore, place these words of Mine upon your heart and upon your soul, and bind them for a sign on your hand, and they shall be for a reminder between your eyes. You shall teach them to your children, to speak of them when you sit in your house and when you walk on the road, when you lie down and when you rise. And you shall inscribe them on the doorposts of your house and on your gates — so that your days and the days of your children may be prolonged on the land which the Lord swore to your fathers to give to them for as long as the heavens are above the earth.

Va-yomer adonöy el mosheh lay-mor. וַיֹּאמֶר יְיָ אֶל מֹשֶׁה לֵּאמֹר:
Dabayr el b'nay yisrö-ayl v'ömartö דַּבֵּר אֶל בְּנֵי יִשְׂרָאֵל וְאָמַרְתָּ
alay-hem v'ösu löhem tzitzis al אֲלֵהֶם וְעָשׂוּ לָהֶם צִיצִת עַל
kan'fay vig'dayhem l'doro-söm, כַּנְפֵי בִגְדֵיהֶם לְדֹרֹתָם,
v'nös'nu al tzitzis ha-könöf, p'sil וְנָתְנוּ עַל צִיצִת הַכָּנָף, פְּתִיל
t'chayles. V'hö-yöh löchem l'tzitzis, תְּכֵלֶת: וְהָיָה לָכֶם לְצִיצִת,
ur'isem oso uz'chartem es köl וּרְאִיתֶם אֹתוֹ וּזְכַרְתֶּם אֶת כָּל
mitzvos adonöy va-asisem osöm, v'lo מִצְוֹת יְיָ וַעֲשִׂיתֶם אֹתָם, וְלֹא
sö-suru acha-ray l'vav'chem v'acharay תָתוּרוּ אַחֲרֵי לְבַבְכֶם וְאַחֲרֵי
aynay-chem asher atem zonim עֵינֵיכֶם אֲשֶׁר אַתֶּם זֹנִים
acha-rayhem. L'ma-an tiz-k'ru אַחֲרֵיהֶם: לְמַעַן תִּזְכְּרוּ
va-asisem es köl mitzvo-söy, וַעֲשִׂיתֶם אֶת כָּל מִצְוֹתָי,

217

vih-yisem k'doshim laylo-haychem.

וִהְיִיתֶם קְדֹשִׁים לֵאלֹהֵיכֶם:

Ani adonöy elo-haychem asher

אֲנִי יְיָ אֱלֹהֵיכֶם אֲשֶׁר

ho-tzaysi es'chem may-eretz

הוֹצֵאתִי אֶתְכֶם מֵאֶרֶץ

mitzra-yim lih-yos löchem lay-lohim,

מִצְרַיִם לִהְיוֹת לָכֶם לֵאלֹהִים,

ani adonöy elo-haychem. Emes.

אֲנִי יְיָ אֱלֹהֵיכֶם: אֱמֶת.

The Lord spoke to Moses, saying: Speak to the children of Israel and tell them to make for themselves fringes on the corners of their garments throughout their generations, and to attach a thread of blue on the fringe of each corner. They shall be to you as tzitzit, and you shall look upon them and remember all the commandments of the Lord and fulfill them, and you will not follow after your heart and after your eyes by which you go astray – so that you may remember and fulfill all My commandments and be holy to your God. I am the Lord your God Who brought you out of the land of Egypt to be your God; I, the Lord, am your God. Truth.

Ve-emunöh köl zos, v'ka-yöm ölaynu,

וֶאֱמוּנָה כָּל זֹאת, וְקַיָּם עָלֵינוּ,

ki hu adonöy elo-haynu v'ayn

כִּי הוּא יְיָ אֱלֹהֵינוּ וְאֵין

zulöso, va-anach-nu yisrö-ayl amo,

זוּלָתוֹ, וַאֲנַחְנוּ יִשְׂרָאֵל עַמּוֹ,

hapo-daynu mi-yad m'löchim,

הַפּוֹדֵנוּ מִיַּד מְלָכִים,

mal-kaynu hago-alay-nu mi-kaf köl

מַלְכֵּנוּ הַגּוֹאֲלֵנוּ מִכַּף כָּל

he-öritzim. Hö-ayl hanif-rö lönu

הֶעָרִיצִים: הָאֵל הַנִּפְרָע לָנוּ

mitzöraynu, v'ham'sha-laym g'mul

מִצָּרֵינוּ, וְהַמְשַׁלֵּם גְּמוּל

l'chöl o-y'vay naf-shaynu, hö-oseh

לְכָל אֹיְבֵי נַפְשֵׁנוּ, הָעֹשֶׂה

g'dolos ad ayn chay-ker, v'niflö-os ad

גְדֹלוֹת עַד אֵין חֵקֶר, וְנִפְלָאוֹת עַד

ayn mispör. Ha-söm naf-shaynu

אֵין מִסְפָּר: הַשָּׂם נַפְשֵׁנוּ

bacha-yim, v'lo nösan lamot rag-laynu.

בַּחַיִּים, וְלֹא נָתַן לַמּוֹט

Ha-madri-chaynu al bömos

רַגְלֵנוּ: הַמַּדְרִיכֵנוּ עַל בָּמוֹת

218

o-y'vaynu, vayörem kar-naynu al köl
son'aynu. Hö-ayl hö-oseh lönu
n'kömöh b'far-oh, v'osos umof'sim
b'ad'mas b'nay chöm. Ha-makeh
v'ev-röso köl b'choray mitzrö-yim,
va-yo-tzay es amo yisrö-ayl mi-tochöm
'chayrus olöm. Hama-avir bönöv bayn
giz'ray yam suf, v'es rod'fayhem v'es
son'ayhem bis'homos tiba, v'rö-u
vönöv g'vorösö, shib'chu v'hodu
lish'mo. Umal'chuso v'rötzon kib'lu
alay-hem, mosheh uv'nay yisrö-ayl
l'chö önu shiröh b'sim-chöh
raböh, v'öm'ru chulöm.

אֱלֹהֵינוּ, וַיָּרֶם קַרְנֵנוּ עַל כָּל
שׂנְאֵינוּ: הָאֵל הָעוֹשֶׂה לָּנוּ
נְקָמָה בְּפַרְעֹה, וְאוֹתוֹת וּמוֹפְתִים
בְּאַדְמַת בְּנֵי חָם: הַמַּכֶּה
בְּעֶבְרָתוֹ כָּל בְּכוֹרֵי מִצְרָיִם,
וַיּוֹצֵא אֶת עַמּוֹ יִשְׂרָאֵל מִתּוֹכָם
לְחֵרוּת עוֹלָם: הַמַּעֲבִיר בָּנָיו
בֵּין גִּזְרֵי יַם סוּף, וְאֶת רוֹדְפֵיהֶם
וְאֶת שׂוֹנְאֵיהֶם בִּתְהוֹמוֹת טִבַּע, וְרָאוּ
בָנָיו גְּבוּרָתוֹ, שִׁבְּחוּ וְהוֹדוּ
לִשְׁמוֹ: וּמַלְכוּתוֹ בְּרָצוֹן קִבְּלוּ
עֲלֵיהֶם, מֹשֶׁה וּבְנֵי יִשְׂרָאֵל
לְךָ עָנוּ שִׁירָה בְּשִׂמְחָה
רַבָּה, וְאָמְרוּ כֻלָּם:

And belief is all this; it is established with us that He is the Lord our God, there is no other, and that we Israel are His people. It is He Who redeems us from the hand of kings; our King, Who delivers us from the grip of all the tyrants; the benevolent God, Who avenges us against our persecutors, and brings retribution on all our mortal enemies. He does great things beyond limit, and wonders beyond number. He has kept us alive, and did not allow our feet to falter. He led us upon the high places of our foes, and increased our strength over all our adversaries. He is the benevolent God Who, in our behalf, brought retribution upon Pharaoh, and signs and miracles in the land of the Hamites; Who, in His wrath, struck all the first-born of Egypt and brought out His people Israel from their midst to everlasting freedom; Who led His children through the divided parts of the Sea of Reeds, and drowned their pursuers and their enemies in the depths. As His children beheld His might, they extolled and offered praise to His Name, and willingly accepted His sovereignty; Moses and the children of Israel with great joy raised their voices in song to You, and they all proclaimed:

Mi chö-mochö bö-aylim adonöy,   מִי כָמֹכָה בָּאֵלִם יְיָ,

mi kö-mochö ne-dör ba-kodesh, norö   מִי כָּמֹכָה נֶאְדָּר בַּקֹּדֶשׁ, נוֹרָא

s'hilos, osay fe-le. Mal'chus'chö rö-u   תְהִלֹּת, עֹשֵׂה פֶלֶא : מַלְכוּתְךָ רָאוּ

vö-nechö, bokay-a yöm lif'nay   בָנֶיךָ, בּוֹקֵעַ יָם לִפְנֵי

mosheh, zeh ayli önu v'öm'ru: מֹשֶׁה, זֶה אֵלִי עָנוּ וְאָמְרוּ :

Adonöy yim-loch l'olöm vö-ed.   יְיָ יִמְלֹךְ לְעֹלָם וָעֶד.

V'ne-emar, ki födöh adonöy es   וְנֶאֱמַר : כִּי פָדָה יְיָ אֶת

ya-akov, ug'ölo mi-yad chözök   יַעֲקֹב, וּגְאָלוֹ מִיַּד חָזָק

mi-menu. Böruch atöh adonöy,   מִמֶּנּוּ. בָּרוּךְ אַתָּה יְיָ,

gö-al yisrö-ayl.   גָּאַל יִשְׂרָאֵל :

Who is like You among the supernal beings, O Lord! Who is like You, resplendent in holiness, awesome in praise, performing wonders! Your children beheld Your sovereignty as You split the sea before Moses. "This is my God!" they exclaimed, and declared, "The Lord shall reign forever and ever." And it is said: For the Lord has redeemed Jacob, and delivered him from a power mightier than he. Blessed are You Lord, Who has delivered Israel.

Hash-kivaynu övinu l'shölom,   הַשְׁכִּיבֵנוּ אָבִינוּ לְשָׁלוֹם,

v'ha-amidaynu mal-kaynu l'cha-yim   וְהַעֲמִידֵנוּ מַלְכֵּנוּ לְחַיִּים

tovim ul'shölom, v'sak'naynu   טוֹבִים וּלְשָׁלוֹם, וְתַקְּנֵנוּ

b'aytzöh tovöh mil'fönechö,   בְּעֵצָה טוֹבָה מִלְּפָנֶיךָ,

v'hoshi-aynu m'hayröh l'ma-an   וְהוֹשִׁיעֵנוּ מְהֵרָה לְמַעַן

sh'mechö, uf'ros ölaynu sukas   שְׁמֶךָ, וּפְרֹשׂ עָלֵינוּ סֻכַּת

sh'lomechö. V'högayn ba-adaynu,   שְׁלוֹמֶךָ : וְהָגֵן בַּעֲדֵנוּ,

v'hösayr may-ölaynu o-yayv dever   וְהָסֵר מֵעָלֵינוּ אוֹיֵב דֶּבֶר

v'cherev v'rö-öv v'yögon. V'hösayr וְחֶרֶב וְרָעָב וְיָגוֹן : וְהָסֵר

sötön mil'fönaynu umay-acha-raynu, שָׂטָן מִלְּפָנֵינוּ וּמֵאַחֲרֵינוּ,

uv'tzayl k'nöfechö tas-tiraynu, וּבְצֵל כְּנָפֶיךָ תַּסְתִּירֵנוּ,

ush'mor tzaysay-nu uvo-aynu וּשְׁמוֹר צֵאתֵנוּ וּבוֹאֵנוּ

l'cha-yim tovim ul'shölom may-atöh לְחַיִּים טוֹבִים וּלְשָׁלוֹם מֵעַתָּה

v'ad olöm. Ki ayl shom'raynu וְעַד עוֹלָם : כִּי אֵל שׁוֹמְרֵנוּ

umatzi-laynu ötöh. Böruch atöh וּמַצִּילֵנוּ אָתָּה : בָּרוּךְ אַתָּה

adonöy, shomayr es amo יְיָ, שׁוֹמֵר אֶת עַמּוֹ

yisrö-ayl lö-ad. יִשְׂרָאֵל לָעַד :

Our Father, let us lie down in peace; our King, raise us up to a good life and peace. Improve us with Your good counsel, help us speedily for the sake of Your Name, and spread over us the shelter of Your peace. Protect us and remove from us the enemy, pestilence, sword, famine and sorrow. Remove the adversary from before us and from behind us; shelter us in the shadow of Your wings; and guard our going out and our coming in for a good life and peace from now and for all time. For You, God, are our guardian and our deliverer. Blessed are You Lord, Who guards His people Israel forever.

1. All rise. Leader recites the Half-Kaddish (page 176).
2. Congregation recites the silent *Amidah* (page 177).

The Counting of the Omer

From the second night of Passover until the night before Shavuot, we count the *Omer*. This is done before "*Ölaynu*," the last prayer of the *Maariv* (evening) service. Counting the Omer serves to prepare us to receive the Torah on Shavuot (49 days from Passover). If one forgot to count the Omer on one night, he should count it during the following day without a blessing. He can then continue counting during all remaining nights with a blessing. If he forgets an entire day, he can say the count of the Omer but should not make a blessing beforehand.

The Omer is counted while standing. As long as no days have been missed, one should recite the following blessing before counting:

Böruch atöh adonöy, elo-haynu   בָּרוּךְ אַתָּה יְיָ, אֱלֹהֵינוּ

melech hö-olöm, asher kid'shönu   מֶלֶךְ הָעוֹלָם, אֲשֶׁר קִדְּשָׁנוּ

b'mitzvosöv, v'tzivönu al   בְּמִצְוֹתָיו, וְצִוָּנוּ עַל

s'firas hö-omer.   סְפִירַת הָעֹמֶר:

Blessed are You, Lord our God, King of the Universe, Who has sanctified us with His commandments, and commanded us concerning the counting of the Omer.

Say the counting for today (page 226), followed by the portions below:

Höracha-mön hu yacha-zir lönu   הָרַחֲמָן הוּא יַחֲזִיר לָנוּ

avodas bays hamik-dösh lim'komöh,   עֲבוֹדַת בֵּית הַמִּקְדָּשׁ לִמְקוֹמָהּ,

bim'hayröh v'yö-maynu ömayn selöh.   בִּמְהֵרָה בְיָמֵינוּ אָמֵן סֶלָה:

May the Merciful One restore unto us the service of the Beit Hamikdosh to its place, speedily in our days; Amen, Selah.

Lam'natzay-ach bin'ginos miz-mor shir. Elohim y'chö-naynu vivö-r'chaynu, yö-ayr pönöv i-tönu selöh. Löda-as bö-öretz dar-kechö, b'chöl go-yim y'shu-ösechö. Yodu-chö amim elohim, yodu-chö amim kulöm. Yis-m'chu vira-n'nu l'umim, ki sish-pot amim mi-shor, ul'u-mim bö-öretz tan-chaym selöh. Yodu-chö amim elohim, yodu-chö amim kulöm. Eretz nös'nöh y'vulöh, y'vö-r'chaynu elohim elo-haynu. Y'vö-r'chaynu elohim, v'yi-r'u oso köl af'say öretz.

לַמְנַצֵּחַ בִּנְגִינֹת מִזְמוֹר
שִׁיר : אֱלֹהִים יְחָנֵּנוּ
וִיבָרְכֵנוּ, יָאֵר פָּנָיו אִתָּנוּ
סֶלָה : לָדַעַת בָּאָרֶץ דַּרְכֶּךָ,
בְּכָל גּוֹיִם יְשׁוּעָתֶךָ :
יוֹדוּךָ עַמִּים אֱלֹהִים, יוֹדוּךָ
עַמִּים כֻּלָּם : יִשְׂמְחוּ וִירַנְּנוּ
לְאֻמִּים, כִּי תִשְׁפֹּט עַמִּים מִישׁר,
וּלְאֻמִּים בָּאָרֶץ תַּנְחֵם סֶלָה :
יוֹדוּךָ עַמִּים אֱלֹהִים, יוֹדוּךָ
עַמִּים כֻּלָּם : אֶרֶץ נָתְנָה
יְבוּלָהּ, יְבָרְכֵנוּ אֱלֹהִים
אֱלֹהֵינוּ : יְבָרְכֵנוּ אֱלֹהִים,
וְיִירְאוּ אֹתוֹ כָּל אַפְסֵי אָרֶץ :

For the Choirmaster; a song with instrumental music; a Psalm. May God be gracious to us and bless us, may He make His countenance shine upon us forever; that Your way be known on earth, Your salvation among all nations. The nations will extol You, O God; all the nations will extol You. The nations will rejoice and sing for joy, for You will judge the peoples justly and guide the nations on earth forever. The peoples will extol You, O God; all the peoples will extol You, for the earth will have yielded its produce and God, our God, will bless us. God will bless us; and all, from the farthest corners of the earth, shall fear Him.

Önö, b'cho-ach g'dulas y'min'chö, ta-tir tz'ruröh. Kabayl rinas am'chö, sag'vaynu taha-raynu, noröh. Nö

אָנָּא, בְּכֹחַ גְּדֻלַּת יְמִינְךָ,
תַּתִּיר צְרוּרָה : קַבֵּל רִנַּת עַמְּךָ,
שַׂגְּבֵנוּ, טַהֲרֵנוּ, נוֹרָא : נָא

gibor, dor'shay yichud'chö, k'vövas   גִּבּוֹר, דּוֹרְשֵׁי יִחוּדְךָ, כְּבָבַת
shöm'raym. Bör'chaym taha-raym,   שָׁמְרֵם: בָּרְכֵם, טַהֲרֵם,
racha-may tzid'kös'chö tömid   רַחֲמֵי צִדְקָתְךָ תָּמִיד
göm'laym. Chasin ködosh, b'rov   גָּמְלֵם: חֲסִין קָדוֹשׁ, בְּרוֹב
tuv'chö nahayl adö-sechö. Yöchid,   טוּבְךָ נַהֵל עֲדָתֶךָ: יָחִיד,
gay-eh, l'am'chö p'nay, zoch'ray   גֵּאֶה, לְעַמְּךָ פְּנֵה, זוֹכְרֵי
k'dushö-sechö. Shav-ösaynu kabayl,   קְדֻשָּׁתֶךָ: שַׁוְעָתֵנוּ קַבֵּל,
ush'ma tza-akö-saynu, yoday-a   וּשְׁמַע צַעֲקָתֵנוּ, יוֹדֵעַ
ta-alumos. Böruch shaym k'vod   תַּעֲלוּמוֹת: בָּרוּךְ שֵׁם כְּבוֹד
mal'chuso l'olöm vö-ed.   מַלְכוּתוֹ לְעוֹלָם וָעֶד:

We implore you, by the great power of Your right hand, release the captive. Accept the prayer of Your people; strengthen us, purify us, Awesome One. Mighty One, we beseech You, guard as the apple of the eye those Who seek Your Oneness. Bless them, cleanse them; bestow upon them forever Your merciful righteousness. Powerful, Holy One, in Your abounding goodness, guide Your congregation. Only and Exalted One, turn to Your people Who are mindful of Your holiness. Accept our supplication and hear our cry, You Who knows secret thoughts. Blessed be the name of the glory of His kingdom forever and ever.

Ri-bono shel olöm, atöh tzivi-sönu al   רִבּוֹנוֹ שֶׁל עוֹלָם, אַתָּה צִוִּיתָנוּ עַל
y'day mosheh av-dechö lis-por s'firas   יְדֵי מֹשֶׁה עַבְדְּךָ לִסְפּוֹר סְפִירַת
hö-omer k'day l'taha-raynu   הָעוֹמֶר כְּדֵי לְטַהֲרֵנוּ
mik'lipo-saynu umitum-osaynu,   מִקְּלִפּוֹתֵינוּ וּמִטֻּמְאוֹתֵינוּ,
k'mo she-kösav-tö b'sorö-sechö: כְּמוֹ שֶׁכָּתַבְתָּ בְּתוֹרָתֶךָ:
Us'far-tem löchem mimö-chöras   וּסְפַרְתֶּם לָכֶם מִמָּחֳרַת
ha-shabös mi-yom havi-achem es   הַשַּׁבָּת מִיּוֹם הֲבִיאֲכֶם אֶת

omer ha-t'nuföh sheva shabösos
t'mimos tih'yenöh. Ad mimö-chöras
ha-shabös hash'vi-is tisp'ru
cha-mishim yom, k'day she-yitö-haru
naf'shos am'chö yisrö-ayl
mizu-hamösöm, uv'chayn y'hi rötzon
mil'fö-nechö, adonöy elo-haynu
vay-lohay avosaynu, she-biz'chus
s'firas hö-omer shesöfar-ti ha-yom,
y'sukan mah she-pögam-ti bis'firöh
(say the Sefira for that day) v'etö-hayr
v'eska-daysh bik'dushöh shel ma-löh,
v'al y'day zeh yush-pa shefa rav
b'chöl hö-olömos ul'sakayn es
naf'sho-saynu v'rucho-saynu
v'nish'mo-saynu mi-köl sig uf'gam
ul'taha-raynu ul'kad'shaynu
bik'dushös'chö hö-elyonöh,
ömayn selöh.

עֹמֶר הַתְּנוּפָה שֶׁבַע שַׁבָּתוֹת
תְּמִימֹת תִּהְיֶינָה: עַד מִמָּחֳרַת
הַשַּׁבָּת הַשְּׁבִיעִת תִּסְפְּרוּ
חֲמִשִּׁים יוֹם, כְּדֵי שֶׁיִּטָּהֲרוּ
נַפְשׁוֹת עַמְּךָ יִשְׂרָאֵל
מִזֻּהֲמָתָם, וּבְכֵן יְהִי רָצוֹן
מִלְּפָנֶיךָ, יְיָ אֱלֹהֵינוּ
וֵאלֹהֵי אֲבוֹתֵינוּ, שֶׁבִּזְכוּת
סְפִירַת הָעוֹמֶר שֶׁסָּפַרְתִּי הַיּוֹם,
יְתֻקַּן מַה שֶּׁפָּגַמְתִּי בִּסְפִירָה
(פלונית השייך לאותו הלילה) וְאֶטָּהֵר
וְאֶתְקַדֵּשׁ בִּקְדֻשָּׁה שֶׁל מַעְלָה,
וְעַל יְדֵי זֶה יֻשְׁפַּע שֶׁפַע רַב
בְּכָל הָעוֹלָמוֹת וּלְתַקֵּן אֶת
נַפְשׁוֹתֵינוּ וְרוּחוֹתֵינוּ
וְנִשְׁמוֹתֵינוּ מִכָּל סִיג וּפְגָם
וּלְטַהֲרֵנוּ וּלְקַדְּשֵׁנוּ
בִּקְדֻשָּׁתְךָ הָעֶלְיוֹנָה,
אָמֵן סֶלָה:

Master of the universe, You have commanded us through Moses Your servant to count Sefirat HaOmer, in order to purify us from our evil and uncleanness. As You have written in Your Torah, "You shall count for yourselves from the day following the day of rest, from the day on which you bring the Omer as a wave-offering; [the counting] shall be for seven full weeks. Until the day following the seventh week shall you count fifty days," so that the souls of Your people Israel may be cleansed from their defilement. Therefore, may it be Your will, Lord our God and God of our fathers, that

225

in the merit of the Sefirat HaOmer which I counted today, the blemish that I have caused in the Sefirah (say the Sefirah for that day) be rectified and I may be purified and sanctified with supernal holiness. May abundant bounty thereby be bestowed upon all the worlds. May it rectify our Nefesh, Ruach and Neshamah from every baseness and defect, and may it purify and sanctify us with Your supernal holiness. Amen, selah.

Continue with "*Ōlaynu*" (page 202).

1- Today is one day of the Omer.

1- הַיּוֹם יוֹם אֶחָד לָעֹמֶר. חסד שבחסד

2- Today is two days of the Omer.

2- הַיּוֹם שְׁנֵי יָמִים לָעֹמֶר. גבורה שבחסד

3- Today is three days of the Omer.

3- הַיּוֹם שְׁלשָׁה יָמִים לָעֹמֶר. תפארת שבחסד

4- Today is four days of the Omer.

4- הַיּוֹם אַרְבָּעָה יָמִים לָעֹמֶר. נצח שבחסד

5- Today is five days of the Omer.

5- הַיּוֹם חֲמִשָּׁה יָמִים לָעֹמֶר. הוד שבחסד

6- Today is six days of the Omer.

6- הַיּוֹם שִׁשָּׁה יָמִים לָעֹמֶר. יסוד שבחסד

7- Today is seven days, which is one week of the Omer.

7- הַיּוֹם שִׁבְעָה יָמִים שֶׁהֵם שָׁבוּעַ אֶחָד לָעֹמֶר. מלכות שבחסד

8- Today is eight days, which is one week and one day of the Omer.

8- הַיּוֹם שְׁמוֹנָה יָמִים שֶׁהֵם שָׁבוּעַ אֶחָד וְיוֹם אֶחָד לָעֹמֶר. חסד שבגבורה

9- Today is nine days, which is one week and two days of the Omer.

9- הַיּוֹם תִּשְׁעָה יָמִים שֶׁהֵם שָׁבוּעַ אֶחָד וּשְׁנֵי יָמִים לָעֹמֶר. גבורה שבגבורה

10- Today is ten days, which is one week and three days of the Omer.

10- הַיּוֹם עֲשָׂרָה יָמִים שֶׁהֵם שָׁבוּעַ אֶחָד וּשְׁלשָׁה יָמִים לָעֹמֶר. תפארת שבגבורה

11- Today is eleven days, which is one week and four days of the Omer.

11- הַיּוֹם אַחַד עָשָׂר יוֹם שֶׁהֵם שָׁבוּעַ אֶחָד וְאַרְבָּעָה יָמִים לָעֹמֶר. נצח שבגבורה

12- Today is twelve days, which is one week and five days of the Omer.

12- הַיּוֹם שְׁנֵים עָשָׂר יוֹם שֶׁהֵם שָׁבוּעַ אֶחָד וַחֲמִשָּׁה יָמִים לָעֹמֶר. הוד שבגבורה

13- Today is thirteen days, which is one week and six days of the Omer.

13- הַיּוֹם שְׁלשָׁה עָשָׂר יוֹם שֶׁהֵם שָׁבוּעַ אֶחָד וְשִׁשָּׁה יָמִים לָעֹמֶר. יסוד שבגבורה

14- Today is fourteen days, which is two weeks of the Omer.

15- Today is fifteen days, which is two weeks and one day of the Omer.

16- Today is sixteen days, which is two weeks and two days of the Omer.

17- Today is seventeen days, which is two weeks and three days of the Omer.

18- Today is eighteen days, which is two weeks and four days of the Omer.

19- Today is nineteen days, which is two weeks and five days of the Omer.

20- Today is twenty days, which is two weeks and six days of the Omer.

21- Today is twenty-one days, which is three weeks of the Omer.

22- Today is twenty-two days, which is three weeks and one day of the Omer.

23- Today is twenty-three days, which is three weeks and two days of the Omer.

24- Today is twenty-four days, which is three weeks and three days of the Omer.

25- Today is twenty-five days, which is three weeks and four days of the Omer.

26- Today is twenty-six days, which is three weeks and five days of the Omer.

27- Today is twenty-seven days, which is three weeks and six days of the Omer.

14- הַיּוֹם אַרְבָּעָה עָשָׂר יוֹם שֶׁהֵם שְׁנֵי שָׁבוּעוֹת לָעֹמֶר. מלכות שבגבורה

15- הַיּוֹם חֲמִשָּׁה עָשָׂר יוֹם שֶׁהֵם שְׁנֵי שָׁבוּעוֹת וְיוֹם אֶחָד לָעֹמֶר. חסד שבתפארת

16- הַיּוֹם שִׁשָּׁה עָשָׂר יוֹם שֶׁהֵם שְׁנֵי שָׁבוּעוֹת וּשְׁנֵי יָמִים לָעֹמֶר. גבורה שבתפארת

17- הַיּוֹם שִׁבְעָה עָשָׂר יוֹם שֶׁהֵם שְׁנֵי שָׁבוּעוֹת וּשְׁלֹשָׁה יָמִים לָעֹמֶר. תפארת שבתפארת

18- הַיּוֹם שְׁמוֹנָה עָשָׂר יוֹם שֶׁהֵם שְׁנֵי שָׁבוּעוֹת וְאַרְבָּעָה יָמִים לָעֹמֶר. נצח שבתפארת

19- הַיּוֹם תִּשְׁעָה עָשָׂר יוֹם שֶׁהֵם שְׁנֵי שָׁבוּעוֹת וַחֲמִשָּׁה יָמִים לָעֹמֶר. הוד שבתפארת

20- הַיּוֹם עֶשְׂרִים יוֹם שֶׁהֵם שְׁנֵי שָׁבוּעוֹת וְשִׁשָּׁה יָמִים לָעֹמֶר: יסוד שבתפארת

21- הַיּוֹם אֶחָד וְעֶשְׂרִים יוֹם שֶׁהֵם שְׁלֹשָׁה שָׁבוּעוֹת לָעֹמֶר. מלכות שבתפארת

22- הַיּוֹם שְׁנַיִם וְעֶשְׂרִים יוֹם שֶׁהֵם שְׁלֹשָׁה שָׁבוּעוֹת וְיוֹם אֶחָד לָעֹמֶר. חסד שבנצח

23- הַיּוֹם שְׁלֹשָׁה וְעֶשְׂרִים יוֹם שֶׁהֵם שְׁלֹשָׁה שָׁבוּעוֹת וּשְׁנֵי יָמִים לָעֹמֶר. גבורה שבנצח

24- הַיּוֹם אַרְבָּעָה וְעֶשְׂרִים יוֹם שֶׁהֵם שְׁלֹשָׁה שָׁבוּעוֹת וּשְׁלֹשָׁה יָמִים לָעֹמֶר. תפארת שבנצח

25- הַיּוֹם חֲמִשָּׁה וְעֶשְׂרִים יוֹם שֶׁהֵם שְׁלֹשָׁה שָׁבוּעוֹת וְאַרְבָּעָה יָמִים לָעֹמֶר. נצח שבנצח

26- הַיּוֹם שִׁשָּׁה וְעֶשְׂרִים יוֹם שֶׁהֵם שְׁלֹשָׁה שָׁבוּעוֹת וַחֲמִשָּׁה יָמִים לָעֹמֶר. הוד שבנצח

27- הַיּוֹם שִׁבְעָה וְעֶשְׂרִים יוֹם שֶׁהֵם שְׁלֹשָׁה שָׁבוּעוֹת וְשִׁשָּׁה יָמִים לָעֹמֶר. יסוד שבנצח

28- Today is twenty-eight days, which is four weeks of the Omer.

29- Today is twenty-nine days, which is four weeks and one day of the Omer.

30- Today is thirty days, which is four weeks and two days of the Omer.

31- Today is thirty-one days, which is four weeks and three days of the Omer.

32- Today is thirty-two days, which is four weeks and four days of the Omer.

33- Today is thirty-three days, which is four weeks and five days of the Omer.

34- Today is thirty-four days, which is four weeks and six days of the Omer.

35- Today is thirty-five days, which is five weeks of the Omer.

36- Today is thirty-six days, which is five weeks and one day of the Omer.

37- Today is thirty-seven days, which is five weeks and two days of the Omer.

38- Today is thirty-eight days, which is five weeks and three days of the Omer.

39- Today is thirty-nine days, which is five weeks and four days of the Omer.

40- Today is forty days, which is five weeks and five days of the Omer.

41- Today is forty-one days, which is five weeks and six days of the Omer.

28- הַיּוֹם שְׁמוֹנָה וְעֶשְׂרִים יוֹם שֶׁהֵם אַרְבָּעָה שָׁבוּעוֹת לָעֹמֶר. מלכות שבנצח

29- הַיּוֹם תִּשְׁעָה וְעֶשְׂרִים יוֹם שֶׁהֵם אַרְבָּעָה שָׁבוּעוֹת וְיוֹם אֶחָד לָעֹמֶר. חסד שבהוד

30- הַיּוֹם שְׁלֹשִׁים יוֹם שֶׁהֵם אַרְבָּעָה שָׁבוּעוֹת וּשְׁנֵי יָמִים לָעֹמֶר. גבורה שבהוד

31- הַיּוֹם אֶחָד וּשְׁלֹשִׁים יוֹם שֶׁהֵם אַרְבָּעָה שָׁבוּעוֹת וּשְׁלֹשָׁה יָמִים לָעֹמֶר. תפארת שבהוד

32- הַיּוֹם שְׁנַיִם וּשְׁלֹשִׁים יוֹם שֶׁהֵם אַרְבָּעָה שָׁבוּעוֹת וְאַרְבָּעָה יָמִים לָעֹמֶר. נצח שבהוד

33- הַיּוֹם שְׁלֹשָׁה וּשְׁלֹשִׁים יוֹם שֶׁהֵם אַרְבָּעָה שָׁבוּעוֹת וַחֲמִשָּׁה יָמִים לָעֹמֶר. הוד שבהוד

34- הַיּוֹם אַרְבָּעָה וּשְׁלֹשִׁים יוֹם שֶׁהֵם אַרְבָּעָה שָׁבוּעוֹת וְשִׁשָּׁה יָמִים לָעֹמֶר. יסוד שבהוד

35- הַיּוֹם חֲמִשָּׁה וּשְׁלֹשִׁים יוֹם שֶׁהֵם חֲמִשָּׁה שָׁבוּעוֹת לָעֹמֶר. מלכות שבהוד

36- הַיּוֹם שִׁשָּׁה וּשְׁלֹשִׁים יוֹם שֶׁהֵם חֲמִשָּׁה שָׁבוּעוֹת וְיוֹם אֶחָד לָעֹמֶר. חסד שביסוד

37- הַיּוֹם שִׁבְעָה וּשְׁלֹשִׁים יוֹם שֶׁהֵם חֲמִשָּׁה שָׁבוּעוֹת וּשְׁנֵי יָמִים לָעֹמֶר. גבורה שביסוד

38- הַיּוֹם שְׁמוֹנָה וּשְׁלֹשִׁים יוֹם שֶׁהֵם חֲמִשָּׁה שָׁבוּעוֹת וְשְׁלֹשָׁה יָמִים לָעֹמֶר. תפארת שביסוד

39- הַיּוֹם תִּשְׁעָה וּשְׁלֹשִׁים יוֹם שֶׁהֵם חֲמִשָּׁה שָׁבוּעוֹת וְאַרְבָּעָה יָמִים לָעֹמֶר. נצח שביסוד

40- הַיּוֹם אַרְבָּעִים יוֹם שֶׁהֵם חֲמִשָּׁה שָׁבוּעוֹת וַחֲמִשָּׁה יָמִים לָעֹמֶר. הוד שביסוד

41- הַיּוֹם אֶחָד וְאַרְבָּעִים יוֹם שֶׁהֵם חֲמִשָּׁה שָׁבוּעוֹת וְשִׁשָּׁה יָמִים לָעֹמֶר. יסוד שביסוד

42- Today is forty-two days, which is six weeks of the Omer.

42- הַיּוֹם שְׁנַיִם וְאַרְבָּעִים יוֹם שֶׁהֵם שִׁשָּׁה שָׁבוּעוֹת לָעֹמֶר. מלכות שביסוד

43- Today is forty-three days, which is six weeks and one day of the Omer.

43- הַיּוֹם שְׁלֹשָׁה וְאַרְבָּעִים יוֹם שֶׁהֵם שִׁשָּׁה שָׁבוּעוֹת וְיוֹם אֶחָד לָעֹמֶר. חסד שבמלכות

44- Today is forty-four days, which is six weeks and two days of the Omer.

44- הַיּוֹם אַרְבָּעָה וְאַרְבָּעִים יוֹם שֶׁהֵם שִׁשָּׁה שָׁבוּעוֹת וּשְׁנֵי יָמִים לָעֹמֶר. גבורה שבמלכות

45- Today is forty-five days, which is six weeks and three days of the Omer.

45- הַיּוֹם חֲמִשָּׁה וְאַרְבָּעִים יוֹם שֶׁהֵם שִׁשָּׁה שָׁבוּעוֹת וּשְׁלֹשָׁה יָמִים לָעֹמֶר. תפארת שבמלכות

46- Today is forty-six days, which is six weeks and four days of the Omer.

46- הַיּוֹם שִׁשָּׁה וְאַרְבָּעִים יוֹם שֶׁהֵם שִׁשָּׁה שָׁבוּעוֹת וְאַרְבָּעָה יָמִים לָעֹמֶר. נצח שבמלכות

47 Today is forty-seven days, which is six weeks and five days of the Omer.

47- הַיּוֹם שִׁבְעָה וְאַרְבָּעִים יוֹם שֶׁהֵם שִׁשָּׁה שָׁבוּעוֹת וַחֲמִשָּׁה יָמִים לָעֹמֶר. הוד שבמלכות

48- Today is forty-eight days, which is six weeks and six days of the Omer.

48- הַיּוֹם שְׁמוֹנָה וְאַרְבָּעִים יוֹם שֶׁהֵם שִׁשָּׁה שָׁבוּעוֹת וְשִׁשָּׁה יָמִים לָעֹמֶר. יסוד שבמלכות

49- Today is forty-nine days, which is seven weeks of the Omer.

49- הַיּוֹם תִּשְׁעָה וְאַרְבָּעִים יוֹם שֶׁהֵם שִׁבְעָה שָׁבוּעוֹת לָעֹמֶר. מלכות שבמלכות

About the Counting of the Omer

"When you take this people out of Egypt," said God to Moses, "you shall serve God on this mountain." It took seven weeks to reach the mountain. The people of Israel departed from Egypt on the 15th of Nissan (the first day of Passover) and seven weeks later, on the 6th of Sivan, they received the Torah from God on Mount Sinai.

The Kabbalists explain that the 49 days that connect Passover with Shavuot correspond to the forty-nine powers of the soul. Each day, the Jewish people refined one of these soul-powers. On a national level, refining that particular soul power brought the Jews one step closer to their becoming God's chosen people.

Each year, we retrace this inner journey by "Counting the Omer." Beginning on the second night of Passover, we count the days and weeks: "Today, is one day of the Omer," "Today is two days of the Omer," "Today is seven days, which is one week of the Omer," and so on, until "Today is forty-nine days, which is seven weeks of the Omer."

When we have completed the count, we celebrate Shavuot, the "Festival of Weeks." This holiday not only commemorates the giving of the Torah, it celebrates the methodical 49-step process of self-refinement of our soul-powers.

Mishnayot Study for Mourners

It is a great honor for the departed soul when Torah is studied in its honor. For this reason, it is customary to study sections from the *Mishna* (codified compilation of Jewish law) on each day that Kaddish is said. In addition, the word *Mishna* (study) has the same letters as the Hebrew word *Neshama* (soul), for the soul acquires merit through those that study Torah for its sake.

Throughout the twelve months following the passing of one's father or mother, and on the *Yartzeit* (anniversary) of their passing, it is appropriate to study the Mishnayot of the order *Taharot*, especially the twenty-fourth chapter of the tractate *Kelim* (see below), before each prayer service.

One who has the time should study also chapters of Mishnayot whose initial letters comprise the Hebrew name of the deceased. Some prayer books have an index of the chapters sorted according to the Hebrew alphabet.

Mishnayot "Kelim" - Chapter 24

(א) שְׁלֹשָׁה תְרִיסִין הֵם, תְּרִיס הַכָּפוּף, טָמֵא מִדְרָס, וְשֶׁמְּשַׂחֲקִין בּוֹ בַּקְּנְפּוֹן, טָמֵא טְמֵא מֵת, וְדִיצַת הָעַרְבִיִּין טְהוֹרָה מִכְּלוּם: (ב) שָׁלֹשׁ עֲגָלוֹת הֵן, הָעֲשׂוּיָה כְּקַתֶּדְרָא, טְמֵאָה מִדְרָס, כְּמִטָּה, טְמֵאָה טְמֵא מֵת, וְשֶׁל אֲבָנִים, טְהוֹרָה מִכְּלוּם: (ג) שָׁלֹשׁ עֲרֵבוֹת הֵן, עֲרֵבָה מִשְּׁנֵי לֻגִּין עַד תִּשְׁעָה קַבִּין שֶׁנִּסְדְּקָה, טְמֵאָה מִדְרָס, שְׁלֵמָה, טְמֵאָה טְמֵא מֵת, וְהַבָּאָה בַּמִּדָּה, טְהוֹרָה מִכְּלוּם (ד) שָׁלֹשׁ

תֵּבוֹת הֵן, תֵּבָה שֶׁפִּתְחָהּ מִצִּדָּהּ, טְמֵאָה מִדְרָס, טְמֵאָה טְמֵא מֵת, וְהַבָּאָה בַּמִּדָּה, טְהוֹרָה מִכְּלוּם: (ה) שְׁלֹשָׁה תַּרְבּוּסִין הֵן, שֶׁל סַפָּרִין, טָמֵא מִדְרָס, שֶׁאוֹכְלִין עָלָיו, טָמֵא טְמֵא מֵת, וְשֶׁל זֵיתִים, טָהוֹר מִכְּלוּם: (ו) שָׁלֹשׁ בְּסִיסִיּוֹת הֵן, שֶׁלִּפְנֵי הַמִּטָּה וְשֶׁלִּפְנֵי סוֹפְרִים, טְמֵאָה מִדְרָס, וְשֶׁל דְּלָפְקִי, טְמֵאָה טְמֵא מֵת, וְשֶׁל מִגְדָּל, טְהוֹרָה מִכְּלוּם: (ז) שָׁלֹשׁ פִּנְקָסִיּוֹת הֵן, הָאֲפִיפוֹרִין, טְמֵאָה מִדְרָס, וְשֶׁיֶּשׁ בָּהּ בֵּית קִבּוּל שַׁעֲוָה, טְמֵאָה טְמֵא מֵת, וַחֲלָקָה, טְהוֹרָה מִכְּלוּם: (ח) שָׁלֹשׁ מִטּוֹת הֵן, הָעֲשׂוּיָה לִשְׁכִיבָה, טְמֵאָה מִדְרָס, שֶׁל זַגָּגִין, טְמֵאָה טְמֵא מֵת, וְשֶׁל סָרָגִין, טְהוֹרָה מִכְּלוּם: (ט) שָׁלֹשׁ מַשְׁפֵּלוֹת הֵן, שֶׁל זֶבֶל, טְמֵאָה מִדְרָס, שֶׁל תֶּבֶן, טְמֵאָה טְמֵא מֵת, וְהַפּוּחְלָר שֶׁל גְּמַלִּים, טָהוֹר מִכְּלוּם: (י) שָׁלֹשׁ מַפְּצִים הֵן, הָעֲשׂוּיָה לִישִׁיבָה, טְמֵאָה מִדְרָס, שֶׁל צַבָּעִין, טָמֵא טְמֵא מֵת, וְשֶׁל גִּתּוֹת, טָהוֹר מִכְּלוּם: (יא) שָׁלֹשׁ חֲמָתוֹת, וְשָׁלֹשׁ תּוּרְמְלִין הֵן, הַמְּקַבְּלִין כַּשִּׁעוּר, טְמֵאִין מִדְרָס, וְשֶׁאֵינָן מְקַבְּלִין כַּשִּׁעוּר, טְמֵאִין טְמֵא מֵת, וְשֶׁל עוֹר הַדָּג, טָהוֹר מִכְּלוּם: (יב) שְׁלֹשָׁה עוֹרוֹת הֵן, הֶעָשׂוּי לְשָׁטִיחַ, טָמֵא מִדְרָס, לְתַכְרִיךְ הַכֵּלִים, טָמֵא טְמֵא מֵת, וְשֶׁל רְצוּעוֹת וְשֶׁל סַנְדָּלִים, טְהוֹרָה מִכְּלוּם: (יג) שְׁלֹשָׁה סְדִינִין הֵן, הֶעָשׂוּי לִשְׁכִיבָה, טָמֵא מִדְרָס, טָמֵא טְמֵא מֵת, וְשֶׁל צוּרוֹת, טָהוֹר מִכְּלוּם: (יד) שָׁלֹשׁ מִטְפָּחוֹת הֵן, שֶׁל יָדַיִם, טְמֵאָה מִדְרָס, שֶׁל סְפָרִין, טְמֵאָה טְמֵא מֵת, וְשֶׁל תַּכְרִיךְ (וְשֶׁל) נִבְלֵי בְנֵי לֵוִי, טְהוֹרָה מִכְּלוּם: (טו) שְׁלֹשָׁה פְרַקְלִינִין הֵן, שֶׁל צָדֵי חַיָּה וָעוֹף, טָמֵא מִדְרָס, טָמֵא טְמֵא מֵת, וְשֶׁל קַיָּצִין, טָהוֹר מִכְּלוּם: (טז) שָׁלֹשׁ סְבָכוֹת הֵן, שֶׁל יַלְדָּה, טְמֵאָה טֻמְאַת מִדְרָס, שֶׁל זְקֵנָה, טְמֵאָה טְמֵא מֵת, וְשֶׁל יוֹצֵאת לַחוּץ, טְהוֹרָה מִכְּלוּם: (יז) שָׁלֹשׁ קֻפוֹת הֵן, מְהוּהָה שֶׁטְּלָיָהּ עַל הַבְּרִיָּה, הוֹלְכִין אַחַר הַבְּרִיָּה, קְטַנָּה עַל הַגְּדוֹלָה, הוֹלְכִין אַחַר הַגְּדוֹלָה, הָיוּ שָׁווֹת, הוֹלְכִין אַחַר הַפְּנִימִית. רַבִּי שִׁמְעוֹן אוֹמֵר, כַּף מֹאזְנַיִם שֶׁטְּלָיָהּ עַל שׁוּלֵי הַמֵּיחַם, מִבִּפְנִים טָמֵא, מִבַּחוּץ טָהוֹר. טְלָיָהּ עַל צִדָּהּ, בֵּין מִבִּפְנִים בֵּין מִבַּחוּץ, טָהוֹר:

1. There are three kinds of shields [which differ with respect to the laws of cleanness and uncleanness]: The bent shield [which surrounds the warrior on three sides, and which during a war is used by him to lie upon] is subject to midras uncleanness; a shield used by swordsmen in their sword-play is subject to uncleanness by a corpse; and the small shield used by the Arabs [in festivities and in sports, is not subject to any uncleanness, but] remains altogether clean. 2. There are three kinds of wagons [which differ with respect to the laws of cleanness and uncleanness]: One that is shaped like a chair with three sides is subject to midras uncleanness; one shaped like a bed is subject to uncleanness by a corpse; and one [made for carrying] stones remains altogether clean. 3. There are three kinds of kneading-troughs [which differ with respect to the laws of cleanness and uncleanness]: A kneading-trough with a capacity of two log to nine kab which was cracked [hence unusable as a kneading-trough] is subject to midras uncleanness; if it was whole it is subject to uncleanness by a corpse; and one that holds a large quantity [forty se'ah liquid or sixty

se'ah dry measure] remains altogether clean. 4. There are three kinds of boxes [which differ with respect to the laws of cleanness and uncleanness]: A box whose opening is at its side is subject to midras uncleanness; one that has its opening at the top is subject to uncleanness by a corpse; and one that holds a large quantity remains altogether clean. 5. There are three kinds of leather chests [which differ with respect to the laws of cleanness and uncleanness]: That of barbers is subject to midras uncleanness; that at which people eat is subject to uncleanness by a corpse; and that for [pressing] olives remains altogether clean. 6. There are three kinds of stands [which differ with respect to the laws of cleanness and uncleanness]: That which lies before a bed or before scribes is subject to midras uncleanness; that of a service table is subject to uncleanness by a corpse; and that of a cupboard remains altogether clean. 7. There are three kinds of writing tablets [which differ with respect to the laws of cleanness and uncleanness]: One that is spread over with sand is subject to midras uncleanness; one that has a receptacle for wax is subject to uncleanness by a corpse; and one that is smooth remains altogether clean. 8. There are three kinds of beds [which differ with respect to the laws of cleanness and uncleanness]: That which is used for lying upon is subject to midras uncleanness; that which is used by glass-makers [to put their wares on] is subject to uncleanness by a corpse; and that which is used by net weavers remains altogether clean. 9. There are three kinds of baskets [which differ with respect to the laws of cleanness and uncleanness]: That which is used for manure [to be carried to the field] is subject to midras uncleanness; that which is used for straw is subject to uncleanness by a corpse; and that of rope mesh used on camels remains altogether clean. 10. There are three kinds of mats [which differ with respect to the laws of cleanness and uncleanness]: That which is used for sitting is subject to midras uncleanness; that which is used by dyers [to spread garments on them] is subject to uncleanness by a corpse; and that which is used in wine-presses [to cover the grapes] remains altogether clean. 11. There are three kinds of skin flasks and three kinds of shepherds' skin bags [which differ with respect to the laws of cleanness and uncleanness]: Those holding the standard quantity [seven kab for the flask and five for the bag] are subject to midras uncleanness; those holding less than the standard quantity are subject to uncleanness by a corpse; and those made of fish-skin remain altogether clean. 12. There are three kinds of hides [which differ with respect to the laws of cleanness and uncleanness]: That which is used as a rug [to sit on] is subject to midras uncleanness; that which is used as a wrapper for utensils is subject to uncleanness by a corpse; and that which is prepared for making straps and sandals remains altogether clean. 13. There are three kinds of sheets [which differ with respect to the laws of cleanness and uncleanness]: That which is made for lying upon is subject to midras uncleanness; that which is used as a door-curtain is subject to uncleanness by a corpse; and that which has designs [used as a pattern] remains altogether clean. 14. There are three kinds of cloths [which differ with respect to the laws of cleanness and uncleanness]: Towels for the hands are subject to midras uncleanness; coverings for books are subject to uncleanness by a corpse; and shrouds and covers for the musical instruments of the Levi'im remain altogether clean. 15. There are three kinds of leather gloves [which differ with respect to the laws of cleanness and uncleanness]: Those used by hunters of animals and birds are subject to midras uncleanness; those used by catchers of locusts are subject to uncleanness by a corpse; and those used by driers of summer fruit remain altogether clean. 16. There are three kinds of hair-nets [which differ with respect to the laws of cleanness and uncleanness]: That of a girl is subject to midras uncleanness; that of an old woman is subject to uncleanness by a corpse; and that of a woman when she goes outside remains altogether clean. 17. There are three kinds of receptacles [which differ with respect to the laws of cleanness and uncleanness]: If a worn-out receptacle was placed over a sound one as a patch [to make it stronger, the cleanness or uncleanness of the combined receptacle] is determined by the sound one; if a small receptacle was placed over a large one [and both are either sound or worn out, the cleanness or uncleanness of the combined receptacle] is determined by the large one; if both were equal [in size and both are either sound or worn out, the cleanness or uncleanness] is determined by the inner one. Rabbi Shimon said: If an [unclean] pan of a balance was patched on to the bottom of a [clean] boiler on the inside, it becomes unclean, but if on the outside, it is clean; if it was patched on to its side, whether on the inside or on the outside, it is clean.

Mishnayot "Mikvaot" - Chapter 7

Our sages taught that by reciting this chapter of the Mishna, one brings a great spiritual elevation to the soul of the departed. It is further explained that the first letters of the first three paragraphs form the word אי״ה, which in Hebrew is an acronym for "by God's Will." The remaining paragraphs form the word נשמה (Neshama), which means "soul." One should bear this in mind while studying this chapter.

(א) יֵשׁ מַעֲלִין אֶת הַמִּקְוֶה וְלֹא פוֹסְלִין, פּוֹסְלִין וְלֹא מַעֲלִין, לֹא מַעֲלִין וְלֹא פוֹסְלִין, אֵלּוּ מַעֲלִין וְלֹא פוֹסְלִין, הַשֶּׁלֶג, וְהַבָּרָד, וְהַכְּפוֹר, וְהַגְּלִיד, וְהַמֶּלַח, וְהַטִּיט הַנָּרוֹק. אָמַר רַבִּי עֲקִיבָא, הָיָה רַבִּי יִשְׁמָעֵאל דָּן כְּנֶגְדִּי לוֹמַר, הַשֶּׁלֶג אֵינוֹ מַעֲלֶה אֶת הַמִּקְוֶה, וְהֵעִידוּ אַנְשֵׁי מֵידְבָא מִשְּׁמוֹ, שֶׁאָמַר לָהֶם צְאוּ וְהָבִיאוּ שֶׁלֶג וַעֲשׂוּ מִקְוֶה בַּתְּחִלָּה. רַבִּי יוֹחָנָן בֶּן נוּרִי אוֹמֵר, אֶבֶן הַבָּרָד כַּמָּיִם. כֵּיצַד מַעֲלִין וְלֹא פוֹסְלִין, מִקְוֶה שֶׁיֶּשׁ בּוֹ אַרְבָּעִים סְאָה חָסֵר אַחַת, נָפַל מֵהֶם סְאָה לְתוֹכוֹ וְהֶעֱלָהוּ, נִמְצְאוּ מַעֲלִין וְלֹא פוֹסְלִין: (ב) אֵלּוּ פוֹסְלִין וְלֹא מַעֲלִין, הַמַּיִם בֵּין טְמֵאִים בֵּין טְהוֹרִים, וּמֵי כְבָשִׁים וּמֵי שְׁלָקוֹת, וְהַתֶּמֶד עַד שֶׁלֹּא הֶחֱמִיץ. כֵּיצַד פוֹסְלִין וְלֹא מַעֲלִין, מִקְוֶה שֶׁיֶּשׁ בּוֹ אַרְבָּעִים סְאָה חָסֵר קַרְטוֹב וְנָפַל מֵהֶן קַרְטוֹב לְתוֹכוֹ, לֹא הֶעֱלָהוּ, וּפוֹסְלוֹ בִּשְׁלֹשָׁה לֻגִּין. אֲבָל שְׁאָר הַמַּשְׁקִין, וּמֵי פֵרוֹת, וְהַצִּיר, וְהַמֻּרְיָס, וְהַתֶּמֶד מִשֶּׁהֶחֱמִיץ, פְּעָמִים מַעֲלִין וּפְעָמִים שֶׁאֵינָן מַעֲלִין, כֵּיצַד, מִקְוֶה שֶׁיֶּשׁ בּוֹ אַרְבָּעִים סְאָה חָסֵר אַחַת, נָפַל לְתוֹכוֹ סְאָה מֵהֶם, לֹא הֶעֱלָהוּ, הָיוּ בוֹ אַרְבָּעִים סְאָה, נָתַן סְאָה וְנָטַל סְאָה, הֲרֵי זֶה כָשֵׁר: (ג) הֵדִיחַ בּוֹ סַלֵּי זֵיתִים וְסַלֵּי עֲנָבִים, וְשִׁנּוּ אֶת מַרְאָיו, כָּשֵׁר. רַבִּי יוֹסֵי אוֹמֵר, מֵי הַצֶּבַע פּוֹסְלִין אוֹתוֹ בִּשְׁלֹשָׁה לֻגִּין, וְאֵינָן פּוֹסְלִין אוֹתוֹ בְּשִׁנּוּי מַרְאֶה. נָפַל לְתוֹכוֹ יַיִן וּמֹחַל, וְשִׁנּוּ אֶת מַרְאָיו, פָּסוּל, כֵּיצַד יַעֲשֶׂה, יַמְתִּין לוֹ עַד שֶׁיֵּרְדוּ גְשָׁמִים וְיַחְזְרוּ מַרְאֵיהֶן לְמַרְאֵה הַמָּיִם, הָיוּ בוֹ אַרְבָּעִים סְאָה, מִמַּלֵּא בַכָּתֵף, וְנוֹתֵן לְתוֹכוֹ עַד שֶׁיַּחְזְרוּ מַרְאֵיהֶן לְמַרְאֵה הַמָּיִם: (ד) נָפַל לְתוֹכוֹ יַיִן, אוֹ מֹחַל וְשִׁנּוּ מִקְצָת מַרְאָיו, אִם אֵין בּוֹ מַרְאֵה מַיִם אַרְבָּעִים סְאָה, הֲרֵי זֶה לֹא יִטְבּוֹל בּוֹ: (ה) שְׁלֹשָׁה לֻגִּין מַיִם, וְנָפַל לְתוֹכָן קֻרְטוֹב יַיִן, וַהֲרֵי מַרְאֵיהֶן כְּמַרְאֵה הַיַּיִן, וְנָפְלוּ לַמִּקְוֶה, לֹא פְסָלוּהוּ, שְׁלֹשָׁה לֻגִּין מַיִם חָסֵר קֻרְטוֹב, וְנָפַל לְתוֹכָן קֻרְטוֹב חָלָב, וַהֲרֵי מַרְאֵיהֶן כְּמַרְאֵה הַמַּיִם, וְנָפְלוּ לַמִּקְוֶה, לֹא פְסָלוּהוּ. רַבִּי יוֹחָנָן בֶּן נוּרִי אוֹמֵר, (ו) מִקְוֶה שֶׁיֶּשׁ בּוֹ אַרְבָּעִים סְאָה מְכֻוָּנוֹת, יָרְדוּ שְׁנַיִם וְטָבְלוּ זֶה אַחַר זֶה, הָרִאשׁוֹן טָהוֹר, וְהַשֵּׁנִי טָמֵא. רַבִּי יְהוּדָה אוֹמֵר, אִם הָיוּ רַגְלָיו שֶׁל רִאשׁוֹן נוֹגְעוֹת בַּמַּיִם, אַף הַשֵּׁנִי טָהוֹר. הִטְבִּיל בּוֹ אֶת הַסָּגוֹס וְהֶעֱלָהוּ, מִקְצָתוֹ נוֹגֵעַ בַּמַּיִם, טָהוֹר. הַכַּר וְהַכֶּסֶת שֶׁל עוֹר, כֵּיוָן שֶׁהִגְבִּיהַּ שִׂפְתוֹתֵיהֶם מִן הַמַּיִם, הַמַּיִם שֶׁבְּתוֹכָן שְׁאוּבִין, כֵּיצַד יַעֲשֶׂה, מַטְבִּילָן, מַטְבִּילָן וּמַעֲלֶה אוֹתָם דֶּרֶךְ שׁוּלֵיהֶן:

The final paragraphs of this chapter are recited aloud, followed by Kaddish D'Rabannan (page 170). During Shiva, the Mishnayot are recited by a non-mourner.

1. There are things [which when added to or fall into a mikvah of less than the prescribed measure of forty se'ah] serve to raise the mikvah [to its prescribed measure] and do not render it unfit [for ritual immersion]; some make it unfit and do not serve to raise it; and some neither raise it nor make it unfit. The following raise it [to the prescribed measure] and do not make it unfit: snow, hail, frost, ice, salt, and soft mud. Rabbi Akiva said: Rabbi Yishmael took issue with me, saying that snow does not serve to raise the mikvah [to its prescribed measure]. But the men of Medeva testified in his name that he told them: Go and bring snow and make with it [even] a completely new mikvah. Rabbi Yochanan ben Nuri said: Hailstones are like [drawn] water [which disqualifies the mikvah.] How do the [aformentioned] serve to raise [the mikvah to its required measure] and not render it unfit? If into a mikvah of forty se'ah less one fell a se'ah of any of these and increased it [to forty] – it is thereby raised [to its prescribed measure] and not rendered unfit. 2. These render a mikvah unfit and do not serve to raise it [to the prescribed measure]: Drawn water, whether [ritually] clean or unclean, water that has been used for pickling or cooking, and wine made from grape-skin, pip or lees before it ferments. How do they render it unfit and do not serve to raise it? If into a mikvah of forty se'ah less one kartov fell a kartov of any of them, it does not serve to raise [the mikvah to forty se'ah]; but it is rendered unfit by three logs of any of them. Other liquids, however, and fruit juices, fish brine, liquid of pickled fish, and wine made from grape-skin, pip or lees that has fermented, at times serve to raise it [to the prescribed measure] and at times do not serve to raise it. How? If into a mikvah of forty se'ah less one fell a se'ah of any of them, it has not raised [the mikvah to its prescribed measure]; but if it contained forty se'ah, and a se'ah of any of them was put in and then one se'ah removed, the mikvah remains kasher. 3. If one rinsed in a mikvah baskets of olives or baskets of grapes and they changed its color, it remains kasher. Rabbi Yosai said: Dye-water renders it unfit by a quantity of three logs, but not merely by the change of color. If wine or olive sap fell into it and changed its color, it makes it unfit. What should one do [to render it kasher again if it contains less than forty se'ah]? He should wait until it rains and its color returns to the color of water. If, however, it already contained forty se'ah, he may fill [buckets of water], carry them on his shoulder and pour it into the mikvah until its color returns to the color of water. 4. If wine or olive sap fell into a mikvah and discolored a part of the water, if it does not contain forty se'ah which has the color of water, one may not immerse himself in it. 5. If a kartov of wine fell into three logs of [drawn] water and its color became like the color of wine, and it then fell into a mikvah [of less than forty se'ah], it does not render the mikvah unfit. If a kartov of milk fell into three logs less a kartov of [drawn] water, and its color remained like the color of water, and then it fell into a mikvah [of less than forty se'ah], it does not render the mikvah unfit. Rabbi Yochanan ben Nuri said: Everything depends upon the color. 6. If two people went down and immersed themselves, one after the other, in a mikvah which contains exactly forty se'ah, the first becomes [ritually] clean but the second remains [ritually] unclean. Rabbi Yehudah said: If the feet of the first were still touching the water [while the second immersed himself], even the second becomes clean. If one immersed a thick mantle in a mikvah [of exactly forty se'ah], and took it out leaving part of it still touching the water, [if another person immersed himself then] he becomes ritually clean. If a leather pillow or cushion [was immersed in a mikvah of exactly forty se'ah], when it is taken out of the water by its open end the water within it becomes drawn water [and if three logs of it flow back into the mikvah they will render it – having now less than forty se'ah – unfit]. How is one to remove them [without making the mikvah unfit]? He should immerse them and take them out by their closed ends.

At the conclusion of prayer services (after "*Al Tirö,*") recite the following verses aloud, followed by *Kaddish D'Rabbanan*. During Shiva, these verses are not recited by the mourner, but by a non-mourner on his behalf.

Hit-bil bo cs ha-mitöh, af al pi	(ז) הִטְבִּיל בּוֹ אֶת הַמִּטָּה, אַף עַל פִּי
she-rag-lehö sho-k'os ba-tit he-öveh,	שֶׁרַגְלֶיהָ שׁוֹקְעוֹת בַּטִּיט הָעֲבֶה,
t'ho-röh, mi-p'nay she-hama-yim	טְהוֹרָה, מִפְּנֵי שֶׁהַמַּיִם
m'kad'min. Mik-veh she-may-möv	מְקַדְּמִין: מִקְוֶה שֶׁמֵּימָיו
m'ru-dödin, ko-vaysh afilu chavi-lay	מְרֻדָּדִין, כּוֹבֵשׁ אֲפִלּוּ חֲבִילֵי
ay-tzim, afilu chavi-lay kö-nim, k'day	עֵצִים, אֲפִלּוּ חֲבִילֵי קָנִים, כְּדֵי
she-yis-p'chu hama-yim, v'yo-rayd	שֶׁיִּתְפְּחוּ הַמַּיִם, וְיוֹרֵד
v'to-vayl. Ma-chat she-hi n'sunöh al	וְטוֹבֵל: מַחַט שֶׁהִיא נְתוּנָה עַל
ma-alos ham'öröh, hö-yöh mo-lich	מַעֲלוֹת הַמְּעָרָה, הָיָה מוֹלִיךְ

237

ma-alos ham'öröh, hö-yöh mo-lich	מַעֲלוֹת הַמְּעָרָה, הָיָה מוֹלִיךְ
umay-vi bama-yim, kay-vön she-övar	וּמֵבִיא בַּמַּיִם, כֵּיוָן שֶׁעָבַר
öle-hö ha-gal, t'horöh	עָלֶיהָ הַגַּל, טְהוֹרָה:

7. *If one immersed a bed [that is too tall to be immersed all at one time in a mikvah of forty se'ah], even if its legs sank into the thick mud, it nevertheless becomes ritually clean because the water touched them before [they sank into the mud]. A mikvah whose water is too shallow [for proper immersion], one may press down even bundles of sticks, even bundles of reeds, so that the level of the water is raised and then he may go down and immerse himself. A needle which is placed on the step [leading down to a mikvah] in a cave, and the water is moved back and forth, as soon as a wave has passed over it, it becomes ritually clean.*

Rabi cha-nan-yö ben akash-yö omayr:	רַבִּי חֲנַנְיָא בֶּן עֲקַשְׁיָא אוֹמֵר:
rötzö haködosh böruch hu l'zakos	רָצָה הַקָּדוֹשׁ בָּרוּךְ הוּא לְזַכּוֹת
es yisrö-ayl, l'fi-chöch hir-böh lö-hem	אֶת יִשְׂרָאֵל, לְפִיכָךְ הִרְבָּה לָהֶם
toröh umitz-vos, shene-emar: Adonöy	תּוֹרָה וּמִצְוֹת, שֶׁנֶּאֱמַר: יְיָ
chö-faytz l'ma-an tzid-ko, yag-dil	חָפֵץ לְמַעַן צִדְקוֹ, יַגְדִּיל
toröh v'ya-dir.	תּוֹרָה וְיַאְדִּיר:

Rabbi Chananyah ben Akashya said: The Holy One, blessed be He, wished to make the people of Israel meritorious; therefore He gave them Torah and mitzvot in abundant measure, as it is written: The Lord desired, for the sake of his [Israel's] righteousness, to make the Torah great and glorious.

Some have the custom to pass the left hand over the forehead and say:

V'nefesh ha-shay-nis b'yisrö-ayl hi	וְנֶפֶשׁ הַשֵּׁנִית בְּיִשְׂרָאֵל הִיא
chay-lek elo-ka mima-al ma-mösh.	חֵלֶק אֱלוֹהַּ מִמַּעַל מַמָּשׁ:

The second, uniquely Jewish, soul is truly "a part of God above."

Recite Kaddish D'Rabanan (page 170)

238

The Last Day of Shiva

The seventh and final day of Shiva is calculated from the date of burial. If, for example, the burial was on Tuesday, Shiva concludes the following Monday, right after the morning services.

We are reminded that "the living should take to heart," i.e., that ultimately everyone passes before God, and it is an appropriate time to commit ourselves to improving our observance of His Torah, and the performance of His Mitzvot. This ensures a positive and enduring outcome out of what may otherwise remain only a sad and negative experience.

Formally Ending the Shiva

The term "getting up" from Shiva refers to the conclusion of the Shiva observances. This informs the family that it is time to move on to the less intense mourning period of the *Shloshim* (thirty days), and they can slowly emerge into society.

On the last day of Shiva, it is customary to begin the morning services earlier than usual. Following the services, the mourners sit on low stools or crates while members of the Minyan or visitors console them (as on page 159). After the consolation, the members of the Minyan or visitors leave the room, allowing the mourners to sit by themselves.

After a brief moment, the members of the Minyan or visitors return to the room where the mourners are sitting and console the mourners again, as follows:

Ha-mökom y'na-chaym es-chem הַמָּקוֹם יְנַחֵם אֶתְכֶם
b'soch sh'ör a-vaylay בְּתוֹךְ שְׁאָר אֲבֵלֵי
tzi-yon viy'rushö-lö-yim. צִיּוֹן וִירוּשָׁלָיִם:

Ha-mökom Yig-dor Pir-tzos הַמָּקוֹם יִגְדּוֹר פְּרָצוֹת
Amo Yisrö-el. עַמּוֹ יִשְׂרָאֵל:

May the Almighty comfort you among the mourners of Zion and Jerusalem. May the Almighty heal the breaches of His people Israel.

They then verbally "reproach" the mourners, telling them to get up (i.e. "Stand up from your mourning"), and bless them with "long and healthy years."

After the Mourners "Get Up"

Once the mourners get up, many of the restrictions of Shiva cease and the mourners enter the period between Shiva and *Shloshim* (the thirtieth day). The mourners change into their regular clothing, and may discard the garments upon which

Kriah (traditional rending of the garment) was made. If the Kriah garment was highly valuable and one does not wish to discard it, one should ask a competent rabbi if one may repair it. If the mourner was overly sweaty or dirty, he may take a basic shower.

Various Customs

• Some offer a *L'Chayim* (some kosher schnapps or whiskey and cake) after the morning service, in memory of the deceased.

• It is customary for the mourners to walk around the block of the Shiva home, starting from the right side. One reason given is that with this walk, they accompany the soul on its path. Another is that it symbolizes the family's return to society following their intense mourning period.

• Some have the custom to visit a non-Jewish store, for the Satan cannot rule over two nations at once, and will thus be compelled to depart.

• Some have the custom to place a stone on the place where the mourners sat, for a few hours. Others hammer a nail using a stone into the floor where they sat. The reasons for these two customs are not very clear.

Erecting the Tombstone
and Visiting the Cemetery

Many erect the tombstone on the day following Shiva (the 8th day). Others wait until thirty days, and still others wait until twelve months (see following chapter).

Some visit the gravesite of the departed on this day, in order to recite prayers and Psalms. Some specifically do not visit the gravesite for the entire twelve months. One should follow the custom of his community, or ask a competent rabbi for guidance.

Setting the Tombstone

We are taught that the soul is brought into *Gan Eden* (the Garden of Eden) when the tombstone is erected. For that reason, many erect the tombstone on the day following Shiva (the 8th day). Others wait until thirty days, and still others wait until twelve months. One should follow the custom of his community, or ask a competent rabbi for guidance.

In many communities, the stone is set privately by the *Chevra Kaddisha* (Jewish Burial Society). In other communities, family members gather at the gravesite for the stone setting to recite prayers and Psalms. (Important details concerning the tombstone and its inscription can be found on page 95).

Some Customs

• One who has not been to a Jewish cemetery for thirty days recites a special blessing upon arrival (page 110).

• There is no set service for setting a headstone. Some people recite Psalms, including Psalm 91 (page 103), and some add Psalms 33, 16, 17, 72, 104, and 130.

• Some also recite verses from Psalm 119 (page 42) that begin with the letters of the Hebrew name of the deceased, and the word נשמה (Heb. soul).

• Some recall the deceased's good qualities and traits, and encourage the visitors to honor the memory of the departed by increasing their commitment to repentance and good deeds.

• Some light a candle at the grave once the tombstone is erected.

• Some have the custom to place a pebble or stone on the tombstone, showing that the grave has been visited.

Between Shiva and Shloshim

Even though the *Shiva* (first seven days of mourning) has ended, one is considered a mourner for twelve months for a parent, and until the *Shloshim* (the thirtieth day from burial) for other relatives. During these twenty-three days, the intensity of mourning is reduced. However, some restrictions continue to remain in effect. One should consult a competent rabbi for complete guidance in all of these matters.

Notable restrictions that are lifted:

- Mourners are no longer confined to the Shiva home.

- One may change out of the clothing worn during Shiva.

- One may greet others with customary greetings ("Hello," "How are you," etc.), but others should not greet him in this manner. If they do, he may respond in kind.

- One may sit on regular chairs.

- One may wear leather shoes.

- One may return to work and engage in business.

- One may use cosmetics, lotions, oils, perfumes, makeup, and wear jewelry.

- One may study Torah.

- One may resume marital relations.

- One may attend a *Brit Milah* (circumcision of a child), *Pidyon Haben* (redemption of the firstborn son), Bar Mitzva, *T'noim* (engagement), and a *Siyum* (celebration upon completion of a tractate of Mishna or Talmud), but one should not remain for the meal.

Restrictions that carry over:

- One may not wear new, freshly laundered, or ironed clothing. In the case of great need, one may have the clothing worn by someone else for a few moments and then they are permitted to him. This does not apply to shirts, underwear, and socks or stockings, which may be changed as required.

- One may still not take a luxurious bath or shower during this period.

- If one became dirty or sweaty, he may shower in the usual manner; however, he should do it as quickly as possible.

- One may not take a haircut, shave, or cut one's nails. (A woman preparing for the Mikvah may do all her usual preparations.)

- One may not listen to music or attend a concert, nor go on pleasure trips and tours. This also includes attending social events such as dinners, parties, and so on. One who is mourning his parents may not do so for the entire year.

- One may go into a wedding hall to wish a close relative or friend "Mazal Tov," before the meal is served and while no music is being played. Consult a competent rabbi for guidance.

- One should avoid activities that are not in the spirit of mourning. For example, one may not buy a new home, nor redecorate, renovate, or purchase new furniture, and so on, unless one will suffer great financial loss if it is delayed past the Shloshim.

- One may not marry during the Shloshim. Nowadays, when preparations for the wedding begin months in advance, and postponing the wedding will result in great financial loss, some permit it during the Shloshim, but not during Shiva. Consult a competent rabbi for complete guidance.

- If one's profession is such that he must attend festive events for his income (musician, photographer, caterer, etc.), he may attend them. Some relatives and friends rely on this leniency after Shiva and act as a "waiter" by serving a few dishes so that they may attend a wedding of a relative or close friend.

This should only be done when one's lack of attendance will cause the celebrants great pain. In general, consult a competent rabbi for guidance.

Shloshim - The Thirtieth Day

The *Shloshim* is the thirtieth day from burial. When mourning all relatives except one's parents, the mourning period concludes following the morning service on this day. When mourning parents, the mourning continues for a full twelve months, until the first Yartzeit.

Traditionally, families gather on the eve of the Shloshim to share support, recite prayers and Psalms, and to give charity in the merit of the deceased. Many will also make a *Siyum*, celebrating the completion of the *Mishnayot* studied to merit the soul of the deceased, as well as a meal.

When Shloshim is Not Thirty Days

Sometimes Shloshim can be less than thirty days. This happens when a Jewish holiday occurs during Shiva and thus annuls the remaining days of Shiva mourning. One then calculates the Shloshim day as follows:

Passover and Shavuot: Fifteen days after the holiday ends.

Sukkot: Eight days after the holiday ends.

Rosh Hashana: Between Rosh Hashana and Yom Kippur one

observes those days as one does between Shiva and Shloshim, then Yom Kippur annuls the remaining part of Shloshim.

Yom Kippur: Between Yom Kippur and Sukkot one observes those days as one does between Shiva and Shloshim, then Sukkot annuls the remaining part of Shloshim.

Also, if a Jewish holiday occurs between Shiva and Shloshim, it annuls the remaining days of Shloshim, and one conducts himself as if Shloshim is complete.

Between Shloshim and Yartzeit

The last stage of mourning covers the period between the *Shloshim* (thirty days after burial) and the *Yartzeit* (anniversary of the passing.). These dates are calculated following the Jewish calendar.

When mourning a parent, all mourning restrictions continue as during the Shloshim, except for some exceptions as noted below. When mourning all other relatives, the mourning period concludes with the Shloshim.

Between the end of Shloshim and the Yartzeit:

• One may bathe and shower for pleasure.

• One may take a haircut after his friends reprimand him and tell him to cut his hair (approximately three months from his last haircut).

• One may attend a *Brit Milah* (circumcision of a child), *Pidyon Haben* (redemption of the firstborn son), Bar Mitzva, *T'noim* (engagement), and a *Siyum* (celebration upon completion of a tractate of Mishna or Talmud), but one should not remain for the meal. Consult a competent rabbi for complete guidance.

• One may attend the wedding of a relative, but should not sit at the head table, nor remain in the room when music is playing or when people are dancing. Consult a competent rabbi for complete guidance.

Additional Observances

• Males mourning a parent are obligated to recite the Mourner's Kaddish during the daily prayer services for eleven months, less one day (a month and a day before the Yartzeit).

• One should incorporate a new mitzva or commit to better his observance of a mitzva, in honor of the soul of the deceased.

• One should also inspire his children to do the same. The merit of this is so great that it is even considered more beneficial to the departed soul than reciting mourner's Kaddish. When performing any deed in honor of the departed, some have the custom to say "I am doing this in merit of the soul of [his/her Hebrew name, and that of the father]."

• Some have the custom to donate Jewish books to the local synagogue or Jewish school and to inscribe in them the Hebrew name of the deceased and that of his or her father. This is so that all who learn from the books will bring merit to the soul of the loved one.

• One should give extra charity during the year of mourning. It is also customary to place several coins in a charity box before and after prayers each day.

• Some make sure to have a candle lit in the synagogue or home every day for the first year, to honor the soul of the deceased.

• At the conclusion of the eleventh month, some offer a *L'Chayim* in the synagogue (some kosher schnapps or whiskey and cake) for we are taught that the soul's judgment is concluded on that day.

• Some have the custom when writing the name of the deceased in a letter, to add הריני כפרת משכבו, or הכ״מ (I accept to be an atonement for his passing).

The Yartzeit - Anniversary

The anniversary of the date of passing is very significant in Judaism. Kabbalah teaches that all the spiritual achievements of one's life, including every positive thought, word, or deed, radiate and are revealed in the world and in the Heavens on that day.

On the *Yartzeit* (Yid. anniversary), the soul is at its greatest strength and in its fullest glory. With each ensuing year, this radiance again shines forth in the world and in the Heavens, as the soul is elevated to a higher spiritual level and drawn even closer to God.

While the spiritual radiance from above can influence those below, children of the deceased (as well as students, friends, relatives, even strangers) can similarly benefit those above. On this day, every mitzva performed and every effort to improve one's spiritual life brings great merit to the deceased. This is especially true for one's father and mother.

A Deeper Perspective

A Yartzeit is generally associated with two mixed feelings. On one hand, we learn from our sages that the soul of the departed rises from one spiritual world to a higher one. This is, therefore, a day of rejoicing for the soul, hence a day of corresponding joy for the near and dear ones left behind. On the other hand, the Yartzeit naturally emphasizes the loss sustained by the family, which results in a feeling of sadness. In truth, however, the Yartzeit should not call forth feelings of sadness, but rather a feeling of reflection, self-examination, and repentance.

During this day, one should work to align one's life on this earth to the path followed by the soul above, which is constantly on the ascent. This is to say, just as the soul continuously rises year after year, going from strength to strength, so must those associated with the soul steadily rise in their advancement in Torah knowledge and observance of mitzvot. By doing so, they give the soul of the departed the greatest possible joy.

This approach underlines the basic view of Judaism that, in reality, there is no "death" in matters of Godliness. Rather, the Yartzeit, and even the very day of passing, represents a transition. But this transition is unique for it goes in only one direction — higher and higher, from strength to strength — first in this world, and later in the following world.

Calculating the Date of the Yartzeit

The date of the Yartzeit follows the Jewish calendar, and is generally calculated from the time of passing, not the time of burial. For example, if the person passed away on the twenty-fourth day of Av, the Yartzeit is observed each year on the twenty-fourth day of Av. Some calculate the date of the second (and every future) Yartzeit from the date of burial. One should follow the custom of his community, or ask a competent rabbi for guidance.

If the time of passing was during the twilight (either between sunset and dusk, or between dawn and sunrise), one should consult a competent rabbi, since Jewish law determines dates from sunset to sunrise (i.e. Monday night is considered to begin Tuesday's date).

According to the Jewish calendar, the months of Cheshvan and Kislev sometimes have twenty-nine days and sometimes thirty days. If the passing occurred on the thirtieth day of either of these months, consult a competent rabbi to ascertain the correct date to observe the Yartzeit.

The same applies in leap years. According to the Jewish calendar, leap years have two months of Adar. If the passing occurred during Adar in a regular year, or if the passing

257

occurred on the first day of Rosh Chodesh or during "Adar II," consult a competent rabbi to ascertain the correct date to observe the Yartzeit.

If one does not know the date of passing (and cannot find out), he should consult a competent rabbi and designate a day on the Jewish calendar to be observed every year as the Yartzeit.

Some Customs

• It is customary for men to arrange to be called up to bless the Torah during the Shabbat services of the week prior to the Yartzeit, and to recite the Half-Kaddish after the Torah reading. Some arrange to read the *Maftir* (special portion recited after the Torah reading) as well.

• If the Yartzeit is on a Monday or Thursday, men should arrange to be called up to bless the Torah during the services, and to recite the Half-Kaddish after the Torah reading.

• On the eve of the Yartzeit, each mourner kindles a candle that should remain lit for the entire twenty-four hour period.

• Some take upon themselves to fast on the day of the Yartzeit (beginning at dawn) in order to be aroused to repentance and self-examination. If one is fasting, he adds the

"*Anaeinu*" portion in the *Amidah* (silent prayer) when praying on the day of the Yartzeit. One may not fast on days when *Tachnun* is not recited, as well as on the day of one's son's *Brit Milah* (circumcision of a child) or *Pidyon Haben* (redemption of the firstborn son). Also, a bride and groom may not fast during the week following his wedding.

• If possible, a man observing a Yartzeit should lead all the prayer services of the Yartzeit day (*Maariv*, *Shacharit*, and *Mincha*). If one does not lead the services, one should at least pray with a *Minyan* (quorum of ten Jewish males over age thirteen) and recite the Mourner's Kaddish at the designated times during the service.

• One kindles five candles on the prayer leader's stand in the synagogue when leading the prayer services.

• Some put out cake, schnapps or whiskey after the morning service. Those present say *L'Chayim*, and state a wish that "the soul should be elevated in the heavenly spheres."

• Many study *Mishnayot* (Mishna laws) in honor of the soul, especially the chapters that begin with the letters of the Hebrew name of the departed. They also study the chapters that begin with the letters of the word *Neshama* (soul).

• Some visit the gravesite on this day (see page 267) to recite prayers and Psalms. Some people recite Psalms, including Psalm 91 (page 103), and some add Psalms 33, 16, 17, 72, 104, and 130. Some also recite verses from Psalm 119 (page 42) that begin with the letters of the Hebrew name of the deceased, and the word נשמה (Heb. soul). Some recite additional prayers and supplications (see page 273 and 275, for selections).

Yizkor - The Memorial Prayer

Yizkor, a special memorial prayer for the departed, is recited in the synagogue four times a year, following the Torah reading on the last day of Passover, on the second day of Shavuot, on Shemini Atzeret and on Yom Kippur.

Yizkor, in Hebrew, means "Remember." It is not only the first word of the prayer, it also represents its overall theme. In this prayer, we implore God to remember the souls of our relatives and friends that have passed on.

When we recite Yizkor, we renew and strengthen the connection between us and our loved one, bringing merit to the departed souls, elevating them in their celestial homes.

The main component of Yizkor is our private pledge to give charity following the holiday in honor of the deceased. By giving charity, we are performing a positive physical deed in this world, something that the departed can no longer do.

The soul gains additional merit if the memory of its good deeds spur their loved ones to improve their ways.

It is customary for those with both parents alive to leave the synagogue during the Yizkor service. A mourner during the first year remains in the synagogue, but does not recite the Yizkor. Some kindle a 24-hour Yizkor candle (before the holiday).

The Yizkor Prayer

In addition to reciting Yizkor for one's parents, one may recite Yizkor for any Jew who has passed on, including relatives and friends. When reciting Yizkor for more than one person, repeat the Yizkor paragraph each time, and substitute the words "*Aböh Mori*" (my father), or "*Imi Morösi*" (my mother), with the appropriate title, as follows: For a Husband: "*Ba-ali.*" Son: "*B'ni.*" Brother: "*Öchi.*" Uncle: "*Dodi.*" Grandfather: "*Z'kainy*". Wife: "*Ishti.*" Daughter: "*Biti.*" Sister: "*Achosi.*" Aunt: "*Dodosi.*" Grandmother: "*Z'ken-ti.*"

For a father (and all males) say:

Yizkor elo-him nish'mas aböh mori	יִזְכּוֹר אֱלֹהִים נִשְׁמַת אַבָּא מוֹרִי
(mention his Hebrew name and that of his	(פלוני בן פלונית)
mother) she-hölach l'olömo, ba-avur	שֶׁהָלַךְ לְעוֹלָמוֹ, בַּעֲבוּר
sheb'li neder e-tayn tz'dököh ba-ado,	שֶׁבְּלִי נֶדֶר אֶתֵּן צְדָקָה בַּעֲדוֹ,
bis'char zeh t'hay naf-sho tz'ruröh	בִּשְׂכַר זֶה תְּהֵא נַפְשׁוֹ צְרוּרָה
bitz'ror hacha-yim, im nishmas	בִּצְרוֹר הַחַיִּים, עִם נִשְׁמַת
avrö-höm yitz-chök v'ya-akov, söröh	אַבְרָהָם יִצְחָק וְיַעֲקֹב, שָׂרָה רִבְקָה
riv-köh rö-chayl v'lay-öh, v'im sh'ör	רָחֵל וְלֵאָה, וְעִם שְׁאָר

tza-dikim v'tzid-köni-yos she-b'gan
ayden, v'nomar: Ömayn.

צַדִּיקִים וְצִדְקָנִיּוֹת שֶׁבְּגַן עֵדֶן,
וְנֹאמַר: אָמֵן:

May God remember the soul of my father, my teacher (mention his Hebrew name and that of his mother) who has gone to his [supernal] world, because I will — without obligating myself with a vow — donate charity for his sake. In this merit, may his soul be bound up in the bond of life with the souls of Abraham, Isaac and Jacob, Sarah, Rebecca, Rachel and Leah, and with the other righteous men and women who are in Gan Eden; and let us say, Amen.

For a mother (and all females) say:

Yizkor elo-him nish'mas imi mo-rösi
(mention her Hebrew name and that of her
mother) she-höl'chöh l'olö-möh,
ba-avur sheb'li neder etayn tz'dököh
ba-adöh, bis'char zeh t'hay naf-shöh
tz'ruröh bitz'ror ha-cha-yim, im
nishmas avröhöm yitz-chök
v'ya-akov, söröh riv-köh rö-chayl
v'lay-öh, v'im sh'ör tza-dikim
v'tzid-köni-yos she-b'gan ayden,
v'nomar: Ömayn.

יִזְכּוֹר אֱלֹהִים נִשְׁמַת אִמִּי מוֹרָתִי
(פְּלוֹנִית בַּת פְּלוֹנִית)
שֶׁהָלְכָה לְעוֹלָמָהּ,
בַּעֲבוּר שֶׁבְּלִי נֶדֶר אֶתֵּן צְדָקָה
בַּעֲדָהּ, בִּשְׂכַר זֶה תְּהֵא נַפְשָׁהּ
צְרוּרָה בִּצְרוֹר הַחַיִּים, עִם
נִשְׁמַת אַבְרָהָם יִצְחָק
וְיַעֲקֹב, שָׂרָה רִבְקָה רָחֵל
וְלֵאָה, וְעִם שְׁאָר צַדִּיקִים
וְצִדְקָנִיּוֹת שֶׁבְּגַן עֵדֶן,
וְנֹאמַר: אָמֵן:

May God remember the soul of my mother, my teacher (mention her Hebrew name and that of her mother) who has gone to her [supernal] world, because I will — without obligating myself with a vow — donate charity for her sake. In this merit, may her soul be bound up in the bond of life with the souls of Abraham, Isaac and Jacob, Sarah, Rebecca, Rachel and Leah, and with the other righteous men and women who are in Gan Eden; and let us say, Amen.

Continue here:

Öv höracha-mim sho-chayn
m'romim, b'ra-chamöv hö-atzumim,
hu yif-kod b'ra-chamim,
ha-chasidim v'ha-y'shörim
v'ha-t'mi-mim, k'hilos ha-kodesh
she-mös'ru naf-shöm al k'dushas
ha-shaym, ha-ne-ehövim v'han'imim
b'cha-yay-hem, uv'mosöm lo nif-rödu.
min'shörim kalu, umay-arö-yos
gö-vayru, la-asos r'tzon konöm
v'chay-fetz tzuröm. Yizk'raym
elo-haynu l'tovöh, im sh'ör tzadikay
olöm, v'yin-kom nik'mas dam avödöv
ha-shöfuch. Ka-kösuv b'soras mosheh
ish hö-elohim: Har-ninu go-yim amo,
ki dam avödöv yikom, v'nököm yöshiv
l'tzöröv, v'chiper ad'möso amo. V'al
y'day avödechö han'vi-im kösuv
lay-mor: V'nikaysi dömöm lo nikaysi,
va-donöy sho-chayn b'tziyon.
Uv'chis'vay hakodesh ne-emar: Lömöh
yom'ru ha-go-yim a-yay elo-hayhem,
yivöda ba-go-yim

אָב הָרַחֲמִים שׁוֹכֵן
מְרוֹמִים, בְּרַחֲמָיו הָעֲצוּמִים,
הוּא יִפְקֹד בְּרַחֲמִים,
הַחֲסִידִים וְהַיְשָׁרִים
וְהַתְּמִימִים, קְהִלוֹת הַקֹּדֶשׁ
שֶׁמָּסְרוּ נַפְשָׁם עַל קְדֻשַּׁת
הַשֵּׁם, הַנֶּאֱהָבִים וְהַנְּעִימִים
בְּחַיֵּיהֶם, וּבְמוֹתָם לֹא נִפְרָדוּ:
מִנְּשָׁרִים קַלּוּ, וּמֵאֲרָיוֹת
גָּבְרוּ, לַעֲשׂוֹת רְצוֹן קוֹנָם
וְחֵפֶץ צוּרָם: יִזְכְּרֵם
אֱלֹהֵינוּ לְטוֹבָה, עִם שְׁאָר צַדִּיקֵי
עוֹלָם, וְיִנְקוֹם נִקְמַת דַּם עֲבָדָיו
הַשָּׁפוּךְ: כַּכָּתוּב בְּתוֹרַת מֹשֶׁה
אִישׁ הָאֱלֹהִים: הַרְנִינוּ גוֹיִם עַמּוֹ,
כִּי דַם עֲבָדָיו יִקּוֹם, וְנָקָם
יָשִׁיב לְצָרָיו, וְכִפֶּר אַדְמָתוֹ
עַמּוֹ: וְעַל יְדֵי עֲבָדֶיךָ הַנְּבִיאִים
כָּתוּב לֵאמֹר: וְנִקֵּיתִי דָמָם לֹא
נִקֵּיתִי, וַיְיָ שֹׁכֵן בְּצִיּוֹן:
וּבְכִתְבֵי הַקֹּדֶשׁ נֶאֱמַר:
לָמָּה יֹאמְרוּ הַגּוֹיִם אַיֵּה
אֱלֹהֵיהֶם, יִוָּדַע בַּגּוֹיִם

l'aynaynu nik'mas dam avödechö ha-shöfuch. V'omayr: Ki doraysh dömim osöm zöchör, lo shö-chach tza-akas anövim. V'omayr: Yödin ba-go-yim mölay g'vi-yos möchatz rosh al eretz rabö. Mi-nachal ba-derech yishteh, al kayn yörim rosh.

לְעֵינֵינוּ נִקְמַת דַּם עֲבָדֶיךָ הַשָּׁפוּךְ: וְאוֹמֵר: כִּי דֹרֵשׁ דָּמִים אוֹתָם זָכָר, לֹא שָׁכַח צַעֲקַת עֲנָוִים: וְאוֹמֵר: יָדִין בַּגּוֹיִם מָלֵא גְוִיּוֹת מָחַץ רֹאשׁ עַל אֶרֶץ רַבָּה: מִנַּחַל בַּדֶּרֶךְ יִשְׁתֶּה, עַל כֵּן יָרִים רֹאשׁ:

May the All-Merciful Father Who dwells in the supernal heights, in His profound compassion, remember with mercy the pious, the upright and the perfect ones, the holy communities who gave their lives for the sanctification of the Divine Name. They were beloved and pleasant in their lives, and [even] in their death were not parted [from Him]; they were swifter than eagles, stronger than lions to carry out the will of their Maker and the desire of their Creator. May our God remember them with favor together with the other righteous of the world, and avenge the spilled blood of His servants, as it is written in the Torah of Moses, the man of God: O nations, sing the praises of His people, for He will avenge the blood of His servants, bring retribution upon His foes, and placate His land – His people. And by Your servants the Prophets it is written as follows: I will cleanse [the nations of their wrongdoings,] but for the [shedding of Jewish] blood I will not cleanse them; the Lord dwells in Zion. And in the Holy Writings it is said: Why should the nations say, "Where is their God?" Let there be known among the nations, before our eyes, the retribution of the spilled blood of Your servants. And it is said: For the Avenger of bloodshed is mindful of them; He does not forget the cry of the downtrodden. Further it is said: He will render judgment upon the nations, and they will be filled with corpses; He will crush heads over a vast area. He will drink from the stream on the way; therefore [Israel] will hold its head high.

Visiting the Gravesite

Visiting the gravesite expresses respect for the departed, shows that their memory has not been forgotten, and reinforces one's connection to them.

It is considered a great merit to pray at the gravesite of a loved one and that of a great Torah sage, for we are taught that a portion of the soul is always present at the gravesite.

Throughout Jewish history, in times of need, trouble or distress, people would go to a Jewish cemetery and pray to God, invoking the merits of the deceased and requesting that they intercede in the Heavens, and carry the prayers to God.

One also visits the gravesite to pray for the elevation of the departed soul.

It is also customary to visit on days when prayer is especially appropriate. This includes the *Shloshim* (thirtieth day from burial), on every *Yartzeit* (anniversary of passing), and on the days leading into Rosh Hashana and Yom Kippur. Some also visit on the day before *Rosh Chodesh* (start of the new Hebrew month), and on the fifteenth day of each month.

Days on which it is customary not to visit a gravesite include Shabbat, Jewish holidays, Rosh Chodesh, and the intermediate days of Sukkot and Passover (*Chol Ha-moed*).

It is customary to limit visits to, and prayers at, a new grave for the first twelve months, except for erecting the tombstone and on the *Shloshim* (thirtieth day from burial). This is because during this period the soul is undergoing its judgment, and one does not desire to add any additional "burdens" to the tribulations of the soul.

• One who has not been to a Jewish cemetery for thirty days recites a special blessing upon arrival (page 110).

• Some people recite Psalms, including Psalm 91 (page 103), and some add Psalms 33, 16, 17, 72, 104, and 130. Some also recite verses from Psalm 119 (page 42) that begin with the letters of the Hebrew name of the deceased, and the word נשמה (Heb. soul).

• Some recite additional prayers and supplications (see page 273 and 275, for selections).

• Some have the custom to place a pebble or stone on the tombstone, showing that the grave has been visited.

Readings and Meditations

A Completed Mission

To what can life be compared? To a bucket that is dropped in a pond. When it first enters the water, it is empty. But when it is drawn back up to the owner, it returns full. So too, when we enter the world, we have no mitzvot to our name. But when we return, we have a lifetime full of good thoughts, kind words, and noble deeds. (*Kohellet Rabba*)

Pearls from Our Sages

"The ultimate foundation and pillar of wisdom is the realization that there is a first Being, without beginning or end, who brought everything into existence and continues to sustain it. This Being is God." (Maimonides, *Yesodei HaTorah* 1:1)

"The sum of all evidence is this: Revere God and keep His commandments; for this is the purpose of the life of man." (Ecclesiastes 12:13)

"God has compassion like a father and comforts like a mother." (*Pesikta Rabbati* 139a)

"Every Jew is full of mitzvot like a pomegranate is full of seeds." (*Beraishit Rabbah* 32:10)

"The Holy One, Blessed be He, does not withhold reward from any creature, for any positive act." (*Talmud-Bava Kama* 38)

Returning Safely Home

Once upon a time, a wise man went to the docks to watch as ships entered and left the port. He noticed that, as one ship sailed out toward the open sea, all the people on the dock cheered and wished it well. Meanwhile, another ship entered the port and docked. By and large, the crowd ignored it.

The wise man addressed the people saying, "You are looking at things backwards! When a vessel leaves, you do not know what lays ahead or what its end will be. So there really is no reason to cheer. But when a vessel enters the harbor and arrives safely home, that is something to make you feel joy."

Life is that journey and we are the vessel. When a child is born, we celebrate. When a soul returns home, we mourn. Yet if we viewed life on earth the way the wise man viewed the ship, perhaps we too could say, "The vessel has gone on its journey, it has weathered the storms of life, it has finally entered the harbor and now it is safely home." (*Midrash, Shemot Rabbah*)

Complete in the World Above

Once after World War II, a Chassid visited his Rebbe and began crying bitterly. The chassid had lost everything during the war: his wife, his children, his home, and his hope. He felt incapable of going on. In desperation, he begged the Rebbe for a *Bracha* (blessing) and an *Eitza* (advice); anything that could help him face the future.

The Rebbe, who had also lost his wife, children, and community during the war, listened in silence. He then bent his head in quiet contemplation, searching his own soul for words comfort. After a few moments, he spoke.

"The Torah is the Torah of truth. Not one word, not one letter is extraneous. And yet we find an amazing thing. The Torah ends with, 'And there has not ever arisen a prophet in Israel like Moses, whom God knew face to face; for all the signs and wonders that God sent him to perform in Egypt to Pharaoh and to his slaves and to his entire land; and for the strong hand and for the entire great display that Moses performed in view of all Israel.'"

The chassid stared down at the table, as his Rebbe continued "The scholar Rashi comments, 'In view of all Israel' refers to Moses' act of shattering the tablets with the ten

Commandments before their eyes.' Yet why does the Rash add the words, 'before their eyes?' Why doesn't Rashi just say 'it refers to Moses' act of shattering the tablets?'"

The chassid was silent. The Rebbe looked at him and whispered, "It is because the Tablets were only shattered before their eyes. In the World Above, the Tablets remain complete, holy and pure. So too, the loves of your life have only been shattered before your eyes. Above, they too remain complete, holy and pure, waiting for the day when we will be reunited with Moshiach, may that day arrive speedily in our time."

An Enduring Legacy

The main connection between one person and another whom he loves is not a connection of the physical body, but one involving the qualities of the soul, which is the essential element of the person and indeed his essence. However, this connection between human beings is expressed by means of the body and its limbs, the eyes, ears, hands, power of speech etc., in which a person expresses his thoughts, emotions and the particular characteristics of his soul, his essential element. It is therefore understood that illness, although it may damage the body, can never damage or detract from the soul.

The death that is caused by sickness or accident only separates the body from the soul, but the soul continues to live eternally, and continues its connection with the family members, especially with those to whom it is closest. It grieves together with them in their sorrow and rejoices in their family celebrations. (*Adapted from a talk of the Lubavitcher Rebbe*)

Meditation at a Gravesite

Peace be unto you, may you have peace from now until eternity. May you lie in peace on your resting places without being pained at the distress of those who are close to you.

May you dwell in the holy cloud, and may you rest in the shelter of the Most high, in the shadow of the Omnipotent. May the great and holy King, blessed be He, hasten and speed your resurrection, and your rising with all the other righteous and pious men of the world. May He cause you to merit the world of which is all good and unending.

May it be the will of our Father in heaven that I be worthy — in your merit and in the merit of the other righteous and pious men who rest here — that God Almighty, the Pardoner, will forgive all my sins, iniquities and transgressions. For it is for the sake of your glory that I have come here to praise His great and

Awesome name, and to ask that you pray for me that He should deliver me from difficult travail and from trying times.

May my deeds be endowed with blessing and success, my afflictions be healed, and all sickness removed from my midst. May I, and all of Israel, be granted a generous gift and generous sustenance. May I be granted long days, and years of life and peace, tranquility and security. May I complete my days in good old age.

May I be granted increased wisdom, knowledge, understanding, grace, kindness, and mercy before Him, and before all the created beings. May my heart be focused to love Him and fear His name, to fulfill His will with a complete heart.

May it be Your will, God, that my work lead to blessing and not to poverty, to life and not to death. Grant me merit so that the Name of heaven will not be desecrated by my deeds, and that I be one of those who are always useful and who provide goodness to all men. Lead me on a straight path before You and create a pure heart within me.

May Your Torah fill our home throughout our entire lifetime, and focus our hearts to revere Your name. Draw us close to all that You Love. Grant us a good heart, a good portion, a good inclination, a good friend, a good reputation, a good disposition, a good character, a humble soul, and a meek spirit.

In the merit of the righteous buried here, and throughout the entire world, and the good deeds that they have performed in this world, may they all be worthy intercessors before You and before Your throne of glory to carry out my petition and fulfill my request.

Supplication and Prayer at a Gravesite

I beseech You, Lord of the worlds, Merciful One Who is full of compassion: If I have erred, sinned, transgressed, or committed iniquity, performing this or that forbidden deed, God, hear; God, forgive; God, listen and act, do not delay. Do not see me shunned and ignore me. You will surely help and surely raise me up. It is only in Your great kindness that You created me, so that I could achieve merit. You brought me into being from nothingness.

If my deeds have caused a separation between holy and holy, choose me, draw me close, and renew me. Return us to You, God and we will return. Grant my heart the desire to return to You in complete repentance, so that I will not be put to shame before my ancestors in the World to Come.

Remove the yoke of the evil inclination from my heart. Help me to subdue its desires, so that I can make Your will my will, for You have created me to fulfill Your will.

I implore You God of mercy, Master of forgiveness: Forgive me, pardon me, grant me atonement. Cleanse my sins in Your great mercy, but not through suffering or illness. Do not turn me away empty-handed from Your presence, for You listen to prayers — for the sake of all the righteous resting here and for the sake of Your great glory. Blessed be He who hears prayer.

May it be Your will, God our Lord, and Lord of our ancestors, to grant us long life, a life of peace, a life of goodness, a life of blessing, a life of sustenance, a life of prosperity and honor, a life imbued with the love of the Torah and the fear of heaven. A life in which You will fulfill all the desires of our hearts for good. May my prayer be accepted so that You deal kindly with me and my descendants and their descendants, in this world, for long days and years of life and peace, and in the World to Come.

May the meditation of my mouth and my words be acceptable before You, God, my Rock and Redeemer.

Ways to Honor the Soul of the Deceased

• Ensure that the deceased receives a proper Jewish burial, consisting of a *Tahara* (purification of the body), a *Shomer* (a Jewish person to stay with the deceased until burial), *Tachrichim* (traditional shrouds), a "traditional kosher" casket, and proper burial in the ground, by the Chevra Kaddisha.

• Male mourners should recite the Mourner's *Kaddish* with a *Minyan* (quorum of ten Jewish males over age thirteen) at the gravesite after the burial, and for eleven months following the passing.

• Mourn the departed in full accordance with Jewish law and tradition.

• Give additional charity by placing several coins in a charity box before and after prayer each day in honor of the departed soul.

• Men should lead the three daily prayer services in the Shiva home and recite the Mourner's Kaddish. Following Shiva, men should lead the three daily prayer services in the synagogue for eleven months, if mourning parents.

• Light a candle in the synagogue every day for the first year, in honor of the departed soul.

• Commit to improving one's observance of a mitzva, and to inspiring one's children to do the same.

• Donate Jewish books to the local synagogue or Jewish school, inscribing in them "In honor of..." the Hebrew name of the deceased, and that of his or her father, "...of blessed memory."

• Study as many tractates of the *Mishna* (codified compilation of Jewish law) as possible, dividing the rest between volunteers. If possible, the entire Mishna should be completed by the *Shloshim* (thirty days from the burial). A chart for its division between several people is provided on page 279.

• Recite the *Yizkor* (memorial prayer) in the synagogue on the last day of Passover, on the second day of *Shavuot*, on *Shemini Atzeret*, and on Yom Kippur.

• Visit the gravesite to recite prayers and Psalms.

• Place a pebble on the gravestone to mark your presence.

• Care for the gravesite. Make sure it does become overgrown with weeds or fall into disrepair.

• Name a new baby with the Hebrew name of the departed.

278

Mishnayot Division Chart

Section	Num. of Chapters	Learner's Name	Section	Num. of Chapters	Learner's Name
ZERAIM			Rosh Hashanah	4	
Berachot	9		Taanit	4	
Peah	8		Megillah	4	
Demai	7		Moed Katan	3	
Kila-yim	9		Chagigah	3	
Shevi-it	10		**NASHIM**		
Terumot	11		Yevamot	16	
Maasrot	5		Ketubot	13	
Maaser Sheni	5		Nedarim	11	
Chalah	4		Nazir	9	
Orlah	3		Sotah	9	
Bikurim	4		Gitin	9	
MOED			Kidushin	4	
Shabbat	24		**NEZIKIN**		
Ayruvin	10		Bava Kama	10	
Pesachim	10		Bava Metzia	10	
Shkalim	8		Bava Batra	10	
Yuma	8		Sanhedrin	11	
Sukkah	5		Makot	3	
Baytzah	5		Shevuot	8	

Section	Num. of Chapters	Learner's Name	Section	Num. of Chapters	Learner's Name
Aydiot	8		**TAHAROT**		
Avodah Zarah	5		Kaylim I	1-15	
Avot	6		Kaylim II	16-30	
Horiot	3		Oholot	18	
KODASHIM			Nega-im	14	
Zevachim	14		Parah	12	
Menachot	13		Taharot	10	
Chulin	12		Mikvaot	10	
Bechorot	9		Niddah	10	
Erchin	9		Machshirin	6	
Temurah	7		Zavin	5	
Keritot	6		Tevul Yom	4	
Meilah	6		Yada-yim	4	
Tamid	7		Uktzin	3	
Midot	5				
Kinim	3				

Recommended Reading

Below are some works that one may find useful during the period of mourning. Some of these books have also served as sources for this companion.

Bridge of Life, Gesher Hachaim, HaRav Yechiel M. Tucazinsky, translated by HaRav Nissan A. Tucazinsky, Moznaim Publishing.

Consolation, The Spiritual Journey Beyond Grief, Rabbi Maurice Lamm, JPS Publishing

Death and Bereavement, Rabbi Abner Weiss, Mesorah/UOJCA

Halachos of Aveilus. The Laws of Mourning, Feldheim Publishing

It's All a Gift, Dealing with Loss, Miriam Adahan, Feldheim Publishing

Jewish Way in Death and Mourning, Rabbi Maurice Lamm, Jonathan David Publishers

Kitzur Shulchan Oruch, Code of Jewish Law, Rabbi Shlomo Gantzfried, translated by Rabbi Eli Touger, Moznaim Publishing

Mourning and Remembrance, Rabbi Aaron Felder

Mourning in Halacha, The Laws and Customs of the Year of Mourning, Rabbi Chaim Binyomin Goldberg, Mesorah Publishing

Nitei Gavriel (Hilchot Aveilut), Rabbi Gavriel Zinner

Searching for Comfort, Rabbi Meir Munk, Mesorah

To Comfort the Bereaved, A Guide for Mourners and Those Who Visit Them, Aaron Levine, Jason Aronson Publishing

Towards a Meaningful Life, Rabbi Simon Jacobson, William Morrow & Company

Glossary

Aliyah Going up to bless the Torah

Aninut Time period for mourners from passing until burial

Aron Casket

Avel; Aveylim One who is in mourning

Bikur Cholim Visiting the sick

Chesed Shel Emet "True Kindness," referring to those caring for the deceased

Chevra Kaddisha Jewish Burial Society

Eretz Yisroel The Land of Israel

Gan Eden The Garden of Eden

Gartel Prayer sash

Gehinom Purgatory; spiritual cleansing process

Hagomel Thanksgiving blessing, recited when the Torah is read

Halacha, Halachic Jewish law, in conformance with

Hamakom Yenachaim Condolence declaration

Havdallah Prayer at the conclusion of Shabbat and holidays

Hesped Eulogy for a deceased

Kaddish Prayer of praise for God

Kaddish Yatom Mourner's Kaddish

Kaddish-D'Rabannan Recited at the conclusion of studying a portion of Talmud or Mishna

Kaddish-Titkabel Recited after completing major sections of the daily prayer services

Kel Molay Rachamim Memorial prayer recited at a funeral

Kever Grave

Kvurah Burial

Kohain; Kohanim Member(s) of Priestly tribe

Kriah Obligatory rending of the garment by mourners

Levaya Funeral

Maariv Evening prayer service

Maftir Special portion recited after the Torah reading on Shabbat and Jewish holidays

Matzeivah Tombstone

Mi Shebayrach Special prayer for the sick

Mincha Afternoon prayer service

Minhag Jewish custom, often becoming normative practice

Minyan Quorum of 10 Jewish men over 13, required for service

Mishnah; Mishnayot Codified compilation of Jewish law

Mitzva; Mitzvot Divine commandments

Mourner's Kaddish See Kaddish

Nechama Condolence

Ner Light or candle

Neshama Soul

Nichum Avaylim Comforting the mourners

Niftar One who passed away

Olam Habah World to Come
Olov Hasholom; **Oleha Hasholom** May he/she rest in peace
Onain Mourner's state, from the time of passing until burial
Rosh Chodesh First day of the month on the Jewish calendar
Seudat Ha-Avarah Condolence meal
Seudat Hoda-Ah Meal of thanksgiving
Shacharit Morning prayer service
Shana Year; applies to the eleven months of Kaddish
Shiva Seven day mourning period that begins after burial
Shloshim The thirtieth day from burial; Mourning milestone
Shmirah Guarding or attending (the deceased until burial)
Shomer Person who guards or attends (the deceased)
Siyum Celebration upon completion of a section of Torah
Tachnun Supplications of Forgiveness, recited in daily prayers
Tachrichim Simple, traditional shrouds
Tahara Washing, purifying, and preparing the body for burial
Tallit Prayer shawl worn by men during prayer
Tehillim Book of Psalms
Tzedaka Act of righteousness; the giving of charity
Tziduk Hadin Prayer recited after passing and following burial
Viduy Confessional prayers (recited before passing)
Yartzeit Anniversary of passing, based on the Jewish calendar
Yizkor Memorial prayer recited in the synagogue on holidays

For bulk orders please contact

The Jewish Learning Group
1-888-56-LEARN

www.JewishLearningGroup.com

לזכות

הרב יוסף בן חי׳ מלכה
מרת חנה פריווא בת אלטער יהושע הכהן ע״ה
הרב שניאור זלמן בן חנה פריווא
מרת דבורה גבריאלה בת רייזא פייגא
מנחם מענדל בן מרים שרה
מניא שיינא בת מרים שרה
חנה פריווא בת דבורה גבריאלה
ומשפחתם